D1520823

LACAN WITH THE PHILOSOPHERS

Lacan with the Philosophers

RUTH RONEN

Translated from Hebrew by Michal Sapir

UNIVERSITY OF TORONTO PRESS
Toronto Buffalo London

ISBN 978-1-4875-0281-2

Library and Archives Canada Cataloguing in Publication

Ronen, Ruth, 1958–
[Lacan im ha-philosophim. English]
Lacan with the philosophers / Ruth Ronen ; translated from
Hebrew by Michal Sapir.

Translation of: Lacan im ha-philosophim.
Includes bibliographical references and index.
ISBN 978-1-4875-0281-2 (hardcover)

1. Lacan, Jacques, 1901–1981.   2. Psychoanalysis and philosophy.
3. Philosophers, Ancient.   I. Title.   II. Title: Lacan im ha-philosophim.
English.

BF109.L32R6613 2018   150.19′5092   C2017-906772-9

This book was published with the support of the Israel Science
Foundation (ISF).

University of Toronto Press acknowledges the financial assistance to its
publishing program of the Canada Council for the Arts and the Ontario
Arts Council, an agency of the Government of Ontario.

Canada Council   Conseil des Arts
for the Arts   du Canada

ONTARIO ARTS COUNCIL
CONSEIL DES ARTS DE L'ONTARIO
an Ontario government agency
un organisme du gouvernement de l'Ontario

Funded by the   Financé par le
Government   gouvernement
of Canada   du Canada

Canadä

Contents

1 Lacan with the Philosophers   3

2 The Love of Truth: Lacan with Plato   25

3 Soulove: Lacan and Aristotle "On the Soul"   52

4 To Think or Not to Be: Lacan with Descartes   83

5 Lacan Wagers with Pascal   111

6 The Erotics of the One: Lacan with Kant   145

7 Beyond Good and Evil: Lacan and
Kantian Morality   178

8 Lacan and Hegel in Three Steps: Otherness,
Death, Singularity   205

Conclusion   247

Glossary of Lacanian Terms   251

Notes   263

Bibliography   281

Index   285

LACAN WITH THE PHILOSOPHERS

Chapter 1

Lacan with the Philosophers

People may find that I am busying myself here a little bit too much with what are called – God's curse on the name – the great philosophers. The fact is that perhaps not they alone, but they in an eminent way, articulate what one may well call a pathetic research because it always returns, if one knows how to consider it throughout all its detours, its more or less sublime objects, to this radical knot that I am trying to undo for you namely desire; it is to this that I hope, by enquiring into it if you are willing to follow me, to restore decisively its property as an unsurpassable point, unsurpassable in the very sense that I mean when I tell you that each one of those who can be described by this name of great philosopher cannot be surpassed on a certain point.

– Lacan, *Seminar IX, Identification*, 28.2.62[1]

In David Lodge's comic novel *Small World*, a perennial literature student works on a study of "T.S. Eliot's influences on Shakespeare." This absurd topic reflects some of the spirit of the present book, which wishes to show, among other things, how Lacan "invented" the philosophers he referred to in his writings and lectures. Lacan, who was accused by many psychoanalysts and psychologists of reading Freud in a way that was foreign to Freud himself, took a similar liberty with the philosophers whose thought is so markedly present in his writings.

When Lodge published his novel (in 1984), however, his academic/literary project reflected not only the spirit of the absurd, but also the spirit of post-structuralist freedom that in those years flew the flag of interdisciplinarity. Indeed, if we forget for a moment the arbitrary burden of time, that is, the principles of linear time that our thinking about events is usually subject to, we immediately face a range of possibilities that assume a different relationship between, say, the Russian Revolution and the French Revolution, the post-technological age and the rise of the bourgeoisie, Surrealism and Renaissance painting, atonal music and Bach. Is it not possible, setting aside temporal realism, to retrospectively find the foundations of atonality in Bach? The shoots of Marxism in Robespierre, and so on? It was the absolute freedom of a discourse committed to nothing essential outside itself that sustained the idea of interdisciplinarity. The freedom that manifests itself in the spectrum of questions discussed in the interdisciplinary context is made possible by the permission to pursue an atemporal discourse. It is true that Homer wrote his epic poems before Freud; even so, what prevents us from wondering about Odysseus's unconscious? It is true that in antiquity the distinction between the master and the slave was inscribed on their bodies; even so, what prevents us from discussing the master's law in a pragmatic context, as a kind of speech act? Sometimes, it seems, the "realness" of discourse gets lost among the disciplines, the difference between one historical moment and another gets blurred, truth becomes relative and elastic due to the discursive freedom made possible by interdisciplinarity.

The question of Lacan and the philosophers could (but should not) be approached from the perspective of discursive freedom. As already noted, Lacan himself seems to take a similar liberty in referring to the philosophers: he uses the Aristotelian soul to frame his conception of masculine and feminine sexuality, he uses Plato to formulate his understanding of the transference relationship, and the Heideggerian Thing to develop the concept of *jouissance*. But can the slippage of philosophy into the psychoanalytic discourse really be examined in this vein? Is Lacan's use of philosophy merely another case of skipping from one discourse to another, from one framework of discussion to another, from one set of concepts to another? In this book I will try to trace Lacan's movement into philosophy and characterize the nature of his engagement with philosophy. Not coincidentally, this inquiry will also reveal a completely different form of "interdisciplinarity," one that is very far from what has been perceived, in the academic history of the last decades, as the need to do away with disciplinary borders.[2]

In Seminar XVI of 1969, Lacan says about the couple "Freud and me" that the question is "where I place myself in this couple. Well then," he continues, "reassure yourselves, I place myself always at the same place, at the place where I was, and where I still remain, alive. Freud does not need to see me in order to look at me. In other words, as a text I already quoted here states, 'a living dog is worth more than the discourse of a dead person.'"[3] How are we to understand this deadly effect of the coupling?

Although these words refer to the couple Freud and Lacan, there seems no better way to describe Lacan's relationship with the philosophers.[4] In this couple the positions are equally fixed. It is the dead philosophers who are looking at Lacan without seeing him, whereas he, Lacan, is in the position of the living. The philosophers, just like Freud, do not need to see Lacan in order to look at him, but in this blind gaze of the dead they create a place for Lacan, they make room for him as someone who is alive, from his point of view, of course. Moreover, it seems that just as Lacan, as the living pole in the couple, managed to breathe life into Freud, he also managed to inject a different spirit into the dead philosophers he chose to engage with. But since we are not dealing with reincarnations, it must quickly be emphasized that this life that Lacan has breathed into the dead is his own life, which in a sense he gives in order to ostensibly resuscitate those who do not and cannot see him – the philosophers.

For readers of Lacan today, however, the surviving member of the couple is himself no longer alive. Now that Lacan too has passed away, we come full circle and say that it is both sides of the couple, both positions, that one looks at but does not see – thus, they make room for each other. Again, we are dealing not with the harmony of reciprocal relations but rather with something that touches on the nature of invention. It is Freud who invented Lacan just as Lacan reinvented Freud, and this circumstance contains no reciprocity or reflective relations. As Derrida says when he refers to his and Lacan's love for each other: the moment someone speaks for a "we," it is a form of guesting that is also a violation of the other's ability to resist. This kind of love reveals a violent asymmetry.[5] Indeed, the philosophers invented Lacan just as Lacan invented the philosophers.[6] The philosophers invented Lacan because Lacan resides deep in the heart of the humanist discourse, where he is perhaps more welcomed than he is in the company of those who engage with mental health. Lacan invented the philosophers by developing an approach to reading philosophy and an intimate and close employment of it while opposing, critiquing, sometimes negating its existence.

"Lacan and the philosophers" is a match sponsored by more than one pair: Lacan and Plato, Lacan and Aristotle, Lacan and Descartes, Lacan and Hegel, Lacan and Kant, Lacan and Heidegger. But in approaching any of these pairs, in order to read Lacan reading Plato or Hegel, we must begin with the first coupling on the agenda, that of Lacan and the philosophers, and ask how we should understand the conjunction "and" in this context. For this is not a simple or random conjunction, but a real and indispensable one. Just like in a love relationship, we can say about this couple in retrospect: Lacan and the philosophers were meant for each other – thus pointing to the necessity, to the inevitability of the relationship.

But to suppose a necessity with regard to the coupling of Lacan and the philosophers is to assume what we are trying to prove. This necessity must be proven, and at the start of this path to the proof we must ask a preliminary, more modest question: What does Lacan have to do with philosophy? The analogy between this question and the question about the couple Freud–Lacan may be useful again in this context if we focus our question thus: Does Lacan, in his philosophical act, continue in the footsteps of the philosophers he cites? Lacan continued in the footsteps of Freud; that said, Lacanian psychoanalysis is a discourse that reinvents Freud, creating a different Freud from what Freud is without Lacan. Lacan's psychoanalysis is stamped with Lacan's uniqueness, but it also preserves, to the very end, an irreducible affinity with Freud's thought. Lacan was an inventor whose invention had a father, and Lacan did everything he could to mask the originality of his formulation of psychoanalysis by presenting himself, almost until the last days of his teaching, as a Freudian (rather than a Lacanian). That is, Lacan presented his own teaching as completely derived from Freud, while walking a tightrope in his reading of Freud. Lacan imparted the psychoanalysis that he invented in Freud's wake in a way that for many readers is almost impenetrable. It seems that as much as Lacan placed Freud's texts under the X-ray of his incisive, lucid reading, he also somewhat obscured those texts, rendering Freud's original and masterful teaching less accessible.

The utter originality of Lacan's thought can only be perused through the lens of Freud and his psychoanalytical legacy. Lacan re-creates Freud in a way that embodies some kind of leap, some shift, some revolutionary change of direction with regard to how Freud was understood *before* Lacan. Lacan interprets originality (i.e., the dimension of invention) and mastery (i.e., his teaching's affinity with the history of psychoanalysis and the principles of analytical discourse) in his own way. Between the Freudian idea of the unconscious and the moment of Lacanian invention, Lacan seems to move invention from its obvious place in his teaching. If the moment of invention is an absolute moment that often occurs outside knowledge – with no one, including the inventor himself, understanding how it happens – Lacan almost completely rules out the possibility of this kind of invention in his teaching; indeed, until the late stages in his teaching, Lacan presented himself as a mere interpreter of Freud. But even in the dimension of invention, Lacan when "reinventing" psychoanalysis avoids turning it into a creed, a transmittable doctrine. Lacan transmits his invention through a teaching that seems "unfriendly" to his listeners and readers, a teaching that resists appropriation. This initial characterization of the masterful originality of Lacanian psychoanalysis is crucial, because Lacan's position vis-à-vis the Freudian legacy manages to create an unfamiliar position in the relationship that forms between a thinker and his disciplinary "forefathers." While Lacan is a Freudian, his teaching refuses to become a psychoanalytic doctrine or to establish a defined discipline of thought. We encounter one expression of this refusal in the way in which he uses philosophy.

Lacan's masterful originality in relation to the father of psychoanalysis can be seen as a kind of inverse analogy of the way in which he approaches philosophy. Lacan's use of philosophy often takes on an anti-philosophical, resistant guise, creating a rift between psychoanalysis and philosophy. That is, he makes his appeal to philosophy while strongly emphasizing the psychoanalytical *invention* in relation to the philosophical discourse. But while maintaining this divergence, Lacan makes crucial use of the logic, the motivations, and the ways of thinking that inform this discourse. In short, Lacan uses philosophy to create an "anti-philosophical" discourse that is in many ways distinctly philosophical.[7]

"Lacan is not a philosopher," says Alain Badiou,[8] and "there is no philosophy of Lacan." This sweeping statement is based on the fact that Lacan himself believed that his thinking stemmed solely from his clinical experience. Such an experience is "radically external and foreign to philosophy," continues Badiou. But it is not only Lacan's clinical orientation that classifies him as a non-philosopher, but also the fact that he declares himself to be an *anti*-philosopher. According to Badiou, however, what we have here is not an anti-philosophical ideology, but rather a position derived from the way in which Lacan reads philosophy. To say, then, that Lacan is an anti-philosopher is unhelpful and does not clarify his position towards philosophy, since Lacan not only "transverses, reads, comments, revolves around the great philosophers,"[9] but also erects a hurdle that any brave philosopher should be able to cross.[10]

In order to decipher the couple Lacan and the philosophers, I therefore propose to view Lacan's appeal to philosophy as a way to *use* it.
This constitutes a unique and original way of establishing interdisciplinary relations. In his use of philosophy, Lacan develops one of the most
complex and difficult-to-characterize ways in which one practice makes
use of another, thereby changing both psychoanalysis and philosophy
in some way. So when characterizing the couple Lacan and the philosophers we cannot simply dismiss the whole thing as "anti-philosophy,"
for that term purports to locate psychoanalysis outside what is relevant
for the philosophical concern with truth. Badiou, as already mentioned,
believes that the relevance of psychoanalysis lies precisely in the fact
that it is *not* driven by a love of truth for its own sake, though it is
concerned with truth. In the present study I will indeed explore the
possibility that the relevance of psychoanalysis to philosophy, and that
of philosophy to psychoanalysis, is related to the way in which Lacan
uses philosophy in order to establish the psychoanalytic concern with
truth. He thereby reveals the deep meaning of *the link between use and
invention*, the way innovation is produced when use is understood as
intimate connection through resistance (rather than as a form of assimi-
lation and absorption).

The following chapters examine how Lacan uses philosophy, and the
question is, what is the purpose of this use? If we accept Badiou's view
that what has always defined philosophy is the demand not to accept
any opinion without first examining its causes and its fundamental
purpose, then we can say that psychoanalysis embraces this position
through its approach to the unconscious – it relentlessly struggles with
the question of the cause and purpose of assuming there is an unconscious. Thus, although according to Badiou's criteria psychoanalysis
is not a philosophy, because as a theory it is derived from the clinic
(and therefore psychoanalysis has no interest in formulating a meta-
language or a theory for its own sake, of the type that follows from the
Socratic "philosophizing" – *philosophein*), in practice the philosophical
inquiry is not foreign to psychoanalysis.[11]

But philosophy is not just philosophizing; it is also a wager on truth.
Philosophy, even when it is sceptical about the possibility of getting to
the truth, sees truth as a stopping point for thought. For philosophy
there is something that stops thought, that prevents it from following
the mechanisms of discourse alone, because philosophy's purpose is an
object that itself is not subject to the principles that govern the organization of language or the progress of thought. For the philosopher – as

opposed to the sophist, for example – thought (or discourse) encounters something that is not itself. As we will see later, for psychoanalysis, a central question is how to articulate the logic of the unconscious through a language that will never escape the equivocation that stems from the encounter with an object. The same is true for the philosopher, whose anguish is related to a truth that is not given or that has to be strived for. It is the truth that defies thought and resists articulation that separates the philosopher from the sophist, since for the latter nothing stops the play of language, nothing turns philosophical pathos into *full speech* (which is speech that, for Lacan, articulates the truth about the subject's desire).

This is the point at which psychoanalysis is put to the test, according to Badiou. Here, with regard to the wager on truth, and even with regard to belief in the irreducible existence of the truth, psychoanalysis in general and Lacanian psychoanalysis in particular pose a challenge for the philosopher, because it has its own way of deciphering the relationship between thinking and being, that is, between thinking and being where the truth of being cannot turn into thought.

Badiou sees Lacanian psychoanalysis as a practice that makes it possible to return to a pure philosophical position, one that recognizes truth and only truth as that which thought necessarily encounters. With regard to this philosophical striving, we must not be fooled by the absence of a common object shared by psychoanalysis and philosophy. Even if the place where psychoanalysis finds being (as speaking in the clinic) has different characteristics from those of the philosophical field, and even if psychoanalysis is interested in the unconscious (in the subject's desire) while philosophy is interested in the subject of cognition, this difference in object does not necessarily indicate a different position towards truth. When we examine the link between philosophy and psychoanalysis, we should not be misled by the singular object of inquiry that psychoanalysis puts at the centre of its concern. A universal object is not what guarantees thought's encounter with truth, and Badiou uses psychoanalysis to remind us of the core of philosophical ethics and to position it against any version of sophism. That is, psychoanalysis can be used precisely to reconstitute the voice that is unique to philosophy, the voice that enables (and commits) it to tie together being, the subject, and truth.

Badiou examines how Lacan uses psychoanalysis in the service of philosophy. We too will have to embark on the same path and examine Lacan's use of philosophy – not, however, in order to revive a philosophical practice, but in order to examine what is productive and fertile in this encounter for its two parties. This is the context in which this book's core question should be examined: What does Lacan seek with the philosophers? How, why, and to what end does Lacan read, comment on, and use philosophy? For both philosophy and psycho-analysis, what can be derived and deduced from Lacan's way of using philosophy?

While Lacan's fundamental attitude towards philosophy seems anti-philosophical, an attitude of criticism, opposition, rejection, his read-ing of the philosophers paints a more complex picture than this. In the following chapters we will be examining how Lacan approaches each philosopher in turn; here, in these introductory remarks, we address Lacan's position with regard to philosophy *in general*. As we will see presently, even Lacan's firm, diagnostic statements about philosophy make no unequivocal judgment; in fact, they make no judgment at all. Let us examine this through a few examples.

Our first example is found in Seminar XIX from 1971–2, and its importance lies in the fact that it suggests the place Lacan assigns to philosophical discourse and his diagnosis of the effects on which this discourse relies. Here, as elsewhere, Lacan explicitly claims that only through psychoanalytical practice can we recognize the effects that result from the structure of any discourse, because psychoanalysis exposes the discourse's hidden logic, the very logic that turns a discourse into the ground for any practice, into the condition for any social bond. Psy-choanalysis describes the logic of the discourse not only through fixed relationships (such as between S1 and S2) but also through the move-ment that any discourse generates even before it becomes associated with a system of concepts or values, or with a certain ideology.

What is that movement generated by discourse, any discourse? Dis-course always posits an agent, that is, an element from which and by virtue of which the reality of that discourse will be created. There is a difference between a discourse that posits in the place of the agent a signifier of some meta-principle, a signifier that denotes the discourse's *source of validity* (e.g., "truth," "beauty," "justice," "power"), and a dis-course that posits in the place of the agent a signifier of a *subject* (such as *the hysteric subject*), or a discourse that posits in the place of the agent some *overall knowledge* (scientific, legal, philosophical, etc.). Lacan's claim is that the mere positing of something in the place of the agent produces a *circulation* whose effects will be shown in the discourse's structure, and it is psychoanalysis that points to these effects.

In the following example, Lacan locates philosophy within the University discourse, that is, as a discourse assigning *a body of knowledge, any knowledge,* the status of the discourse's agent:

> Before a signifier is really put in place, namely, precisely mapped out from the ideology for which it is produced, it always has effects of circulation. Meaning precedes, in its effects, the recognition of its place, the place that it establishes.
>
> If the University discourse is defined by the fact that in it knowledge is put in the position of the semblance, this can be monitored, this is confirmed by the very nature of teaching in which you see what? A false ordering of what could be displayed, as I might say, throughout the centuries, in terms of different ontologies. Its high point, its culmination is in what is gloriously called "the history of philosophy," as if philosophy did not have ... its source in the adventures and misadventures of the discourse of the Master, that must be renewed from time to time. (Seminar XIX, 153[VI7–18])[12]

When knowledge is posited as an agent of discourse, and this knowledge is examined in isolation from its effects, it is possible to think that knowledge in and of itself has an objective meaning (even before it has been enlisted to give validity to a world view, to a research program, or to an ideology). The University discourse is built on granting knowledge such validity, as complete, autonomous, neutral, and objective. But what produces the University discourse, Lacan says, is precisely the fact that the knowledge that appears as the agent of the discourse, and that generates the circulation that is responsible for what is the discursive world of the University, is always revealed to be a *semblance.* Knowledge is a semblance in the sense that the circulation it generates is related neither to the content of this knowledge, nor to the question of whether this knowledge exists anywhere, nor to whether it is true or false. The University discourse is thus based on positing knowledge (which is no more than a semblance of knowledge), in the place of the agent of the discourse. In this way, knowledge can sustain a world view, create an outlook, and establish an entire ontology.

The fact that the place of agent is occupied by a semblance is not unique to the University discourse. In the case of the other discursive structures Lacan alludes to, the element that appears in the place of the agent is also a semblance (the semblance of an object in the analyst's discourse, the semblance of authority in the master's discourse, and a semblance of the subject in the hysteric's discourse). But the important question with regard to the University discourse is what stands *behind* the semblance of knowledge, and here, since the Age of Enlightenment, we find that knowledge is supposed to replace the arbitrary authority of the master with what appears under the guise of neutral and objective knowledge. However, as Slavoj Žižek puts it: "The master reappears in the guise of ... an object which embodies S2, the chain of knowledge ... the semblance of a neutral 'objective' knowledge" (Žižek, *For They Know Not What They Say*, 235).

The logic of the University discourse, as Lacan formulates it, thus shows that knowledge (S2) posited in the place of the agent generates a movement towards truth; at the end of this circuit what we find in the place of truth is the master (S1 – as shown in the scheme below). The diagnosis for philosophy therefore emerges as follows: philosophy positions itself around a signifier of knowledge about truth (throughout its history, philosophy has posited various signifiers for what advances the philosopher towards truth – God, reason, common sense, nature, Being, consciousness); but what psychoanalysis shows us with regard to the University discourse is that knowledge as an agent generates a movement that ultimately reveals the University discourse as governed by a master, and this revelation takes place even before (and outside) the subjection of knowledge to the portraying of a world view, to the construction of an ontology, or to the formulation of an ideology.

We can clarify the meaning of Lacan's diagnosis with the example of the signifier "liberalism," which can be taken as a signifier of a body of knowledge. As such, "liberalism" dictates a world view, laws, rules of behaviour and governance, a set of values (equality, freedom of choice and of action, etc.). "Liberalism," as body of knowledge, nourishes a certain ontology, it serves as the basis for a world view. In this context, liberalism can appear as a historical and current knowledge that can support, for example, political struggles for equal rights. But such a view of knowledge, Lacan claims, is *a false ordering*. It ignores the fact that the discourse of "liberalism" is controlled by a master who manipulates liberal values in order to augment its mastery. Hence, it is not the liberal world view that decides the effects of "liberalism": the master is there to promote and maintain the liberal world view that has been created only as a semblance of dominance (according to the place it occupies):

$$\frac{S_2}{S_1} \rightarrow \frac{a}{\$}$$

The University discourse is based on positing knowledge as something in whose name and by virtue of which the discourse is founded and applied. However, Lacan tells us, what the University discourse locates in the place of the agent of the discourse is no more than a semblance, which leads the knowledge's addressee to think that fluctuations in knowledge and frequent innovations in what is perceived as the heart of knowledge stem from the development of knowledge itself: from the constant quest for true knowledge. Not so, claims Lacan; rather, the "knowledge" that is at the heart of the University discourse is knowledge whose changes stem from fluctuations in the status of a master in whose name this knowledge was formulated in the first place (political changes of government, the rating of opposing world views such as Marxism, etc.), and therefore if we move clockwise from the place of the signifier of knowledge S2 (which appears in the place of the agent), we will arrive at the final place in the discursive structure, on the lower left, the place of truth, where we find the signifier of the master S1.

This is the structure through which philosophy should be understood, Lacan contends – the structure of the University discourse, which gives extra weight to the semblances of knowledge and uses them as the basis for a glorious history of changing ontologies. Philosophy interprets the signifier of knowledge as referring to the substance of truth, thus assigning it premature weight (missing the fact that these ontologies constructed by philosophy are merely the result of fluctuations in the discourse of the master, who determines the truth or falsity of knowledge).

Lacan returns to this location of philosophy under the wings of the University in various places. This scathing criticism of philosophy – that it is a discourse that posits, in the constitutive place, knowledge that is built on confusing the real effect of an (undisclosed) signifier with the false effect of a signifier given unduly ontological weight – characterizes only one line of arguments that he makes with respect to philosophy at large. We will now examine two other references, which in a certain sense represent two additional positional strategies that Lacan adopts in relation to philosophy. Beyond the critical approach outlined above, Lacan imputes to philosophy a desire for truth that leads to the philosophical mirage that truth is attainable. Another approach sees philosophy as an authentic and distinct expression of a question that psychoanalysis is similarly engaged in seeking appropriate ways to formulate.

Lacan's diagnosis of philosophy's relation to truth will be now examined through the opening session of Seminar IX, which deals with "Identification":

> Psychoanalysis presented itself at first to the world as being that which brought the real truth [*la vraie vérité*]. Naturally, one falls quickly into all sorts of metaphors which allow the thing to escape. This real truth is what is concealed. There will always be one, even in the most rigorous philosophical discourse: it is on this that there is founded our credit in the world and the stupefying thing is that this credit still persists even though, for a good while now, not the least effort has been made to give even the slightest start to something which would respond to it.
>
> Under these circumstances I feel myself quite honored to be questioned on this theme: "where is the real truth of your discourse?" And I can even, after all, find that it is precisely indeed in so far as I am not taken for a philosopher, but for a psychoanalyst, that I am posed this question. Because one of the most remarkable things in philosophical literature, is the degree to which among philosophers, I mean in so far as they are philosophizing, when all is said and done the same question is never posed to philosophers ...
>
> There is one thing, in any case, which has never seemed to shake for anyone the credit of philosophers, which is that it has been possible to speak, with respect to each of them, and even the greatest, about a double truth. That then I who, entering into psychoanalysis, put my feet in the platter by posing this question about truth,[13] should suddenly feel the aforesaid platter getting warm under the soles of my feet, is something about which after all I can rejoice, since, if you reflect on it, I am all the same the one who turned on the gas.[14]

On the face of it, Lacan's diagnosis refers to two different dimensions of truth: the one answering the philosophical abstract question about knowing what is true (to which the Cartesian answer will be: "I think therefore I know that I am"), the other answering the question posed by the subject in analysis: "Who am I?" If Lacan had placed the philosophers and the psychoanalysts in two distinct camps, the question about Lacan and the philosophers would have had very different and less far-reaching consequences. The point, however, is that both tread the same route towards truth yet regard the effects of this route differently. When the philosopher speaks the truth, a concealed facet of truth is necessarily revealed by the mere endeavour to speak it. Surprisingly enough, it is the psychoanalyst, who holds no claim to knowing truth as such, who is challenged to reveal the hidden side of truth, the real truth always lurking behind the one spoken. This is a curious situation, given that it is the philosopher who has defined his occupation as that of discovering truth, who has taken it on herself to be a guarantor of truth. So why is it the psychoanalyst who is being asked about the "real truth"? Is this "other truth" unknown to the philosopher? Lacan suggests that the *real* truth is demanded from the psychoanalyst who answers this demand in a way that distinguishes his position from that of the philosopher. The real truth, for which the analyst has put his feet to the fire, was produced by the philosopher in his quest for truth, and as an effect of his discourse. This truth, which is produced by the philosopher and which stands as the object of the philosopher's desire to speak it, is brought before the analyst to challenge him. Curiously, the philosopher wants to know nothing about this truth, whereas the psychoanalyst stakes his being (i.e., his feet) on it in order to make it clear that this truth can be known even if it cannot be possessed or held.

Language, by striving to articulate truth, produces a truth that evades articulation. The philosopher wants to know nothing about the concealed truth that constitutes the other side of the truth he has spoken. At the most, Lacan says later, the philosopher will agree to say that truth is not one, or is not unequivocal. Thus, for example, he will admit that although Descartes summons God to vouch for the existence of true knowledge, the way in which this Cartesian God guarantees truth remains unknown. The object of Descartes's faith is ambiguous and cannot clearly negotiate the way of the cogito to true knowledge. In other words, the philosopher is able to articulate the clear and distinct truth of the cogito without burning his feet on the other side of this (Cartesian) truth; even if God creates a hole in Descartes's argument, it is still posited as a final remedy for doubt.

We will discuss Descartes in one of the next chapters, but at this stage let us point to the way in which Descartes's case serves here as the basis for a general diagnosis of philosophy. And the general diagnosis is that it is the psychoanalyst who is entrusted with the real truth (even if it is part of his role to refuse to stand as its possessor), and it is the philosopher who is entrusted with the unconcealed (articulated) face of the truth even if he produces an inconsistency in the very act of articulating truth. However, as we will see later, this truth that is produced by the mere attempt to philosophically speak it is the very truth the patient asks about. It is the truth produced as the effect of discourse – the real truth that is the object of both the philosopher and the psychoanalyst.

Lacan's position towards philosophy and its truth can by no means be easily dismissed as critical or judgmental. At the opening to his yearly seminar about the subject of identification, Lacan turns to philosophy in order to set up the initial coordinates through which the question of identification can be approached. And why does Lacan appeal to philosophy for this purpose? It is because, according to Lacan, philosophy since and even before Descartes has been engaged in an effort to understand the constitution of the subject through the signifier, and this is precisely the guidance required in order to approach the question of identification in psychoanalysis. For example, for Descartes the constitution of the subject takes place in and is conditional on the statement: "I think." It is philosophy that puts the question "Who am I and what is my Being?" in the centre and tries to answer this question by examining the effects of language and the signifier on our understanding of what the subject is.

But Lacan claims that philosophy, the philosophy of Descartes and of Kant and Hegel after him, not only uses the signifier and its effects to infer a reply to the question "Who/what am I?," but also identifies Being with what stems from the fact that thought is built like a language. That is, what explains Being for philosophy is the self-same as thinking, and when the subject asks "Who am I" he can easily say "I am the one who says: I think." It is in the self (*selbst*) – that is, the self that is identical to itself – that Being and thinking converge. This is Descartes's formula, which, since its introduction, philosophy has made relentless efforts to discard, while keeping its fundamental logic as a point of departure. Lacan suggests that philosophy identifies Being with a structure of thought because it views the subject as the effect of a signifier or of a structure/logic of discourse.

It is thus the identification of Being with thinking through the signifier or through the structure of speech that leads Lacan straight to the first thesis that guides him throughout this seminar on identification: *Nothing supports the traditional philosophical idea of the subject except the existence of a signifier and its effects*, from Descartes's *Meditations* to Heidegger's "What Is Called Thinking?"[15] The philosophical position is vital in order to begin to examine the effects of the "self-same" relation of thought to language. This relation also constitutes the essence of identification where Being is identified with a signifier (of thought, of cognition, or of consciousness). Identification is all about equating A with A; it examines the identification of a subject with the one who thinks, with his body, his reflection, his titles, his social affiliations, and so on.

Lacan is occupied in this seminar with the question of what makes Being more than the image or the sign with which it is identified. How does identification create a difference between A and A, thus lending reality to the subject? In this context, in which Lacan is dealing with the possible values of the identity equation, what does he deduce from the philosophical idea that "pins" Being to what the signifier tells us about it? The crucial case that is examined in this context is that of the Cartesian subject and the equation that supports it.

When we examine the effects of the cogito we find that although "I think" does not indicate thinking or a thinker, it nonetheless creates a moment of certainty in the subject. As already shown by Immanuel Kant, who made the first serious attempt to revise the cogito argument, "I think" is not a thought, and the thinker's characteristics are not necessary in order to talk about thinking. "A thought," says Lacan, "in no way requires that one thinks about the thought."[16] Descartes, therefore, offers the most radical distinction between the speech act and the (content of) the proposition, but in practice he uses the speech act as a carrier of a proposition about the thinker and about thinking, since for him that which thinks exists as a thinking substance. This is why, if we return to the starting point of this discussion, Lacan claims that philosophy, more than any other practice, regards the subject as an effect of the signifier – it is because it begins by perceiving the subject's Being as the result of the very fact of its being the one who says "I think." For Descartes, the subject who is identified with the statement "I think" immediately takes on characteristics of realness: "therefore I am." After Descartes, philosophy would ponder how to overcome the gap revealed in Descartes's thought between the signifier and Being – or, in fact, how to overcome this *double-truth* (about the subject, whose Being depends on the statement, but about whom the statement says nothing beyond the fact that it is the one who states "I think") – but its solutions to that gap would stem from the force of the signifier and its effects. Bertrand Russell, for example, would resolve the revealed distance through the notion of a meta-language, that is, through a meta-linguistic distinction between two planes (the formal statement on the one hand, and the reference or the reality constituted by it on the other), thus avoiding the paradox of a proposition such as "I am lying."

Lacan thus uses the identity created by Descartes to point to, on the one hand, the philosophical subject's inherent dependency on the signifier, a dependency that also impinges on psychoanalysis, and, on the other hand, the double-truth that necessarily derives from the relation of identity. From the moment Descartes pinned Being to the signifier of thought, he created a double-truth by trying to suppress the incongruence between A ("I think") and A (the one who thinks). Those who will follow him will reveal this double-truth only to create another in its stead.

If Lacan's position can be called critical, it is critical in the sense used by Kant, that of articulating the *a priori*, preliminary knowledge that lies at the basis of every inquiry. Lacan asks about philosophy the same question that Kant asked about the basic preliminary conditions that enable the creation of knowledge: What are the conditions that underpin philosophy as a practice of thinking? We have to ask why the clarification of these conditions is necessary for psychoanalysis, but we must not infer from this that Lacan holds a philosophical position or that he positions himself in any sense as a critic of the philosophical discourse. What can be the position of a psychoanalyst towards a discourse in which he does not take a position, but which displays a great affinity with the questions that occupy psychoanalysis, most notably: What is the subject? Lacan takes up a position that is necessarily external to the philosophical field, while simultaneously making use of that field as if there were no division between the two practices.

Since Lacan, as a psychoanalyst, positions himself outside the philosophical field, we cannot say that he has a philosophical position: he is not part of this field, neither is he a critic of philosophy, nor what is called in Lacanianese the "not all" of philosophy, that is, the boundary marker of the philosophical discourse. Even if it sometimes seems that Lacan positions himself as the exception to the philosophical rule, or as the one who points to the inherent lack in the philosophical discourse (philosophy cannot say "all," and psychoanalysis embodies its "not-all"), it seems that we are dealing with a different kind of self-positioning, which should be properly described. That is, to clarify what Lacan's position towards philosophy might be, if he does not see himself as a philosopher but uses philosophy to formulate fundamental elements in his approach, we need to define the type of use he makes of philosophy, a use that, as noted above, is not critical in the usual sense. If in order to classify Lacan's position in relation to philosophy we need to see why philosophy is necessary for the formulation of psychoanalysis, then philosophy is not foreign to psychoanalysis, even though it operates in a different and separate field. Yet however much we emphasize the relevance and necessity of the philosophical discourse for psychoanalysis, bringing them together can only be done under the caveat that the analytical discourse is subject to a different logic than the philosophical discourse. Psychoanalysis cannot be integral to the structure of philosophy, because such a position presupposes their being part of the same discursive logic. Philosophy and psychoanalysis cannot be seen as a couple; here, the conjunction "and" serves a different role.

From our first example it could thus be inferred, at this stage, that Lacan *uses* philosophy not to diagnose the failures of the philosophical discourse in its approach to truth, but to point out why the recipient of the question about the "real truth" is the psychoanalyst rather than the philosopher, although this real truth punctures holes in the discourse of both the one who approaches it as a subject to engage with, and the one who at the most enjoys scorching his feet in its fire. The real truth, as that which is hidden from view, is not a matter of discipline, but a real presence in the discourse itself. The very fact that the articulation of Being is subordinate to language already causes the question about the real truth to be raised in relation to every discourse that concerns the truth. For the psychoanalyst, the real truth is the name given to the effects of the signifier in the linguistic practice, be it philosophical or analytical – the practice that is called a practice of constituting a subject.

If we have already touched on the difference between *critique* and *usage*, we can formulate another fundamental principle that will qualify Lacan's position towards philosophy. Lacan talks about "Philosophy" in general, yet *philosophy for him is not a type of discourse, but rather a position with regard to discourse.* This is perhaps why Lacan can say in Seminar XVII that in its essence philosophy belongs to the discourse of the master[17] (although it mainly engages the university), but also recognize that the separation of philosophy from the discourse of psychoanalysis does not protect the analyst from it; there is no choice but to contend that the analyst's discourse is a philosophical occurrence, albeit a problematic one.[18]

Philosophy, of course, does not present psychoanalysis with a single field, nor is it of one piece. Nevertheless, for Lacan, one can say that philosophy is a singular position, as is psychoanalysis; a position is tested by the manner in which it registers the effects of the signifier and its employment on the subject. There is a difference between a position that rejects the effects of the signifier on the subject and a position that acknowledges them. Over and above these two distinct and separate positions, the fate of the philosophical position is equally sealed once language and thought are equated, once Being is bound with the signifiers of language and thought in philosophy's striving for truth. Philosophy is inevitably trapped in this impossible bond, even if different philosophies will seek to explain, unravel, resolve, or repress this double-bind in various ways.

Philosophy is therefore close to psychoanalysis in that it accepts the logic of discourse as what determines the placement of the subject, which can also be said of the psychoanalytical position. Therefore, despite the vast range of possible philosophical positions, Lacan can point to something fundamental in what he calls "philosophy," something fundamental that indicates an absolute difference from psychoanalysis as well as an essential affinity with it. Thus, while philosophy presents a position that is distinct from the psychoanalytical one, Lacan is able to use texts that with regard to discipline belong to a philosophical context in order to formulate a psychoanalytical propositions, such as for example Plato's "Symposium" in order to formulate the relation of the analyst to knowledge, or Sartre's *L'être et le néant* in order to formulate the notion of gaze (as one of the objects of the drive). Although these and other texts occasionally appear in the role of "primary professional literature" and as intimate as Lacan's use of philosophy may be, it never evens out or reduces the radical difference between a philosophical position and a psychoanalytical one, between a philosophical discourse and the discourse of an analyst.

It is too early to characterize what philosophy is from the point of view of psychoanalysis, or how psychoanalysis understands what philosophy tries to register from the effects of language. At this stage we will confine ourselves to Lacan's portrayal of psychoanalysis in Seminar XVII, "The Other Side of Psychoanalysis" (1969–70), as that which serves as the other side for other discursive structures, which reveals the logic of the other discourses, yet without serving as their truth. From Lacan's point of view, the role of psychoanalysis is to make use of the ways in which the effects of the signifier are perceived philosophically as delineating the place of truth. That is, there is something in philosophy's path to the truth that is necessary for psychoanalysis, because it is through philosophy that the effects of the signifier on the articulation of truth are revealed.

The analytical discourse, claims Lacan, solves nothing relating to other areas of knowledge. It is woven into the discourse, committed to revealing the limit of the word and the signifier. In this sense, to be the other side does not mean to come full circle or to reveal the truth. One can say that psychoanalysis points to something that is present in the philosophical discourse anyway, and that can be recognized from the analytical position: it is the effect of the signifier on thought and the way the signifier creates a disruption in thought. From this starting point one can say that psychoanalysis is interested in philosophy in order to expose these effects precisely in a discourse that assumes relations of congruence between Being and thinking, and where the unconscious is not assumed at all. To be the other side of philosophy means to point to the inconvenient, sometimes agonizing effects of this encounter of thought with the signifier, even when the philosopher refuses to do so.

Rather than exposing the truth about philosophy, psychoanalysis therefore points to the way in which the philosophical image of thought comes up against a language that is revealed as its "other," but from a position that seems to overlap with and even be integral to the philosophical discourse itself. That is, *the psychoanalytical discourse has to adopt the philosophical object*, to look at philosophy from the point of view of this object, in order to appear as philosophy's other side. The analytical discourse must, for example, adopt the Aristotelian psyche and examine the effects of the signifier "anima" in Aristotle, in order to approach the question of the psycho-soma in the psychoanalytical context. It is a necessary step because Aristotle posited the signifier "anima," as the signifier that explains life, spirit, and thought of Being, at the same time that "anima" will appear as conflicted with Being. The question we will have to answer at each and every stage is therefore: What is the object from the position of which the analytical discourse can speak, and in relation to which psychoanalysis positions itself as the other side of philosophy? The other question that emerges in this context is: Why does psychoanalysis appear from this point of view as a separate discourse from the philosophical one, rather than as realizing the analyst's position in relation to the philosopher's?

Regarding this last question, it should be said that if psychoanalysis is the other of other discourses, as well as of philosophy, it cannot be a supplement or an addition to what is missing in the other discourse. To be the other side of the philosophical discourse means to point to a *relation* even if this relation cannot be defined in advance. To be the other side is equivalent to an act or a move that psychoanalysis performs in relation to philosophy, but being the other side of it, the psychoanalytical move cannot be a parallel or a separate move. That is, the second fundamental principle that emerges from Lacan's general propositions about philosophy is that Lacan uses it to clarify the structure, the logic, of the analytical discourse itself, as necessarily derived from what philosophy is. The other side of philosophy is not the site of an alternative, specific, and defined discursive world. Psychoanalysis is not a set of concepts (the unconscious, the drive, the repressed, transference) that applies to the dark area of language and human consciousness, while philosophy deals with the overt, bright side of thought. Lacan does not examine philosophy as a demarcated discursive world, and his move in reading philosophy is not a deconstructive one. Psychoanalysis itself also refuses the possibility of being a discursive world because in its practice it offers a lens through which one can look at logic, language, and any other scientific or contemplative practice without contradicting, refuting, or negating any of them. It never presents itself as an alternative, but neither does it turn the other discourse into an object of inquiry.

To further clarify this last point, let us look at another "diagnostic" quotation from the seminar "The Other Side of Psychoanalysis." Again, and not incidentally, the subject is truth:

> The transcendental I is what anyone who has stated knowledge in a certain way harbors as truth, the S_1, the I of the master. It is, very precisely, out of the I identical to itself that the S_1 of the pure imperative is constituted. It is, very precisely, in imperatives that the I is displayed, for they are always in the second person.
>
> The myth of the ideal I, of the I that masters, of the I whereby at least something is identical to itself, namely the speaker, is very precisely what the university discourse is unable to eliminate from the place in which its truth is found. From every academic statement by any philosophy whatsoever, even by a philosophy that strictly speaking could be pointed to as being the most opposed to philosophy, namely, if it were philosophy, Lacan's discourse – the I-cracy[19] emerges, irreducibly.
>
> Of course, no philosophy is ever reducible to this. For philosophers the question has been a lot more supple and pathetic. Remember what is in question, everyone acknowledges it more or less, and some of them, the most lucid, do so clearly – they want to save truth. This has taken one of them, good heavens, a long way – to the point where, like Wittgenstein, by making it the rule and the foundation of knowledge, there is nothing left to say, at least nothing that concerns truth as such, so as to refuse, to avoid, this rock. Surely the author has something close to the analyst's position, namely, that he eliminates himself completely from his own discourse.[20]

Philosophy is diagnosed as positioning the I as the foundation of discourse, an irreducible foundation. It is the I that appears as the speaker of the discourse and as the guarantor of knowledge: the I states knowledge while also appearing to master the utterance. From the psychoanalytical standpoint, such a structure is opposed to that of the imperative, because the imperative spoken by an "I" traps the speaker in an utterance in which he himself is not included, nor can the speaker control the consequences of the utterance. The split logic of the imperative manifests itself in the explicit or implicit use of the second person (Thou). One can say that the imperative denies the speaker knowledge and denies meaning from the one to whom the imperative applies. From the point of view of psychoanalysis, the imperative is connected to the object of absolute gratification, which can never be obtained but which leaves the subject always guilty, always lacking.[21] The subject is therefore the agent split by the imperative, while the I is the agent of the statement that seems to obscure the presence of such a split. Unlike the split subject assumed by the imperative, philosophical discourse is concerned with knowledge that is attainable, and is therefore centred on the I in which knowledge and Being overlap. As Lacan says in several places, the I that says "I think" or "I speak" and defines the position of the philosopher embodies the only place in the structure of the proposition that cannot be reduced or represented. I = I, with no remainder. In other words, the "I" of philosophy is someone who masters the gap between saying and being, who overcomes the division between the I who speaks and the I who thinks. The agent of philosophy's discourse is exempt from positing an "other" and is not split by his own utterance. "The truth speaks 'I'," says Lacan, because "I," as the one who masters speech, as the one who gives unity to the discourse, does not create a cut in language but rather, indivisibly and irreducibly, carries its truth.[22]

But as can be learned from Lacan's words, the "I" that acts as a master-signifier that stipulates and governs the discourse is merely a myth, an ideal that guarantees nothing. To believe that discourse can reduce itself to truth, one must posit an I identical to itself, and being identical to itself means that I is a signifier that carries no meaning or propositional content. This is the ideal and the illusion that every discourse that wishes to speak the truth relies on. But philosophy, unlike the "university discourse"[23] in general, is not content with having the I serve as an ideal that guarantees that truth will be spoken; rather, indeed and with full pathos, it wishes to speak the truth, wishes to rescue truth from the chains of the empty signifier. And when it fails to do so, it pushes someone like Wittgenstein to a place where it is no longer possible to say anything. This is the place where the philosopher, just like the analyst, completely abandons the discourse in order to allow truth to appear, unless it is someone like Wittgenstein, who no longer believes there is anything to say, certainly not anything that concerns the truth.

Psychoanalysis is the other side of philosophy although it too, even when it is Lacan's psychoanalysis, is trapped under the rule of the I. Psychoanalysis is the other side of philosophy although it too, albeit from a different position, wants to rescue truth. One can say that psychoanalysis is the other side of philosophy in the sense that for the psychoanalyst, the emptying of the I is not a desperate reason to eliminate himself from his discourse (since to begin with, the analyst should avoid appearing as the I of the analytical discourse[24]), but its acting reason. One can say that for the philosopher, the emptying of the I as an ideal of discursive mastery causes nostalgia or resignation, while for the psychoanalyst the emptying serves as the logical basis for determining the analyst's place – a place where in order to position himself as analyst he needs the philosophical belief about discourse and truth.

In the following chapters we will see how Lacan uses the philosophers by finding in their work the foundations of psychoanalytical thought. But once Lacan turns the philosopher into an analyst he positions himself as a philosopher; at this point he aims to return the philosopher to the point from which he is obliged to wonder about causes and purposes, as Badiou says, that is, to the point of recommitting to the philosophical task. Lacan's use of the philosophers is a psychoanalytical one, designed to extract from the philosopher a philosophical proposition in order to point to this proposition's affinity with the psychoanalytical truth. The analyst and the philosopher, it appears, constantly encounter each other, and this encounter seems immeasurably productive.

Chapter 2

The Love of Truth:
Lacan with Plato

In Seminar XVII, Lacan relates philosophy to the discourse of the master. Philosophy is portrayed as a practice dealing with "the theft, the abduction, the removal from the slave of his knowledge, through the operations of the Master."[1] How can we understand Lacan's radical description of the way philosophy realizes its desire for knowledge and truth by robbing the slave of his knowledge?

The key to understanding this relationship between the philosopher and the master can be found in Plato, and in the way Plato posits Socrates as someone who actualizes the position of the philosopher. For even if philosophy, in all the stages of its development, uses the master's methods to gain knowledge, in Socrates, the practice of stealing knowledge is established as a necessity that stems from the desire for truth. As we will see, Lacan posits Socrates – unlike Descartes, for example – as someone who desires knowledge, but not in order to appropriate this knowledge. Rather than wanting to appear as the owner of knowledge, Socrates seeks knowledge so that it will take him closer to the truth. It is this desire for knowledge that makes Socrates centre his philosophical practice on the act of extracting knowledge from the slave. Like the ancient master, even when Socrates purports to know something he does not appear as the owner of that knowledge, or as someone who is able to appropriate this knowledge, but at most as someone who can extract this knowledge from another, an other in whom knowledge is present without him knowing anything about it. Although Socrates is presented as someone who is supposed to know or who supposes himself to know, he only formulates this knowledge after having extracted it from the slave. The signs of this Socratic position can be found in the various dialogues written by Plato, and its essence, as Lacan shows, is revealed in the *Symposium*. Lacan reads the *Symposium* in order to expose the fundamental fact about the position of the Platonic philosopher: that in order to be said, truth requires desire and love, and that in order to be said, truth requires the position of someone who has no knowledge. Therefore Socrates's position is the position of someone who shows that love (or beauty, virtue, justice, eternity, or any other topic) can only be talked about from the point of not knowing – or, more precisely with regard to Socrates, from the position of someone who knows, but who knows that he must speak without assuming to himself knowledge.

When considering philosophy's relationship with knowledge, as it is presented by Lacan with regard to Plato, remember that in ancient times the slave did more than define an inferior social status; the slave was also the one with the know-how within the familial-communal structure. The slave's knowledge of how to work the land, his knowledge in the different crafts, was not given or formulated anywhere, but was inscribed in the body of the slave, who knows, without knowing anything about it, how to use this knowledge to do his job. It is knowledge unknown as such, but to the extent that there is knowledge it is found in the slave's possession, and it is by virtue of this knowledge and based on it that the master appears as master. The slave is not only the one who performs the various tasks, but also the one who informs the master what his enemies and friends say about him, who brings him news from other places and so on.

While the slave has knowledge, the master has no knowledge about the slave's work. We can say that the "master" can appear as such only due to *the slave's knowledge*; that the master could not be a master without the slave. Lacan even claims that for this reason the master has the structure of the unconscious itself. That is, the signifiers that constitute a master, such as the counting of crops or of other products of labour, come from the slave's unknown knowledge.

Yet it is the master who turns this knowledge into knowledge *for someone*, for a subject. It is the master who allows the slave's knowledge to be articulated, and it is the slave without whom the signifiers of knowledge could not appear. Thus the master, like the unconscious, can only appear as subject of a knowledge that cannot be known from the master's position, and it is that knowledge whose deployment, whose formulation, is dependent on the master's presence. The master is entirely dependent on and conditioned by his other, the slave, and the knowledge he carries. Only when the master raises himself to the level of knowledge, when knowledge appears in the master's place as knowledge the master possesses, will more and more absolute masters, previously unknown in history, appear. That is, this relationship between the slave's knowledge and the signifier of mastery will be disrupted, and we will encounter a different structure of knowledge. In this new structure the master assumes knowledge and also claims to possess it.

But to understand how this knowledge, which is only inscribed in the slave's body, can be extracted and even stolen, we must consider the master's position within the social relation called by Lacan the *master's discourse*. That is, if the philosopher is situated within the master's discourse, we should ask what derives from the master's place as an agent, as the cause of the discourse. *The master's discourse* is the fundamental discourse in which the dominant place, that of the agent, is occupied by S1 – the master's signifier – standing for the law or the principle that determines what will appear opposite the place of the master, under S2 – the signifier of knowledge. We already know that in the master's discourse it is knowledge, signified by Lacan as S2, that supports the master. In other words, the knowledge possessed by the slave, like anything located in the place of S2, constitutes the master's signifier as such, and thus we can see the relationship between S1 and S2 as a conditional relationship. What emerges from this structure of the master's discourse is that although the discourse is impossible without its agent – that is, the master – the master's signifier constitutes the possibility and the limits of knowledge without itself appearing as a signifier of knowledge, since it appears outside the place of knowledge. Thus it seems that the master's discourse highlights the fact that the agent cannot operate within the discourse without his other – in this case, without the function that possesses and employs knowledge in practice, even though this other who possesses knowledge lacks what it takes to turn this knowledge into an object of knowledge for himself.

At this point, having examined the master's and the slave's relationship with knowledge, we can see that there are two possible positions concerning the knowledge held by the other, that is, by the slave. One position leaves unarticulated knowledge in the hands of the slave, and leaves the master, the master of knowledge, in ignorance. The second position is revealed by the logic of this discourse, which points to a necessary movement between S1 and S2. The movement between these signifiers suggests a wish to formulate the knowledge possessed by the other in order to turn it into a knowledge that can be transmitted through speech or writing. But what can be the reason for the master's interest in articulating the slave's know-how? One reason might be the wish to gain control over the fruits of the slave's labour; another might be the wish to attain theoretical knowledge that is not dependent on any particular subject. That is, the Socratic master sets his eyes on what lies beyond the slave's knowledge as the object of his striving, a striving that leads to the articulation of the unarticulated knowledge possessed by the slave, so that it receives an epistemic status, the status of an object of cognition.

Thus, the master-philosopher moves towards the slave's knowledge so that extracting this knowledge will serve him in his pursuit of truth. Plato himself is concerned in the different dialogues with the relationship between knowledge of apparent things, knowledge that constitutes the realm of opinion (*doxa*) (held by Socrates's various interlocutors), and knowledge that serves the philosopher in his pursuit of the truth. The question that arises is where the Socratic knowledge (*episteme*) is located in relation to the knowledge of visible things or to conjectural knowledge. Or, in Lacan's terms, how does the status of the slave's know-how change when it becomes knowledge formulated by the philosopher? This is where we should define the distinct position of the Socratic philosopher, for whom placing himself in relation to the knowledge of the other (the slave) is necessary for this knowledge to become transmissible. When knowledge is extracted from the slave, it is still opinion (*doxa*), and in its transition from the subject (slave) to the philosopher (master), it is formulated as knowledge, that is, as *episteme*. The removal of knowledge from the slave is therefore a necessary condition for this knowledge to become real knowledge (*episteme* rather than *doxa*), and for that purpose the master must acknowledge the knowledge held by the slave.

What distinguishes Socrates as a master-philosopher is what happens to knowledge once he has succeeded in generating its necessary movement. Lacan claims that at least in some of Plato's dialogues this movement of transmission does not produce theoretical knowledge in the strict sense of the word – that is, it does not create a knowledge independent of a subject. Virtue, justice, Eros, the soul, self-knowledge, or any topic that the dialogues deal with, is extracted from the twilight realm of opinion, but not in order to be formulated as theoretical knowledge in the sense we know from the later history of thought. Philosophy would have to go some way before knowledge appeared as the agent of discourse rather than its object or purpose. But even within the limits of what we can call the master's discourse – that is, even before knowledge itself is turned into an agent (in the discourse that Lacan calls the university discourse)[2] – the master-philosopher appears as different from the masterful master. In contrast to the Hegelian master, who wishes to steal from the slave in order to appropriate the fruits of his labour, the Socratic master wishes to steal from the slave so that the slave's knowledge can become transmissible knowledge, and therefore a necessary link on the way to truth. In the latter case, the knowledge extracted from the slave and formulated by the philosopher is not assimilated as the master's knowledge. The master does not inscribe this knowledge in order to turn it into a practical product or to appear as its owner; rather, he uses it to know the Ideas. Hence the knowledge that is transmitted between the slave and Socrates must undergo a transformation in order to become the master's knowledge, but this change does not result in the master taking the slave's place or vice versa. The status of the knowledge is changed, but that knowledge is still subject to the exchange between the slave and the master, and in the dialogic process the knowledge extracted from the slave never reaches full epistemization.

The Socrates of the *Symposium* thus appears as having no know-how of love (Socrates *ne sait pas faire*), and what he knows about love is obscured by the myths told to him by Diotima. That is, the truth about love remains trapped in what Socrates knows but does not say, and in the act of love that Socrates knows about but cannot (or refuses to) perform.

Here we can formulate the third point that emerges from Lacan's analysis of the Socratic discourse as a master's discourse: the master's desire for knowledge and his wish to make that knowledge transmissible do not mean that any objective, independent knowledge is produced in the Platonic dialogue. That is, the philosopher, as opposed to the scientist born with Descartes and the hysteric born with Hegel, is subject to the master's knowledge because his desire is not a desire *to know* but a desire *for knowledge*; indeed, the philosopher's position does not produce a knowledge that belongs to someone but a knowledge that is *for* someone (as we will see, the Platonic philosopher is not a subject who resists the signifier's split or seeks to suture it, but precisely the one who exposes this split and therefore cannot possess knowledge). But neither can the Socratic philosopher adopt a knowledge that has been stripped of any subjective position (as would happen only with Descartes). The Socratic philosopher's desire for knowledge does not produce knowledge (the Socratic philosopher aspires to knowledge

but, unlike the hysteric, does not lead to knowledge), nor does that
desire generate knowledge for a certain subject (the Socratic philosopher claims knowledge but never appears as possessing knowledge).

This is what Plato's dialogues teach us, says Lacan. When in *Menon*
mathematical knowledge is extracted from the slave by means of the
master's questions, the ridicule directed at the figure who is disarmed
of the knowledge he carries enables Lacan to show that we are indeed
dealing with the serious matter of "robbing the slave of his function at
the level of knowledge";[3] but only when, denying knowledge that is
acquired improperly, someone (Descartes) extracted for the first time
the function of the subject from the relationship between S1 and S2,
would science, in the sense of theoretical knowledge, appear. Only
when something else, outside the subject, appeared as responsible for
the regularity of knowledge, would knowledge become what is considered scientific knowledge.

With the Socratic philosopher we are not there yet, and therefore the
knowledge that Socrates extracts never appears as knowledge from/
of the subject. If the philosopher is the master who wishes to make
knowledge transmissible and therefore extracts it from the slave by
force, cunning, or ridicule, then he does so not as a subject who wishes
to assimilate this knowledge, but as someone who is responsible for
generating the movement between one signifier and another. The role
of the philosopher is to make knowledge move so that the know-how
possessed by the other is relocated to the place where it becomes possible to formulate knowledge about the reality of Ideas. Rather than as a
subject, therefore, the philosopher appears as someone whose role is to
lead knowledge from the place where it is inscribed in the slave's body
to the place where it becomes transmissible. The philosopher's role in
relation to knowledge is connected to the fact that for knowledge to be
transmissible, a philosophical act is required on the part of the one who
knows what this knowledge is designed to discover – the truth. In other
words, the Socratic philosopher is not a subject who determines knowledge and possesses it, but rather someone who operates in the field of
knowledge and who enables knowledge to move.

It seems this is also the Socratic philosopher to whom Lacan refers
in "L'Etourdit," when he talks about the "notsofoolish [*passifou*]" philosopher, who "plays all the better the air of the half-said in that he can
do so with a good conscience. He is entertained to say the truth: like
the fool he knows that it is quite doable, on condition that he does not
suture (*Sutor* ...) beyond his soleness [*semellité*]."[4] Is this not a summary

of what we have seen so far? The soleness, the place where the philosopher's soles stand, is the place where the desire for truth meets the recognition that truth can only be half-said, that the love of truth leaves what does not and cannot fall within the borders of the said as constitutive of truth itself. The not so foolish philosopher is someone who, on the way to articulating the truth, recognizes that he can never articulate this truth as knowledge – that is, truth cannot reside completely within the domain of what the philosopher knows. Knowledge of the truth, like any knowledge, only half-says the truth because knowledge cannot be extracted from the philosopher's position. Although knowledge does not belong to the subject, it is *for* the subject and is therefore not fully universalized. Knowledge of the truth is *for* the philosopher as much as knowledge of how to guard is *for* the guardians in the ideal state and knowledge of love is *for* the lover.

While knowledge is always *for* a subject, the truth has no subject. The truth cannot be *known* because knowledge cannot be stripped from its use. Once truth is articulated as knowledge, knowledge is distanced from the truth it aims at. Consequently, the master-philosopher does not possess the knowledge of the truth, for his role consists solely in allowing the subject's knowledge to appear. Lacan can therefore claim that *the Other knows only insofar as he is not a subject*. Knowledge can be supposed to the Other as long as he is not a subject, and this is precisely the position of the *notsofoolish* philosopher: while causing the appearance of knowledge, he is also other to the knowledge thus appearing because he knows he will never appear as the subject who carries this knowledge. Indeed, when the master is replaced by the subject of science, he will be split in a different way than the split we find in Socrates. In Descartes we find a subject who supposes a momentary lack of knowledge, only to suture himself later with clear and distinct knowledge that is equal to the knowledge, free of limitation, assigned to God. In Socrates we find someone who is attributed with knowledge (because of his desire for truth, because he enables the transition from the slave's know-how to the possibility of knowledge), but who refuses to take on the position of the one who knows. That is, the split here is between the presence of knowledge for a subject and the possibility of formulating this knowledge as truth. The philosopher wishes to articulate a knowledge that he cannot possess and that he does not wish to be identified with.

We can already see, at this point of departure regarding the philosopher as master, that Lacan wishes to define a position that derives from the Socratic desire for truth and the wish to extract the truth from opinion and belief, and bring it into the realm of knowledge as the distinct position of the "notsofoolish philosopher." We can conclude at this point that Lacan meets Plato where Plato outlines a certain way of placing oneself in relation to knowledge, a way that Lacan identifies as necessary for understanding also the position of the analyst. But with regard to the relationship between the philosopher and knowledge, Plato formulates something else that is typical of both the philosophical context and the analyst's position. Both the Socratic philosopher and the analyst are not subjects of knowledge, although their starting point is that of a subject who presents himself as possessing knowledge. Both the philosopher and the analyst do not possess knowledge but wish to extract knowledge so that it serves their purpose, a purpose that is none other than truth itself. Particularly given that this truth can never be said as such. Lacan reads the *Symposium* in such a way that through this radical reading, the analyst can learn from the philosopher something fundamental about his required position in relation to knowledge: the philosopher's knowledge is a knowledge of signifiers, of the signifiers of cognition that capture and recognize "the nature of being," and as such it is subject to the inevitable distance between the signifier of knowledge and truth, a distance whose measure Lacan indicates through his reading of Plato. The analyst can learn from Plato that knowledge is not knowledge owned by a subject, and that knowledge has a troubled relationship with truth, but in order for this lesson to be properly learned from Plato, we need the psychoanalytical lesson of how to read Plato properly. Lacan thus considers Socrates in utmost seriousness to be the first analyst. But even if this is merely a metaphor or another rhetorical device, in order for us to see Socrates as an analyst, we must read Plato with utter seriousness and love, that is, without supposing any prior knowledge.

The *Symposium*, as a speech about love, suggests that the truth about love is a product of the discourse rather than anything *a priori*. However, Plato, and not only in the *Symposium*, indicates that the truth that is created by the discourse is only partial. The truth about love in the *Symposium* turns out to be the hole the discourse creates as it is being unfolded before the reader/listener. That is, the Socratic truth necessarily appears by transmitting a discourse that truth necessarily perforates. Lacan calls this discursive structure, a structure imposed by the discordance between language and truth, "macaroni discourse," referring to the hole in the macaroni tube that – rather than what surrounds it – is what we eat. In the *Symposium* we also realize that the discourse about love is designed only to teach us that without desire or love, truth will not appear. The twists and turns of the *Symposium* are therefore meant to demonstrate the nature of love, which is the love not of the whole but of the part, which is born of lack rather than fullness, which concerns the cause rather than the effect – the love that relates to truth and that enables the possibility of knowing. In other words, we must learn, through psychoanalysis, what is the Socratic love of truth, so that it becomes possible, based on what this love implies, to know why love is necessary for psychoanalysis. In addition we must learn, through psychoanalysis, what the purpose is of the Socratic quest for knowledge, so that it becomes possible, based on what this knowledge implies, to know how knowledge should be employed within analysis. Thus, what emerges from the *Symposium*, and is connected to what conditions the birth of love and causes the appearance of desire, is turned in Lacan's hands into a lesson about the analyst's desire. Lacan performs a Lacanian reading of the *Symposium* in order to extract the position required of the analyst, the analyst who appears here as equal to the philosopher. This position was already known to Socrates but requires the analyst to bring it to light.

In order to trace the outlines of this reading, we will examine three crucial topics in the context of this dialogue and of Lacan's related seminar: the relationship between knowledge and truth, the essence of love, and the relationship between Socrates's position and the tragic hero.

A. Knowledge, Opinion, and Truth

Socrates professed "to understand nothing but matters of love."[5] However, while he claims to know about love, he does not love, or at least his position as a lover (of Alcibiades and Agathon) remains the conjecture of the dialogue's other participants rather than something he declares. In this sense, understanding matters of love is unrelated to the possibility of partaking in love. Socrates, who according to Alcibiades behaves as if he is in love with all the beautiful boys, ill-treats them so that "beginning as their lover he has ended by making them pay their addresses to him."[6] That is, Socrates is not really involved in matters of love, but he knows how to elicit love. What, then, does Socrates understand that allows him to make others fall in love with him?

In Alcibiades's words of praise, Socrates is presented as someone whose speech and appearance are deceiving: Socrates's words sound ridiculous at first, and outwardly he is as ugly as the Satyr. But whoever listens to his words will find that "they are divine"[7] and that Socrates's interior is divine, made of gold and utterly beautiful. That is, it seems that Socrates's understanding in matters of love concerns his ability to make others see in him something that does not concern his appearance or his external attributes, and that elicits love. Lacan will claim that rather than relating falling in love with Socrates to an internal quality, Alcibiades's speech relates it to the presence of an indefinite thing whose very existence is denied by Socrates. For Socrates reacts to being loved by rejecting this love as unjustified: he views himself as someone underserving of love, undeserving of being the wanted one: the *eromenos*. Lacan will show that Socrates's understanding in matters of love is bound up with that essential yet unexplained quality that makes people fall in love with him – or, more precisely, it is bound up with his ability to present himself as a shell enveloping something that is hidden inside; and that whoever loves Socrates sees this hidden thing and desires it. Alcibiades thinks that if he yielded to Socrates's advances he would have the opportunity of "hearing him tell what he knew";[8] yet in this dialogue, what Socrates knows never takes the form of real knowledge, let alone knowledge transmitted through speech from one person to another.

The *Symposium*, Lacan claims, is a dialogue that establishes the Socratic position towards knowledge while undermining its foundations. This undermining of the Socratic position is related to the fact that the discourse about love, which seeks to answer the question what is love, revolves around a topic that cannot become *episteme*, that is, is not knowable. For Lacan, the *Symposium* represents a kind of Platonic laboratory that examines the fundamental place in which the Socratic philosopher situates himself: he is committed to truth, a commitment that is mentioned several times in this text, yet he finds himself engaged in a discourse that constructs truth as unknowable. That is, since the *Symposium* touches on the truth about love without this truth being attained through knowledge, the question that arises concerns Socrates's position in the context in which knowing does not appear as a condition for truth. Lacan claims that in the *Symposium* truth is not knowable, and the rupture between knowledge and truth is posited in all its gravity precisely because this dialogue admits a philosophical discourse in which there is no transformation of opinion (*doxa*) into knowledge (*episteme*). *Symposium* offers a real answer to the question of love, in Diotima's words and in Alcibiades's actions, but this truth does not amount to knowing or knowability of love. Diotima guides

Socrates in matters of love, and at the end of the conversation with her, Socrates *believes her*. That is, in the place where we find the culmination of the participants' discussion about love, we are obliged to recognize that the discourse about love is a discourse located in an intermediate zone between knowledge and ignorance, just as the god of love himself is situated between the divine and the human, the beautiful and the ugly, poverty and plenty. It is a dialogue in which truth, at most, takes the form of right opinion but eludes the possibility of knowledge. Lacan will say at a later point in his teaching that right opinion is the only one that can be taught, because it captures the act of saying in what is said.[9] That is, right opinion does not allow one to extract or strip the sense of what is said from the way it is said (and therefore it is faithful to the subject's place in language), and the truth about love cannot be transmitted without the subject who talks about it being captured in this truth.

Lacan notes that because love does not allow the passage from opinion to knowledge, the floor is handed over to Diotima; the dialogue then ends with the scene of Alcibiades's intervention. Something else is needed in addition to Diotima's speech for the truth about love to turn into knowledge, and such knowledge becomes possible only thanks to Alcibiades's arrival on the scene, and not because Socrates is able to expand on his knowledge about love. Thus, as we will see in the next subsection, Lacan's reading of Plato emphasizes the centrality of Alcibiades's outburst, and it shows how the truth about love is constructed far from the attempt to construct a discourse about love. The words of the speakers in the *Symposium* not only provide the setting for the really important speech in the series – the one handed over to Diotima – but also serve as stages in the process of extracting knowledge of love that never reaches the stage of becoming articulated knowledge.

But what is it that hinders knowledge? Why, in a dialogue dedicated to clarifying the concept of love, do we only reach the threshold of knowledge about this subject matter? In an essay he wrote about Lacan and Plato, Alain Badiou suggests that Lacan does not believe that Plato – and not only in the *Symposium* – believes in the possibility of some worldly being taking part in the atemporal essence of ideas. Badiou agrees that this lure (*leurre*) of participating in the pure world of ideas is rejected by Plato himself, and he claims that this is what makes Plato Lacanian in Lacan's eyes.[10] That is, Plato and Lacan both fundamentally preclude the possibility of knowing the truth. Nevertheless, this Platonic position in itself does not explain the essence of the obstacle that the Socratic method of extracting knowledge from mere opinion faces in the *Symposium*. To explain this we need to look into Socrates's position towards knowledge as it emerges from the *Symposium*, as this position points to an affinity between Socrates and the analyst.

Indeed, in his essay "L'Etourdit," Lacan says that in the *Menon* dialogue Plato is already trying to extract right opinion in a way that can be transmitted and taught, and that what is transmissible is not necessarily understandable, meaningful, or provable. Lacan claims that the Platonic wish is to formulate right opinion as *matheme* (i.e., through a formal representation of the relations between the subject and the object of knowledge/desire); this amounts to him saying that the transmissible formulation always misses the relations among the saying, the one who says, and the said. That is, the wish to convey knowledge reveals that what prevents the (mathematical) transmission of knowledge is the fact that the speaker cannot free himself from the shackles of the saying (*le dire*), from the reality of language, which intervenes in what is said. The place of this missed encounter between being on the one hand, and the possibility of knowing the truth on the other, is occupied by the *matheme*, claims Badiou, because the *matheme* "empties out all the scraps and conveys that which in experience touches the un-known of a truth ... the void is what separates truth and knowledge."[11]

The analyst is the only one who is exempt from what no other discourse liberates from – from the idea that language is an organ of thought and can be used to convey knowledge: "The analyst can be saved from this since his very discourse rejects him, shedding light on him as the waste of language."[12] This position, postulated in regard to the analyst, also applies to the Socrates of the *Symposium*, because the opinion expressed in this dialogue does not bind Socrates as a subject of the discourse, as someone who is chained to language and identified with its discursive structure. Clarifying this Socratic position will therefore shed light on the point of encounter between the analyst and the Socratic philosopher.

Lacan's words suggest that language always remains foreign to those who are located in the psychoanalytical discourse – a seemingly astonishing claim, since it is precisely in analysis that one's dependence on language is total (the analyst and the patient are totally dependent on each other's words). But there is something else in this claim: the analyst is exempt from the possibility of seeing truth as a reality immanent to language; he is located to begin with where truth and language do not coincide. For the analyst, as well as for Socrates, being rejected by language means not only that they are not inscribed in it as subjects, but also that they appear as the refuse that has been cast out of language. The analyst and the Socratic philosopher appear with language in order to point to the impossible relationship between language and truth, to the philosopher's/analyst's rejectedness from language as a condition for the appearance of truth. The analyst who has nothing but language appears as the foreign element that is rejected from it, and it is precisely this positioning that allows truth to appear.

Through the concept of transference, psychoanalysis expresses this distance between the analytical discourse and the images it provides for the analyst and the analysand on the one hand, and for the object rejected by the discourse and embodied by the analyst himself on the other. Transference is therefore linked to the real structure of language, that is, to what is encountered where language does not provide a convenient shelter, where a dialogue is not possible, where the discourse is not given to interpretation and does not offer means for mutual understanding. The analytical legacy associated with this sense of the transference relations is connected by Lacan to Socrates, and especially to Socrates as he is revealed in the *Symposium*.

In the *Symposium*, the truth about Eros is transmitted through Diotima's speech. This speech illustrates the basic tenet of the Socratic speech about love: that without the subtraction from language of the subject who claims to know (i.e., without the subtraction of Socrates who gives the floor to Diotima), we cannot know the truth about love. In the next subsection I will examine how this subtraction takes place, but at this stage we are concerned with the question of what love and the knowledge of love are in relation to the discourse on love. This relation embodies what psychoanalysis calls transference.

Diotima herself displays an authoritative position towards knowledge, so much so that Plato himself says she is "an accomplished sophist."[13] Diotima's name is linked to the theme that Lacan repeatedly underscores throughout his analysis of the *Symposium*: *dioecisme* in Greek means to split, the same division that appears in Aristophanes's speech in connection to the split of the round entity. The motif of the split reappears or is perpetuated through Diotima's speech, which situates Eros at the intersection of two sets, where he should be seen as neither a whole nor a part nor a distinct value ascribed to a certain category (e.g., the beautiful or the good). Eros is located between two worlds and is sectioned off from both, and this location can only be narrated through myth. Lacan uses Diotima's characterization to say that only from this position – that of the split off and the reliance on myth – can

erotic desire (for beauty, for instance) be characterized as "a relationship with something which concerns *not having*, not anything which
can be possessed, *but being*, and being properly speaking in so far as it
is that of the mortal being."[14] Indeed, Diotima describes the vicissitudes
of love as a quest for what always appears in its partial embodiment.
Thus the lover moves from the beauty he finds in the beautiful body of
the beloved, to the desire for the beautiful pursuits and the beautiful sciences, and eventually to the desire to know beauty itself. Diotima connects the love of the beautiful, which proceeds from the concrete realm
of visible things to the abstract realm of ideas, to eternity. Through the
love of the beautiful, mortal being perpetuates itself through generation, which leads to destruction and again to birth in what is not subject
to mortality. Beauty, says Diotima, allows the mortal to aspire to immortality, to that which exceeds life itself.

Thus, according to Lacan's analysis, Diotima's speech ties together
the two points that are crucial to the inquiry about love: love is born in
lack, and the discourse about love is the necessary actualization of this
lack. How do these points become tied together in Diotima's speech?
This speech suggests that to explain what love is, you cannot simply
say something that will be seen as a truth about it. Truth cannot be said
and is therefore said through a (mythical) image that captures some of
the reality of this truth. What myth reveals is the crucial place that lack
has in eliciting love. In order to explain why the description of Eros as
desire demands that we posit lack as the basis of desire, Diotima turns
to the myth related to Eros's birth, the myth about Poverty and Plenty
from whom Eros was born. In the mythological story about Poverty and
Plenty, Poverty – Aporia – shows up at the feast of the gods, but is not
noticed by anyone because she has no assets that would earn her a place
at the gods' table. And when Plenty (Poros) falls asleep and is oblivi-
ous, "poverty, considering her own straitened circumstances, plotted to
have a child by him, and accordingly she lay down at his side and con-
ceived Eros."[15] This is how the moment that precedes love is described,
says Lacan – the moment in which poverty has nothing to offer, she is
resourceless – and it is precisely this moment that is the condition for
the appearance of love. Just as, when Alcibiades is with Socrates, he
discovers that all the qualities he thought made him a beloved object
(his wealth, beauty, youth, brains) are worthless in Socrates's eyes and
mean nothing to him. Only then, when Alcibiades appears as an empty
vessel, unable to say what it is that makes Socrates love him – that is,
when he appears stripped of his assets – is love awakened in him.

In Agathon's speech, the tragedian's speech, Agathon praises love while insinuating that love disrupts the harmony and involves destruction and disaster (fiasco). Thus, love is born in poverty and lack, as Diotima shows, and its nature is failure, as the comic element in Agathon's seemingly tragic speech reveals. Socrates, who connected truth with speech, produces lack and destruction as the condition for articulating the act of love, an articulation that will appear through Alcibiades's act at the end of the dialogue – his bursting onto the scene. After praising love, Agathon fails to answer the question of what it is that Eros desires if he is essentially whole and perfect. The starting point for any knowledge of the truth about love must lie in the dimension of lack, which permeates the words of all the speakers but takes on a growing reality as we approach the last speaker. And when Agathon appears and his words allude to the catastrophe in love, at the end of his speech we can already note that Eros is necessarily the love of the things he lacks.

As already mentioned, the one responsible for this revelation about love in the symposium is Diotima: her speech reveals the necessity of lack in myth: myth is a discourse that describes the moment of creation, the cause of things, as a moment of subtraction. Through the use of myth, Diotima points to the inability of discourse to capture what has been subtracted. Beauty, for example, which at first appeared as an external attribute of the beloved, is subtracted from the field of vision and is eventually displaced into the realm of ideas. Beauty thus remains impossible to know fully – it merely perpetuates itself as the object of the quest for knowledge.

In order to understand what the fact that love is born of lack means for the possibility of knowing what love is, let us return to Diotima's words about the vicissitudes of that thing called "beauty," which, displaced from sphere to sphere, perpetuates man's being in immortality. "What she [Diotima] introduces is the following, that this beauty has a relationship with something which concerns not having, not anything which can be possessed, but being, and being properly speaking in so far as it is that of the mortal being. What is proper to a mortal being is that he perpetuates himself by generation."[16] Although what is perpetuated in the alternations between generation, death, and regeneration has no permanence, something nonetheless recognizes itself, reaffirms itself through these alternations. The permanence of that thing that perpetuates itself is what is ejected from the discourse and displaced onto the next object. That is, Diotima shows that love is not love *for* the beautiful but love *of* the beautiful, of what is subtracted each time and sends man to superior object. Since Eros lacks the good and the beautiful (for otherwise it would not desire them), what results from love is the deferment, the endless suspension of the thing that is desired, a suspension that Diotima calls the everlasting.

The permanent deferment of the object of knowledge is highlighted at the point where Socrates, the founder of a discourse through which truth is supposed to appear, passes the thread of the conversation to Diotima. It is a point at which Socrates seems as stupid as his usual interlocutors, as his question "Is love then evil and foul?" is thrown back at him. This point, Lacan says, is the end result of the method that relies on more or less, yes and no, presence or absence – on everything that adheres to the law of the signifier (what is not beautiful is foul, what is not present is absent). The law of the signifier is what governs the usual course of the Socratic inquiry, revealing the inconsistencies of his interlocutors. But here, faced with the Socratic question that clings to the signifier (if we said that Eros desires what he lacks and if Eros desires the beautiful, does that not mean that Eros is foul?), Diotima answers: "Hush!" That is, in relation to love, the logic of the signifier stops being relevant, and the Socratic method that contests the signifier's consistency in order to replace opinion with knowledge is similarly removed from the stage. Lacan's claim is that the truth about Eros is not a truth that can be reached through the dialectic of the signifier. The truth about love requires something other than the Socratic method in order to be transmitted. Speaking about love requires myth and obliges us to speak from a place that does not posit knowledge as attainable.

Love, like Socrates himself, is demonic – it does not consistently distinguish between the lover and the beloved, the empty and the full, the mortal and the immortal. This is because love is based on a different logic, one that ties the lover and the beloved together in an asymmetrical but necessary reciprocity whose cause is impossible to formulate. Just as the presence of a father means there is someone who is this father's son, so the presence of the lover means there is someone who is loved. With respect to this necessity of love, Socrates and the law of the signifier cease to be relevant (Eros is loved neither for his beauty nor for his foulness, nor for any other attribute surrounding love) and are replaced by a "macaroni" discourse: that is, a discourse that incorporates its own perforation without this perforation being suturable. Diotima's speech has paved the way for establishing the relations among discourse, truth, and the knowledge of love, and has shown us that from poverty's lack, from Socrates's ignorance, and from the split of the speech that supposes knowledge – from all of these the truth about love will be able to appear.

B. Loving with What Is Lacking

If the discourse about love rests on different foundations than those of the signifier's consistency, it is because there is no way of explaining or justifying through signifiers of love what binds the lover to the beloved and vice versa. The nucleus of the riddle of love touches on the awakening of love in the beloved as a result of the lover's love. This is the enigmatic side of love, which is unknowable and can only be expressed through a formula that posits a relation of conversion between the lover and the beloved, and thus reveals something about where the meaning of love lies. Lacan claims that the scene with Alcibiades illustrates the metaphor of love by embodying, through something that borders on myth, the turning of the beloved into a lover. And this is the image Lacan uses:

> This hand which stretches towards the fruit, towards the rose, towards the log which suddenly bursts into flame, first of all to tell you that its gesture of reaching, of poking, is closely linked to the maturation of the fruit, to the beauty of the flower, to the flaming of the log, but that, when in this movement of reaching, of drawing, of poking, the hand has gone far enough towards the object, if from the fruit, from the flower, from the log, a hand emerges which stretches out to encounter your hand, and that at that moment it is your hand which is fixed in the closed fullness of the fruit, the open fullness of the flower ... what is produced at that point is love![17]

This is the enigma of love, illustrated through the hand that miraculously responds to the lover's call, an enigma that can only be described through the metaphor of converting the *eromenos* into the *erastes*: the beloved into the lover. And these are the points that emerge from the scene with Alcibiades, and that represent the elements in the metaphor of love, a metaphor that is merely the formula for transmitting knowledge about love: first, that in love something is transmitted that is not an object of exchange; second, that love is born of lack; third, that love appears in the subject when he (or she) locates in the beloved the object for which he is himself loved, thus turning the other into the one who elicits love. And fourth, that in the act of love, in turning the beloved into a lover, the indifferent object (subject to a relationship of exchange) turns into an object of absolute difference. All of these components characterize the way love operates, and the only way to express them is through a formula (*matheme*) that will show the subtraction that necessarily takes place when someone is located as a beloved, and the dislocation of the object for which someone is loved onto the unknown, agalmatic object that takes its place in the lover and turns him into a beloved.

Alcibiades in Plato's dialogue is already an aging man, bearing only traces of his great beauty and famous exploits, and his words recall his younger years, when with all his beauty and assets he still failed to win Socrates's heart. Love knows nothing of beauty or virtue, and Socrates, who lacks physical beauty, is loved to total distraction by the lover. Socrates is therefore an embodiment of the demon Eros, who was described by Diotima as someone who cannot be described in terms of possessing or lacking beauty. Eros, like Socrates, carries something else for which he elicits desire, and the description of his beauty or foulness will not get us any nearer to knowing the cause of love. "Alcibiades, my friend … truly you must see in me some rare beauty of a kind infinitely higher than any which I see in you. And therefore, if you mean to share with me and to exchange beauty for beauty, you will have greatly the advantage of me; you will gain true beauty in return for appearance … But look again, sweet friend, and see whether you are not deceived in me."[18] These words merely bring into focus the folly of attempting to think about the awakening of desire around an object of exchange or appropriation. They also bring into focus the fact that the object that makes one love is impossible to characterize or know.

Note, however, that once its false partialness has been revealed, beauty is not taken out of the equation. As the above quotation shows, Socrates possesses beauty as well – the beauty attributed to the *agalma*, which is hidden inside a deceptive shell. Socrates's beauty is linked to the divine that lies behind the demonic and ridiculous façade, to the thing that makes Alcibiades desire to be in Socrates's company. That is, beauty appears as a cause of love in Alcibiades's speech as well. The impossibility of saying what it is that turns the beloved into a lover does not mean that the cause of loving is a mirage or a delusion; on the contrary, the *agalma* and the beauty that is persistently attributed to it point to the real status of the object that serves as the cause of love, indicating that love is not imaginary and is not a form of illusory attribution to the other. The *agalma* points to the place in the other, in the lover, where the subject is suspended and the object, the thing, speaks in its place. That is, the *agalma* is outside the law of the signifier (it has no symbolic status) and outside what the other can know or recognize, but it is identified with a cause that cannot be embodied in any other way. The *agalma* is the cause it is impossible to perceive, define, or know, but we must not err in thinking that anyone can carry an *agalma* for the lover. The other is not a container for the cause of the subject's love; rather, the *agalma* he carries has to somehow embody the uniqueness, the irreducibility of the love encounter.

Lacan describes the object that serves as the cause of the lover's love as *agalma*, that is, a treasure, a precious and hidden object; but the image of the *agalma* still fails to encapsulate the real weight the *agalma* carries, because the *agalma* is an undefined, indescribable object that serves as the cause of love.

Lacan says that the Greek gods could reveal themselves to humans only in the *agalma* as what breaks all the laws, as an embodiment of the essence that remains completely hidden and is not subject to any law. Because it is exposed and hidden at the same time, the *agalma* can appear as only partial but also as the complete embodiment of the cause of love. It is partial because it does not reveal the essence of the thing that holds it; yet it is complete because it points to what turns this thing into the object of desire. The *agalma* carries what is unique in the object of desire and hence is the cause that turns this object into what it is. The *agalma* serves as a partial embodiment of the purpose of desire itself, and this purpose, as opposed to its partial embodiment, takes on the absolute uniqueness of the one who carries it.

This means that Lacan uses the Socratic *agalma* to explain the way in which the object changes its status from an object of exchange into the object called *objet a*. For Diotima, beauty appeared in various objects (the beautiful body, the soul, science, etc.), thus making these objects meaningless vehicles on the way to ideal beauty. Beauty, whoever and whatever carries it, takes us closer to the knowledge of ideas. This is what we learned from Diotima. But Alcibiades teaches us that the uniqueness of the loved one is identified with a partial object, the object that causes the advent of love, and this object is the only place in which beauty can reside. Hence one can find completeness in this partial cause, and in the transition from the partial to the complete the object of desire is revealed as a unique object that exists only for the lover. "In a word, if this object impassions you it is because within, hidden in it there is the object of desire, *agalma* ... and in so far as this privileged object of desire is something which, for each person, culminates at this frontier, at this limiting point which I have taught you to consider as the metonymy of the unconscious discourse where it plays a role that I tried to formalise – in the phantasy."[19] The *agalma*, the thing located in the other, that submits and responds to that lack in the lover, is presented as an undefined object identified with the unconscious, with the phantasy that is unique to the subject. This is Lacan's formulation of the logic of love as it is revealed in Socrates. In that formulation, he uses Plato to clarify the relationship between the *indifferent object* and the *particular object*: it is precisely the former that can be defined and conceptualized; the latter is located outside the limits of knowledge yet is necessary in order to come to terms with *eros*.

Loving with what is absent, the formulation of the way love occurs, of the cause of its appearance, becomes possible with Alcibiades's speech. Love arises when what the lover lacks he finds in the beloved (when from the start the lack appears as an undefined lack that concerns what the beloved is for the other/lover, and when what is found in the beloved is *agalma*, that is, a shell enveloping something secret and indemonstrable). Lacan claims, following Plato, that precisely because the dialectic of the signifier is irrelevant for the lovers' discourse or for formulating the truth about love, love elicits the fundamental question of what is the thing that elicits it – who is the one who can be loved and who is the one who can love.

In analysis, the analyst's position elicits love in the patient, but while it is impossible to ascribe this love to the analyst's personal attributes, this does not make transferential love less serious or real. Transference love is love in the full sense of the word, as Freud showed,[20] and therefore should not be dismissed or rejected. Transference relations give rise to a love that is impossible to interpret or explain, and in this sense transference love is no different from what takes place in love in general. Thus in the *Symposium* we find that the love of the lover awakens the miraculous and initially incomprehensible process in which something in the beloved responds to the demand of the lover, without it being possible to say what this thing is. Love is awakened in Alcibiades, who believes himself loved by Socrates. Love is awakened once Alcibiades locates in Socrates the answer to the question of what makes him, Alcibiades, worthy of love. At this moment, the demand to be loved, just like the hand stretched towards the fruit, receives a response from the other side, and a hand is stretched out to meet the lover's hand. The *agalma* of Socrates, the secret he holds of the cause of love, elicits love in Alcibiades just as the knowledge assumed by the analyst of the subject's desire elicits love in the subject. The subject responds with love to the demand assumed when knowledge is located in the other (the analyst).

C. Dying with/for the Object

In order to grasp the proximity of Socrates's position to that of the analyst, we must concern ourselves with death. In the *Symposium*, death comes up in relation to the mirage of beauty, which, while consistently receding away from man (and being displaced from one object to another), also points him towards eternity. Thus Diotima refers to beauty as that which allows the subject to veil its mortality. Rather than aspiring to attain beautiful things *per se*, Eros aspires to generation and procreation "because to the mortal creature, generation is a sort of eternity and immortality."[21] Man can generate only in the beautiful, and this generation is an expression of the desire for beauty as an eternal idea.

Lacan connects this idea of beauty as a veiling of mortality to his suggestion, in the seminar on the ethics of psychoanalysis, that beauty serves as a barrier, an endpoint that veils what is not subject to the symbolic law. Beauty is not an attribute, a concept, or a value, but is the embodiment of what cannot be signified. Beauty is the last line before what Lacan called the zone *between two deaths*, which is the realm beyond the passing of time and the moment of the individual's extinction; beauty assures man's perpetuation, his continuation as a species and as a being. This is also the beauty that, according to Lacan, appears in the *Symposium*: beauty appears in Diotima's speech in order to conceal the fact that "if there are two desires in man which capture him in this relationship to eternity with generation on the one hand, corruption and destruction on the other, it is the desire for death qua unapproachable that beauty is designed to veil."[22] Beauty blocks our way to the heart of the Thing, Lacan says here.[23] In the seminar on ethics[24] he claims that the tragic figure desires death because it wishes to go beyond its relation to the signifier. That is, while the life of the subject depends on the subject's inscription in the signifier (through which the subject gains his identity in the social field), this inscription goes beyond individual life. The subject's death does not obliterate the signifier but only the living being. The signifier, once representing a subject, already exceeds what personal extinction can touch. The tragic figure addresses the place where the signifier inscribes something absolute and unconditioned beyond the fates of the human being. This tragic position is connected to beauty, because beauty marks the point that the tragic figure has reached, a point that goes beyond mortality: "It is when passing through that zone that the beam of desire is both reflected and refracted till it ends up giving us that most strange and most profound of effects, which is the effect of beauty on desire."[25] Beauty is the refraction point of desire, because beauty is both the substitute for the absolute thing that is desired and the barrier against the possibility of reaching it. Therefore beauty is the most impenetrable and glorious barrier against the possibility of knowing anything about what is hidden at the endpoint, at death.

The tragic figure desires a symbolic death, it desires to cross the limit of human order where human destiny is inscribed, that is, to go beyond the constraints of mortality. Thus Antigone crosses the symbolic boundary embodied by the law (whether the social law or the divine one imposed on humans), and outside the protection of the symbolic order, there is nothing but death. Yet in her act she points at the fact that the subject is inscribed in a signifying order that exceeds the limit of life/death.

Lacan points to the tragic nature of this position, which aims at what lies between two deaths and beyond the limit of human life. Diotima describes this desire as what turns the love *for* the beautiful into a love *of* the beautiful, the love for the tangible thing that is with us into the love of what continuously recedes from us. In Diotima's words, the individual's death is prevented by beauty, because beauty signifies the endpoint where the border between mortality and immortality is crossed. For Diotima, the man who desires beauty pins his hopes on the signifier carrying his being beyond the moment of his destruction. This is exactly the desire outlined for us by the tragic hero, who desires to cross the lines of the symbolic order, to cross the limit of the law in order to situate himself in relation to the order that exceeds human mortality. According to Diotima, man crosses the lines not in order to die but in order to attune his life on earth to a different law, the eternal law of the good, and she illustrates this position through the figures of Alcestis and Achilles, who are ready to die for their lovers so that their virtue is inscribed as immortal. But there is a difference between these two mythical examples, as Lacan shows. Alcestis sacrifices her life so that her husband can live, while Achilles decides to avenge his lover Patroclus, who is already dead, knowing that this revenge will lead to his own death. That is, Achilles is the one who wagers only on the signifier, where the signifier loses its hold on the human order and the tragic hero dies for eternity rather than for life under the aegis of eternity. Be that as it may, this is the tragic position, the position of those mortal men or women who cross the limits of human existence by locating their desire in beauty, in what is beyond man's grasp, in what is an incomprehensible barrier – in death as the absolute destruction from which there is no regeneration.

But Socrates's position, Lacan claims, is different, and thus diverges from the typical pursuit of the Platonic philosopher, who relentlessly strives for knowledge of the Ideas (of the beautiful and of the good). One would have thought that the philosopher is someone willing to give up human limitations in order to inscribe an eternal signifier on the history of thought. Indeed, this is how the philosophical minds are described in the *Politeia* [*The Republic*], as those who "always love knowledge of a sort which shows them the eternal nature not varying from generation and corruption."[26] This is not, however, Socrates's position.

Socrates represents a different position towards death, the position of a being for whom the death of the things that are generated and corrupted is not needed in order to cross the lines, because the eternal object is already *in this being*, really in it. Lacan expresses this by saying that Socrates's gods are real rather than symbolic – that is, for Socrates the signifier of the absolute object is not found beyond his boundaries in the realm of an infinite other, but is present in a real way in the Socratic being itself. Lacan justifies this thought about Socrates by returning to the ostensible desire for death that Socrates expresses in *The Phaedo*. Lacan claims that even Socrates's loyal interlocutors in this dialogue that dramatizes Socrates before his execution are not convinced by the arguments he gives to prove the eternity of the soul (and therefore to justify his desire for death and the fact that he does not intend to try and evade the death that awaits him). Socrates offers proof of the immortality of the soul, but it is an immortality that is present in an entirely real way, rather than as something that is aspired to or that is present beyond the life of this world (climaxing in the description of the soul in terms of warmth and cold, that is, as having a material reality). Socrates does not claim but rather states confidently that he is leaving this life for a truer life, an immortal life; Socrates knows something about immortal eternity.

Socrates is not a tragic hero, because eternity is inscribed in him rather than in the gods:

No tragic sentiment, as it is put in our days, sustains this atopia of Socrates. Only a demon … And then, in addition, a message from a god whose function he himself testifies to us in what one can call a vocation, the god of Delphi, Apollo, that a disciple of his had the rather absurd idea of telling him to go and consult. And the god had replied: "There are some wise men, there is one who is not too bad, namely Euripides, but the wisest of all, the best of all … is Socrates." And from that day forward Socrates said: "I must realise the oracle of the god, because I did not know that I was the wisest, but because he said it, I must be." It is exactly in these terms that Socrates presents to us the sharp turn of what one could call his passage to public life. He is in short a madman who believes that he is at the service, at the command of a god, a messiah, and what is more in a society of chatterboxes.[27]

If the god said that Socrates is the wisest of men – that is, that Socrates possesses wisdom in its absolute embodiment – then Socrates cannot but accept the prophecy and act accordingly. The eternal Thing that belongs to another, that constitutes the symbolic order, is not found outside the being called Socrates but is materialized in his very being. For that reason Lacan claims that Socrates's gods are real, since for Socrates the god is not an absolute authority beyond the limitation of human life, but as real as Socrates himself. This is also why Lacan notes that Socrates does not think much of the gods and only occasionally bothers to obey them, on the condition that he himself defines the boundaries of this obedience. Socrates in fact sees himself inscribed in eternity by virtue of being the wisest of men. The divine reality is in him, and the big Other is he himself. Socrates's death is therefore a death *with* the absolute object rather than a death that realizes the desire for this object.

What is the importance of Lacan's claim that Socrates is not a tragic figure and does not desire death? Lacan in this way brings into focus the Socratic position towards knowledge and towards the practice of love. Socrates appears as someone who stands in the place of the object of love itself, thus testifying to the inability of the signifier, of discourse, to maintain its consistency when faced with this object that cannot be known. If love finds in the beloved what has been subtracted from the lover, then Socrates cannot partake in this lure. The Socratic method basically consists of revealing where there is error, where there is failure in the attempt to formulate truth, to capture the object with discourse. This error is usually attributed to others, to the interlocutors, but here, in the *Symposium*, it is attributed to Socrates himself. Socrates is presented as someone who defies the object, who appears with the object as what attests to the misrecognition, to the inevitable failure, the failure to know what love is as well as the failure in love itself. The wisest of men is not someone whose discourse sutures the split between truth (of the object) and knowledge, but someone identified with the absolute object that is outside all knowledge, thus turning the desire to formulate knowledge into a necessary failure.

Is the analyst likewise a madman of the Socratic kind, that is, someone who is identified with the absolute object? If the analyst is identified with the object that is the absolute cause of desire, in what way is he *identified* with it? To answer this question we must understand how Socrates uses the transference relations he maintains with his interlocutors. For Socrates, the wisest of men, says that the beauty others see in him is nothing. At this point, in order to understand the complexity of Lacan's use of the Socrates of *Symposium*, we can turn to the argument that Lacan outlines elsewhere, in a short essay he wrote about transference,[28] where he uses the Socratic logic sketched out in Seminar VIII to describe Freud's position in relation to his patient Dora. In this essay Lacan describes the analysis undergone by the patient Dora (who left the analysis with Freud shortly after it started) as a series of moves – "developments of truth" as Lacan names them – which in the course of the analysis create a chain of dialectical reversals (and eventually lead to Dora leaving the analysis). Freud's analytical moves are in fact a series of interpretations in which the analyst wishes to identify the objects of desire that populate Dora's world: Is it her father? Herr K.? Frau K.? In this essay Lacan identifies transference with those moments in the analysis in which a suspension of the analytic dialectic enables the object of desire to emerge. For that purpose Freud makes three analytical moves, the first of which recognizes Dora as a subject of desire – a necessary step for the analysis to be established. Thus at first, faced with Dora's description of the situation she has found herself in, as the go-between enabling her father's love relationship with Frau K., Freud asks Dora what is her place in this situation. That is, Freud points to Dora herself as a subject whose psychic economy the depicted situation is connected to. Following Freud's question, Dora's discourse shifts to describing her part in advancing her father's love life. The first development of truth has enabled the subject of desire to appear.

In the next stage Freud points to the triangle Dora–Herr K./Dora's father–Frau K. This constellation is rejected by Dora in various ways, but in practice it enables the reversal that reveals Dora's objects of identification. That is, as a result of the different ways in which Freud constructs Dora's place within this configuration of desire, Dora's objects of identification in her psychic economy are exposed.

In the third development, Freud's interpretative move causes Dora to situate herself vis-à-vis the other woman, Mrs K., and thus Dora's object of desire is signified (although Freud fails in his attempt to identify this object's role in Dora's psychic economy), and Lacan will say that this object, once signified, makes the cause that underlies Dora's love life appear.

The crucial point in Lacan's analysis is that it clarifies how the analyst situates himself with respect to the object of desire. Freud appears in Dora's analysis naming the various objects relevant to her psychic life, and out of the different ways to piece together the structure of Dora's desire, the object that is the driving force, the cause of her desire, eventually appears. Moreover, Freud manages to populate Dora's world with the relevant objects of desire because he does not hesitate to be mistaken, to fail in his constructions. It is through Freud's moves in analysis that his position as an analyst is constituted. An analyst is an agent that desires the truth about being; truth is the cause of the analyst's desire, and from this position the analyst does not hesitate to make a mistake, to wager on his/her being in the name of this desire of the analyst. Such a position can bring about effects that are critical for the analysis.

"Transference," says Lacan, "is nothing real in the subject if not the appearance, at a moment of stagnation in the analytic dialectic, of the permanent modes according to which she [Dora] constitutes her objects. What then does it mean to interpret transference? Nothing but to fill the emptiness of this standstill with the lure. But even though it is deceptive, this lure serves a purpose by setting the whole process in motion anew."[29] Transference, therefore, is not a mysterious matter but a dialectical moment in the analysis, which is of no great importance and usually signifies a mistake on the part of the analyst. The analyst's readiness to make a mistake is merely the recognition that the desire for truth does not produce a complete and consistent discourse, that the truth, about the objects of pleasure that occupy the world of the patient, cannot be sutured with the analytic discourse. The desire for the truth that is managed from such a position is equivalent to the transference, that is, to the method that introduces desire into discourse (while the philosophical method removes desire from discourse) – and this is where Freud's position merges with Socrates's.

We must not infer from this that the philosopher and the analyst share the same position. Philosophy, that is, philosophy beyond Socrates, rejects desire precisely because the desire for an object that eludes signification cannot be reconciled with the love of truth. Love is blind to the inevitable deferment of the object that causes desire, and since the philosopher loves truth – that is, takes the object of truth as an object that would meet the hand stretched out to it – philosophical discourse necessarily rejects desire. Desire always entails a certain negation of the object that causes it, because the object is always no longer there (or infinitely deferred) in relation to the desiring subject. The philosopher believes that desire and love are one and the same, whereas the analyst regards desire and love as distinct modes of pursuing the object. The analyst knows that the constant subtraction of the "object-cause"[30] from the thing loved means that the knowledge about truth will never be obtained. Therefore, when the philosopher acts like an analyst he strips himself of the supposition of knowledge. This is precisely how Lacan suggests that Socrates's position is to be understood: as that of an analyst who, for the love of truth, is ready to be stripped of his knowledge.

To sum up: the analyst's discourse is not the discourse of psychoanalysis, just as the Socratic discourse is not the discourse of philosophy, as much as the two come close together in Plato's symposium. This conclusion may shed light on Lacan's words in Seminar XVI, where he says that like an ant colony, Plato's ideal state lacks the presence of a signifier, but that its overall structure, just like that of an anthill or a beehive, is the sublimation of the sexual relation.[31] Plato's horizon, which we think of as idealistic, is a horizon that unites thought with the sphere of ideas. Plato's ideal state is hence a realization of the sexual relation (where the two ends meet), a positioning of a horizon in which knowledge merges with truth. As such it assumes an order that has no signifier, as the signifier marks the necessary split between what is true and what we know about the truth. In the ideal state this radical difference is overcome. That is why on the way to implementing the ideal philosophical state, the philosopher needs to cancel out all the social and symbolic effects of his way to truth. Socrates cannot be the subject of the philosophical beehive, of the ideal state. The Socratic philosopher acts with his desire and hence fails in his love affairs, even if, being Socrates, this is not taken as failure. Socrates stands for the impossible pairing (relation) between thought and truth, between the lover and the loved, as a pairing that always fails to arrive. Similarly, the analyst with his desire can only carry the knowledge of psychoanalysis in order to undermine it, to fail in respect to it, because the truth desired by the analyst is located beyond the limits of the symbolic exchange between the analyst and his/her interlocutor, beyond the discourse of the analyst.

Chapter 3

Soulove: Lacan and
Aristotle "On the Soul"

That is why the soul is the first grade of actuality of a natural body having life potentially in it.

– Aristotle, *On the Soul*, bk II, ch. 1

If psychology, whatever its object may be, but this object itself, as it is vainly sustained, being able to be defined as unique, in some way being able to lead us, along whatever path, to knowledge, in other words, if the soul existed, if knowledge was connected to the soul ...

– Lacan, *Le seminar XII: Problèmes cruciaux pour la psychanalyse*, 16.12.64

A. The Soul, the Body, and Eternity

The quotes at the head of this chapter present two contrasting conceptualizations of the soul or the psyche: one, Aristotle's, sees the soul as the foundation of life itself, as the actuality of the living being. The other, the soul or psyche of psychology, is a mirage: an imaginary, unreal thing that neither carries knowledge nor leads to it. In this chapter, through Lacan's use of Aristotle, we will discover that in psychoanalysis the soul serves as a hybrid object situated between these two poles: on the one hand, the soul appears from the heart of being, from its innermost essence, as it were, and on the other, the soul is a phantasm that provides bodily being with an imaginary shelter, a way to turn living into something a bit more comfortable and less perishable.

This duality of the soul is not surprising, and it inheres in the very concept of a soul. In its Greek origin the term *psyche* means "life," but in the history of thought *psyche* has actually come to signify the possibility of some part of being remaining after the body's *death*.[1] Plato discussed the link between the spirit or the soul and the finality of life in *The Phaedo*, reaching the conclusion (albeit not decisively, according to his commentators) that the soul is the most disembodied of all things. After Plato the possibility emerged that the soul is immortal and that "when death attacks a man, the mortal portion of him may be supposed to die, but the immortal retires at the approach of death and is preserved safe and sound"[2] – that is, the soul not only is connected to the livingness of being but also signifies an element that exceeds life itself and may be said to exist eternally. Plato raises the hypothesis that the soul is what allows man to partake in eternity, in what is beyond the life of the organism, thus pointing to that element of being that is not dependent on the existence of the body and is not limited by it.

Hence, long before the dualism of Descartes, who postulated an essential separation between the mental substance and the extended (corporeal) thing, there existed a distinction between the eternal soul and the ephemeral body, though it should be noted that this distinction did not imply a separation in the same way as in Descartes. Thus, although Plato in some of his dialogues posits a separation between the eternality of the soul and the mortality of the body, in others (e.g., in *The Phaedrus*, *The Republic*, and *The Timaeus*) he claims that the soul is divided,[3] naming parts of the soul that are closely related to the body and even specifying their bodily location (the parts of the soul can be found in the brain, the heart, the stomach area, etc.).

Be that as it may, even given the wider Platonic picture of the relation between the soul and the body, Aristotle does not share this understanding, but rather sees the soul as having a physical presence. In the treatise *On the Soul*, Aristotle shows that the very possibility of thinking about the soul as something that does not require the body stems from a false perception (even though Aristotle sees the mind as a psychic power that is not annihilated with death, as we will see below). The Aristotelian *psyche* or soul is what animates, what breathes life into the body, and is thus identical to life itself.

Although we will not be examining the bifurcation of the psyche as signifying life from the soul as signifying eternity in the history of ideas, or the point where the psyche appears as the foundation of Freudian psychoanalysis, these questions form the backdrop of this chapter's discussion. For the question of the difference between the psychoanalytical psyche and the soul is a complex one, and this chapter will suggest a partial way to approach it through Lacan's reading of Aristotle. Lacan reads Aristotle in order to rescue the soul from its psychological fate, that is, from its fate as a mirage, and the question is what is there in Aristotle that enables Lacan to see him as someone who conceives of the soul in the same way as the analyst conceives of the psyche. That is, even if Aristotle (as opposed to Socrates, for example) is not an analyst in Lacan's eyes, he nevertheless paves the way for constituting the soul in a way that coincides with the psychoanalytical *psyche*.

On the face of it, the very fact that for Aristotle the soul exists in a living body and is the actuality of its livingness puts him close to the psychoanalytical point of departure. Here the psyche and its formations are seen as events that necessarily have a corporeal reality, that are inscribed in the organism. The body appears in psychoanalysis as a site of psychic inscription not only due to Freud's constitutive interest in hysteria and its physical manifestations and to his psychosomatic notion of the drive.[4] The question of body in its relation to psyche concerns the very foundations of thinking about human existence, and the psychoanalytical answer to that question is epitomized in Freud's late formulation that the "psyche is extended."[5] This means that Lacan's interest in Aristotle must stem from the fact that Aristotle's soul is unique in not leaning on a separation from the body.[6] Aristotle then offers psychoanalysis a non-dualistic possibility of locating the soul in the body, of grasping the soul in its bodily existence, which is essential to the foundations of Freud's thinking about the drive and to Lacan's thinking about *jouissance*.

Yet, as this chapter will demonstrate, Lacan's interest in Aristotle is not exhausted, nor does it even explicitly arise from psychoanalysis's refusal to separate the psychic element from the living and extended body. So how can we account for Lacan's interest in the Aristotelian *anima*? Aristotle suggests an approach that lies outside the modern philosophical mode of posing the body–mind problem. Can one side of the dualism, for instance, the psychic element, be reduced to the other side, that is, to neurological, chemical, or other physiological components? Is the thinking substance able to shed light on the extended thing, and vice versa? While we, as descendants of Descartes, are used to forming the psycho-physical question in such terms, Aristotle offers a philosophical possibility of looking at the body–soul question from a totally different vantage point. We can even say that just as with psychoanalysis, it is difficult to clearly enlist Aristotle for or against a dualistic or monistic position towards the body and the soul. Aristotle remains outside the debate.

Aristotle claims that it is meaningless to ask whether the soul and the body are separate from each other, just as it is unnecessary to ask whether the wax and the shape given to it by the stamp, or generally the matter of a thing and that of which it is the matter, are separate from each other. But this does not lead him to conclude that the soul and the body are one. Just as the inability to separate the body and the soul does not imply their unity, psychoanalysis neither opposes dualism nor supports it, and in a certain sense can also be said to be outside this debate. Therefore, if Lacan recruits Aristotle for the service of psychoanalysis, it may be in order to enable a different approach to the question of the body and the soul.

While the psycho-physical dualism establishes a meta-theoretical estrangement between soul and body, for psychoanalysis the radical difference between the physical and the psychical does not in fact estrange them as two separate orders. Thus, the difference of the soul from the body is present for psychoanalysis just as it is present for Aristotle, and note that in both cases the issue is not psychic materialism, that is, an attempt to reduce the psychic to the physical. This is not what is at stake, and Lacan, as we will see, does not use Aristotle as an example of someone who refuses to divide being into body and soul. For both Lacan and Aristotle, the radical difference between the physical and the psychic is as indisputable as the fallacious ascribing of the physical and the psychic to two different and disconnected orders. For this reason the present discussion avoids both poles concerning the question of body and soul: the monistic pole, where soul is body and body is soul, that is, one; and the pole of rigid dualism, which negates any possibility of the soul affecting the body and vice versa, and even the possibility of one explaining something about the other, since they belong to two different orders.[7] Since Lacan, through Aristotle, rejects these two extreme positions, his interest in the object "soul" focuses only on the middle ground between them, where, to begin with, a certain separateness between body and mind is acknowledged. The question, as already mentioned, is not the actual separateness between body and mind, but the possibility of examining its possible consequences for human existence.

In this chapter I will suggest that we read Lacan's references to Aristotle's *On the Soul* as tracing the moment prior to the question of the relationship between body and thought. Through Aristotle, Lacan deals with a critical moment in which the soul can follow two different realizations: on the one hand, it may be the soul that merges with thought, the soul through which philosophy can speak *about the body*, or through which a science of the soul can be created, and on the other hand, it may be the soul that is identified with the psyche, the psyche that psychoanalysis wishes to explore. Locating Aristotle at a crossroads between these two possibilities of using the soul means that the Aristotelian *anima* holds the clue to the difference between them. Aristotle's approach seizes the moment that enacts a critical distinction for psychoanalysis – the one between the psychological soul and the psychoanalytic psyche. Such an understanding of the Aristotelian soul means that Lacan's use of Aristotle precedes (and even rejects) any distinction between dualism and monism, between assuming a duality of the psychic and the physical and perceiving them as one.

Aristotle himself refrains from referring to the soul as an instrument of unification or unity and examines the soul outside the question of its unity with, or split from, the body. He argues that talking about the "one" in relation to matter and the thing it is the matter of, is as unnecessary as asking about the unity of the wax and the shape of the stamp. "For, of all the various meanings borne by the terms unity and being, actuality is the meaning which belongs to them by the fullest right."[8] The question for Aristotle is how the soul is actualized as substance, rather than whether the two are united or separate.

Moreover, the question of unity has no place because it is unclear what the soul unites and which of its parts unite which bodily parts, since "it is difficult even to imagine what sort of bodily part mind will hold together."[9] That is, the soul unites neither the body as a whole nor its parts, because the soul's unity depends on the body just as the body's unity depends on the soul, and moreover, the bodily location of the psychic powers is not always clear-cut and there is even a part, the mind, that is not ascribed to any bodily organ. Aristotle similarly refrains from determining whether the soul is one or divided into parts, although the soul is structured as a kind of hierarchy of powers (from nutrition and sensation to knowledge and thought), which might suggest that something other than the question of the soul's unity is at stake. What is at stake, and what lies at the heart of Lacan's reference to Aristotle, is the *psychic thing* – be it an instrument, a concept, or a sign – that makes it possible to isolate a moment of encounter between thought and body; metaphorically, as we will see below, it is a moment that decides how desire is located in the Other: as soul or as psyche. In any case this means that *the decision concerning the psychic precedes any structuring of the relationship between the body and the soul* (either a dualistic structuring or a unified one). As mentioned above, Lacan through Aristotle isolates the moment in which a split between two positions regarding the psyche is made possible, and this moment should be described as a moment of decision rather than a moment of conceptual choice.

B. The Snivelling Soul

But let us not get ahead of ourselves: in order to capture this moment of split we will examine the contexts in which Lacan uses the concept soul (*âme*) and the way in which soulness and animation work for Aristotle, since we need first of all to examine at what moment, or in relation to which problematics, the soul appears. Why is it necessary to ask at what moment the soul appears? Because the body in itself, Lacan says, is a machine that works in a truly miraculous way, and this is Aristotle's point of departure as much as it is Descartes's. It is the miracles of the body that enable it to operate without interference, like the little miracle that takes place in the body and thanks to which the eye never dries up because there is a tear gland that secretes the fluid that moisturizes it. Where the body is in itself, without psychic interference, "the body is taken for what it presents itself to be, an enclosed body [*un corps fermé*]."[10] In relation to this closure, says Lacan, the soul appears as an element of intrusion or discordance. Inversely, in Descartes the mind is given as a point of departure, and in relation to it, the body introduces an intrusion. Since for Descartes *the body* is the element of incongruity, anything that is found in the human subject but cannot be attributed to thought, is body. In Aristotle the very movement and vitality of the body are ascribed to the soul (wheras in Descartes vitality is ascribed to bodily elements that come from the brain and that travel quickly to move the muscles and the nerves, rather than to the soul, unless these bodily elements interfere with the operation of reason). In Aristotle, the presence of movement, sensation, growth, and decay (of anything identified with the body's vitality) indicates that something has a soul. But if in Aristotle the body is an enclosed and living body, that is, if the soul is already included in the living body, why see the soul as an element of incongruity that supplements the miracle of the body?

While Aristotle, identifying the soul with the very existence of life in the body, seemingly sees the soul as the element that enables the physical mechanism to operate as an enclosed body, Lacan claims that the Aristotelian soul is not simply the movement and operation of the living body in and by itself. The Aristotelian soul, Lacan says, is what the winning side of thought leads to,[11] that is, the soul is a way to understand the body from the place of thought (which, as we will see below, has an ambiguous status with respect to the body: thought is actualized in the body in practice but possesses none of its attributes). That is, to understand the animated body is to understand it from the place of thought, to understand the limits of the body, the obstacles encountered when the body exhibits its small miracles, or the ways in which the corporeal machine in itself fails to work miraculously. Aristotle appears in Lacan in order to describe the moment in which the soul intrudes on the body's efficient operation. When someone steps on our foot and our eyes emit tears, this is the moment in which something interferes with the body's well-oiled machine, where the body is no longer a capsule of miracles operating all by themselves.

Lacan thus claims that, rather than being simply the sum of all the ways in which the body is moved, the Aristotelian soul refers to those incomprehensible aspects of the body where there is discordance between the physical function and its actualization. The psychic site is therefore, for Lacan, where the body snivels for no reason, producing an unexplained excess or lack. Testimony to that can be found in different places in Aristotle – for example, when he describes the power of sensation (which is one of the soul's powers) and says in relation to smell that "the distinguishing characteristic of the object of smell is less obvious than those of sound or color. The ground of this is that our power of smell is less discriminating and in general inferior to that of many species of animals; men have a poor sense of smell and our apprehension of its proper objects is inseparably bound up with and so confused by pleasure and pain, which shows that in us the organ is inaccurate."[12] He goes on to say that there is no necessary correspondence between the smell of things and their taste and that there are objects that have no smell at all. Aristotle's position suggests that for him the soul is on the side of thought, in the sense that the soul appears precisely as a location of discordance between the body and the various psychic faculties, rather than a place where they operate as one unit. These forms of incongruity are what Lacan calls "snivelling," designating the place in which the soul appears in order to explain the uncoordinated action of the body.

C. Thought on the Winning Side

We started by saying that in relation to the body-in-itself, the question arises as to what kind of object the soul is, or what kind of operation the soul performs in relation to the body, and we saw that Aristotle needs the soul in order to describe a discordance between the bodily mechanism and its ways of moving and operating. That is, for Aristotle the soul, rather than continuing to sustain the body unto itself, as enclosed body, *has a different, distinguishing presence in relation to the corporeal reality.* The importance of the Aristotelian position may be appreciated when we contrast it with another way mentioned by Lacan, of thinking about the body with the soul: that of *identifying* the soul with the thinking body. When the soul is *identified* with the thinking body, it can provide congruity in terms of a definite and systematic mechanism to what looks like an incongruity – a thinking body. This is a different way of interpreting the psyche as the bodily thinking that governs the body's actions.[13] This thinking body can be described in terms of bodily fluids, or in terms of DNA or of hormones (e.g., explaining an illness or a physical difficulty in terms of a meta-principle from a different bodily order – neurological, genetic, and so on). In each case it is a way of thinking about the body as encapsulating knowledge, a way of ascribing thought to the body and thus keeping the body self-sufficient. Lacan believes that despite the distance between them, both these positions – Aristotle's position and the "hormonal" one – posit the soul as an instrument of thought, that is, posit the soul as on the "winning side" in relation to the body. Yet Aristotle does not identify body and soul.

Remember in this context that for Aristotle, the mind is distinct from the soul in that only the soul has bodily presence (whereas the mind, which is one of the soul's powers, has a separate status). Thus, while throughout his treatise Aristotle insists that it is impossible to distinguish the soul from its function as a bodily mode of actuality, towards the end of the treatise he reaches a surprising conclusion: "When mind is set free from its present conditions it appears as just what it is and nothing more: this alone is immortal and eternal (we do not, however, remember its former activity because, while mind in this sense is impassible, mind as passive is destructible)."[14] We will return to this firm distinction between the soul in general and the power of the mind within it (when the mind itself is divided into the active mind and the passive mind), but at this point we can say that this distinction merely emphasizes the need to decipher *how the psychic entity appears as part of the body (mortal) yet as separate*, so that this separateness suggests the difference between soul and the corporeal substance.

The first Aristotelian condition that underpins the link between the psyche and the corporeal, Lacan suggests, is the one that puts the soul on the winning side of thought, and the question that arises is whether this condition is inevitably assumed when we approach the soul in the context of philosophy. The triumph of thought in the domain of the soul is unambiguous in Descartes, for example, for whom the soul (which is identified only with the thinking mind) is distinct in every possible sense from the body that exists unto itself, since for him the mind has no spatial (extended) being. When physical perceptions create psychic change (i.e., affects), the mind becomes an instrument of thinking about the excess of the body. Thus joy is described as the overactivity of the nerves around the heart, and sadness as the contraction of passages until they are blocked.[15] That is, in Descartes the triumph of thought manifests itself in the fact that the criterion *for the body's effect on the soul is psychic*, which preserves the autonomy of thought.

But if the triumph of thought is clear in the case of Descartes, how should we understand Lacan's claim that *the soul is on the winning side of thought* with regard to Aristotle? If in Aristotle the soul is on the winning side of thought, it is not because the philosopher takes pains to maintain the body's separateness from the psychic instrument. In Aristotle, as opposed to Descartes and his successors, the soul is presented to begin with as having bodily characteristics (i.e., the criterion for the soul's involvement in the life of an individual is physical). The soul is what enables the body to be actualized as what it is, and is the name given *to bodily occurrences* (such as growth, decay, nutrition, sensation). Since the soul in Aristotle is described in terms of the body, it can only be on the winning side of thought, in the sense that it refers to occurrences that suggest a surplus or a subtraction in the bodily mechanism. Thus, for example, sometimes calamitous events do not give rise to excitement or fear, while at other times even the feeblest stimulations excite the body, and man is affected by feelings of terror even in the absence of anything terrifying. Furthermore, unlike animals, man can block his hearing or sight when he wishes to. Such cases and others suggest to Aristotle that something other than the physical is operating in our body and that the soul is what takes on itself this excess/lack of the bodily reaction. That the soul is something bodily that cannot be explained in terms of corporeal matter alone offers one direction for understanding why the Aristotelian soul signifies the triumph of thought.

But the soul is on the winning side of thought also for another reason. Aristotle *recruits* the soul in order to solve the unknown relationship between vitality on the one hand and the body and its parts on the other, since, if the soul as a whole unites the entire body, then each of the soul's parts must unite some part of the body, but there are parts of the soul that do not unite any body part (e.g., the mind). Therefore, "the soul is inseparable from its body, or at any rate [...] certain parts of it are (if it has parts) for the actuality of some of them is nothing but the actualities of their bodily parts. Yet some may be separable because they are not the actualities of any body at all. Further, we have no light on the problem whether the soul may not be the actuality of its body in the sense in which the sailor is the actuality of the ship."[16] If the soul is the actuality of the body then, as it turns out, we can expect no correlation between the soul and its parts and the body and its parts: there are contexts in which the soul is actualized in a body part or in the body as a whole, and at other times it is impossible to say which bodily part actualizes its essence through the soul (and in the case of the mind there is even a disconnection from the body parts). This complexity leads Aristotle to posit not only the inevitable separation between body and soul, but also a lack of symmetry between them, since the soul, as the first grade of actuality of the body and its parts, concerns the essence rather than the particular entity, and therefore does not necessarily belong to a specific body. The soul is thus a way to come to terms with what is incomprehensible in the body, as well as a way to distinguish between the particular existence of the body and its bodily essence. This is, then, the additional basis for supposing that the soul, on the side of thought rather than of the body, is needed in order to substantiate the corporeality of being (even if the soul is not dependent on the body and its parts in a one-to-one correspondence).

In *On the Soul*, Aristotle thus offers, through the soul, the possibility of recognizing the body as constitutive of being. The psychic dimension in this sense is neither supplemental to nor external to being, but rather determines being as *bodily*. Aristotle uses the soul to substantiate the essence of bodily being as such through a series of psychic powers: from nutrition and growth to thought, which are all modes of actualizing being as corporeal. Thus, rather than introducing the soul in order to think of the body from the outside, or to describe how the body thinks, Aristotle posits that *man as a bodily being thinks with the soul*.

What, then, is the psychic instrument for Aristotle? At the beginning of his treatise, Aristotle asks what the soul is: Is it entity, quality, quantity, or another category? Does it exist potentially (i.e., as a potential held in the organic structure of the body and its parts?), or does it belong to the actuality of a certain body? Is it divided into parts or not? Is the soul always of the same kind, and if it is not, how does one soul differ from another? That is, the questions that trouble Aristotle are these: What is it in the soul that makes it essential to being? And what aspects of being are inscribed in the soul? In the latter context, Aristotle wishes to consider the relationship between the soul and the objects that appear in it, and to examine in what sense the soul itself can be treated as an object.

As already mentioned, one of the main questions that Aristotle contends with concerns the relationship between the soul and its parts (these parts are the different powers of the soul, such as the mind and sensation) and the relationship between the soul and the parts of the body (does the soul have an organ in the same way that the sense of sight has an organ?). Should the soul be examined as a whole, or should it be examined through its parts? Are there different relations between the different psychic powers and the bodies in which they are actualized? What is the nature of the dependency and the independency between the soul and the body parts?

Let us examine, for example, the issue of old age. Aristotle claims that while old age destroys the body, it does not change the soul: "The incapacity of old age is due to an affection not of the soul but its vehicle, as occurs in drunkenness or disease. Thus it is that in old age the activity of mind or intellectual apprehension declines only through the decay of some other inward part; mind itself is impassible."[17] In old age the activity of the mind and intellectual apprehension decline because the body parts that have sustained being as thinking have been damaged, while the mind itself, which does not reside in the body part, remains unchanged. Aristotle highlights the difficulties that arise when the soul "cannot be without a body, while it cannot be a body; it is not a body but something relative to a body."[18] Since for Aristotle, as already noted, there are different psychic faculties (each of which produces a different kind of movement in the body), and since it can be said with regard to all faculties that although they can be partly connected to a body part, they are not identical to it, Aristotle faces a crucial question: Is there an aspect of the soul that is not dependent on the living body? The mental capacity and the faculty of intellectual apprehension, which have no related body parts or any attributes of their own, give rise to the hypothesis that the soul has its own special affection, which it does not share with the body.

If Aristotle sees thinking as the only activity[19] that is unique to the soul, and that in this sense does not belong to a body part and is not related to physiological changes, then he equally takes pains to connect thinking to the human being as a whole, even if it is not connected to a specific corporeal system. Thinking has faculties devoid of physical attributes, yet it too is a way of organizing the body. Furthermore, like all the other psychic faculties, thinking is not only actualized in the body, but also necessarily actualized in a specific body (rather than in a random body encountered by chance). If there were indeed a psychic affection that is unique to the soul and devoid of physical attributes, or if the body and the soul had chanced upon each other by accident, then the soul could have existed separately from the body. The psychic affection is therefore meaning embodied in matter, and this meaning must be found in matter of a certain kind.

This suggests that Aristotle discusses the body/soul relationship only insofar as it sustains the bodily essence of being. The soul is neither the body nor separate from the body, but is rather "something relative to a body"[20] – the actuality of a living body "of a definite kind." Aristotle does not see the soul as a separate essence or as a form added to physical matter, but rather as the actuality that becomes possible between the corporeal and the psychic: the soul is the way in which the actuality and the meaning of a certain body are determined by its potential to be what it is. For Aristotle, the actualization of a living body of a certain kind takes place through the power to originate movement and change that are actualized in that body (for Aristotle the different faculties, from the nutritive, the sensory, and the appetitive to the faculty of thinking – all constitute the living body's forms of movement, and different beings are examined according to the power they possess to originate movement).

The soul defines the way in which bodily being exists in the individual. "The soul is the cause or source of the living body"[21] in three senses: it is the source of the body's movement, the end of this movement, and the essence of the whole living body. The soul is form, and the body is ground, but the form can only exist as an actualization of the ground (since the soul must exist and sustain a body, in Aristotle we do not find the demand, which we will encounter later on, that thought be devoid of material limitations).

We have seen that in its Lacanian version, the Aristotelian soul is introduced in order to designate what exists in bodily being but is not identified with bodily matter. That is, Lacan reads the Aristotelian soul as that which enables the body to be what it is but bars us from the possibility of knowing what it is in itself. Therefore, as already mentioned, Lacan says that in Aristotle the soul is on the side of thought. Indeed, in Seminar XX Lacan identifies the soul with that bodily surplus value that appears in the shape of snivelling or any other affection that arises from the body and has no physical explanation. How do we explain it when a child cries on seeing his mother's alarm, rather than because of his actual fall? How do we explain cheeks blushing when no one is looking, terror gripping the body without the presence of something terrifying, and so on? But even if in Aristotle the soul is on the side of thought, it does not, as we have seen, serve to distinguish the movement of the soul from the change in the body, but rather to carry this change. The soul is destined to bear what constitutes surplus value in relation to corporeality; the soul works against the possibility of identifying the psyche with abstract thought, independent of objects or of the body in which it operates.

D. The Soul as One and as a Divide

As the above description of the psychic instrument makes clear, the treatise *On the Soul* does not investigate the essence of the soul, nor does it turn the soul into an object of inquiry that stands on its own. If we ask what kind of object the soul is for Aristotle, we find that Aristotle does not try to characterize the psychic object in itself, nor does he see the soul as governing the body's unity and regularity, but rather describes its role in relation to bodily existence. In this sense the Aristotelian soul, despite being a form, cannot be seen as a gestalt; that is, the soul is not a pattern that makes human existence one and whole or even "possessed of form." Ultimately for Lacan, therefore, Aristotle adheres to the same agenda that underpins psychoanalysis. According to this agenda, the interpretation given to the various functions of the body in relation to the power of the soul, forgoes any attempt to distinguish the psychic entity from the physical one or to impose the unity of the soul on the multiplicity of the body. As Lacan says in Seminar XVII, what can be known, as Freud has shown, always comes piecemeal. Knowledge cannot be counted; it arrives in fragments and speaks itself (rather than being spoken by someone).[22] This is also the type of knowledge that Aristotle ascribes to the animating soul – piecemeal knowledge that corresponds to the function assigned to it.

The soul proposed by Aristotle is close in spirit to the Freudian psyche because of the link he posits between thought and bodily existence: thought, which has the potential to become a universal form, in practice will be actualized in a specific bodily existence. In fact, Aristotle is close to the psychoanalytic position that identifies the psychic with a moment of division between body and thought, a moment that in psychoanalysis is identical to subjectivity itself. From Lacan's perspective, Aristotle understood that when I speak or think I do not speak or think *about* my body but *with my soul*; thought is itself a mode of animating the body. It was Aristotle who located the soul at the site of the divide between body and thought, a divide that appears as a body event, as animation. The soul can therefore be considered a site of inversion where thought is actualized as body (just as evil is a point of inversion within the good, and the ugly is the reversal that exists within the beautiful).

Psychoanalysis identifies the drive with a psychical sign of a body event (originating from within the organism) reaching the mind, and Freud stresses that this sign is a representative of what cannot be represented. Lacan refers to Aristotle as someone who does not attempt to interpret the mental element in itself or to read the body as a sign for the mind, thus paving the way for the psychoanalytic position. In Seminar XX, Lacan says that while Aristotle's soul is what thought leads to – that is, to thought *about the body* – nonetheless in Aristotle this stems from the recognition that "if there is something that grounds being, it is assuredly the body. On that score, Aristotle was not mistaken. But he doesn't manage, if we read him carefully, to link it to his affirmation … that man thinks with – instrument – his soul, that is, as I just told you, the presumed mechanisms on which the body is based … 'man thinks with his soul' means that man thinks with Aristotle's thought. In that sense, thought is naturally on the winning side."[23] Lacan claims here that *Aristotle does not manage to reconcile that fact that thought is actualized in a body with the triumph of thought*. Now that we have explained these two aspects in Aristotle, the question that arises is what we can infer from this irreconcilability.

We can say that for Lacan, Aristotle's position is comprised of several separate aspects that allow him to ascribe to Aristotle *a bodily conception of being*. First, Aristotle senses very well, although he lacks the terms for it, that when the soul overlaps with a body, the subject is not to be found in this conjunction. That is, if the body is described in imaginary terms as a complete image, and if this body image is perceived as a meaningful sign of a unified position (e.g., snivelling in the body is described as signifying the presence of a melancholic character type or alternately as signifying a pathological syndrome described in the psychiatric "statute book"), the subject will "get the hell out of" this place of overlap between the soul and the body. This is the first thing that Aristotle understood. Second, Aristotle understood that the bodily remainder always tempts us to strive to isolate an autonomous psychic element, abstracted from the body (an option that Aristotle examines but accepts only in regard to the mind).[24] And third, Aristotle recognized that the soul must take on the specific nature of the bodily being. Aristotle, to use Lacan's words, does not manage to resolve this conflicted set of positions regarding the soul but in fact we can say that these propositions inaugurate the psychic dialectic in relation to the body.

Moreover, Aristotle does not presume to transmit knowledge about the soul itself. Although the soul is a sign, and a sign always exists for something (thus sound cannot be its own thing but is always "of something on something and in something [which produces it]," and the same goes for colour, which is the actualization of light),[25] Aristotle nevertheless proposes the psychic sign without proposing a signified for it. We can say that the Aristotelian soul is a sign without meaning, a sign that carries itself for another sign. The crucial questions concerning the soul that Aristotle's treatise raises thus remain without a decisive answer, because it is not conclusive knowledge about the soul that Aristotle is after.

To examine what it means to claim that Aristotle does not turn to the soul in order to gain knowledge about being, let us return to Aristotle's wavering around the connection between the soul and its vessel (the body), and to his question whether the soul has its own special affection. If the soul has its own special affection, such as thinking, which seems the closest to offering such a possibility, then the soul will be able to exist without a body, but if there is no such affection, the soul will not be able to exist separately. The possible existence of an affection that is unique to the soul means that in relation to the intellectual power, the soul is not affected (passively influenced) by the object, but merely absorbs or takes on its form (when this form is being thought in practice). Note that even if Aristotle ultimately concludes that the mind has the necessary dimension to be considered the soul's own special affection, we must not forget that the mind does not exist without the lesser powers, such as the power of sensation, the power of movement, and so on. For Aristotle the soul has different faculties and powers that are built on one another, and therefore, even if the soul is separate from the body at the moment of its mental activity, this moment is built on prior affections materialized in the body.[26]

In the third and last part of his treatise on the soul, Aristotle discusses the status of the mind in relation to affections such as sensation, in terms of the relationship of each of the psychic faculties to its object, and in terms of the relationship between the faculty of knowing and understanding things and the way in which the things themselves, the objects, implicate and influence the soul. In this context he distinguishes between the mind, which is connected to what is thinkable, and is therefore infallible, and sight, for example, which is connected to the sensible object. Sight is a faculty that can err if the eye, the mediating organ, is dazzled. Aristotle distinguishes between the mind, which is the power of thinking in itself, and which has no nature or attributes of its own until it thinks about a certain thing, and other powers, which have a specific quality according to the body part or the attribute of their object. The mind in this sense has no attributes (it is not affected/influenced by the object of thought) and can therefore think of anything at all, and the moment it thinks of something, it and its object are identical. The mind "can have no nature of its own, other than that of having a certain capacity. Thus that in the soul which is called mind (by mind I mean that whereby the soul thinks and judges) is, before it thinks, not actually any real thing."[27] While the active mind is therefore described as not implicated in the body (otherwise it would carry some quality of the organ or the thing that is its object), the soul itself is described by Aristotle as "the place of forms," as maintaining its objects in potentiality since it has the power to absorb any object's form.

These questions about the soul as the actualized form of a bodily being, about the possibilities of attributing objects to the soul, and about the characterization of the psychic as action and affection, are discussed mainly in a notoriously vague chapter (bk III, ch. 4) in which Aristotle makes contradictory claims about the relationship between the soul and the intellectual power (in chapter 5 he goes on to distinguish between active and passive mind, which will resolve some of the contradictions). This whole discussion is mentioned here in order to suggest why, instead of turning the soul into an object of knowledge, the soul's bodily reality turns it into a kind of ungraspable site: on the level of forms the soul carries the forms, and on the level of the objects being thought in practice, the soul is described as lacking characterization, but also as being affected by these objects. The soul in Aristotle becomes a kind of vanishing point that disappears under the body on the one hand and under the potential form of the material object – on the other.

We can therefore say that in *On the Soul*, Aristotle does not turn the psyche into a site of knowledge from which it is possible to think about what is incomprehensible in the body; rather than formulating knowledge about the soul, Aristotle's text points to the impossibility of grasping the soul as such through thinking. This is because "the mind of the soul," that is, thought *about* the body, is incapable of describing the psychic reality, which is itself implicated in the body. As opposed to contemporary psychologists, Aristotle understood that you cannot associate knowledge with the psyche, that the psychic object is not one, and that any attempt to devise a theory of the psyche, to say what the psyche is, to categorize it and monitor its field of activity, is bound to fail. We can say that where there is a wish to constitute a field of knowledge about the psyche – for example, in the science of the psyche – this wish signifies precisely the inevitable failure to capture the psyche. The object of psychology, as Lacan goes on to say after the words quoted above, is neither one nor whole, and the attempt to turn the psyche into the object of theory – about mental development, for example – cannot fulfil its purpose and runs into a paradox. Whoever tries to know and govern the soul, to turn it into knowledge, is forced to recognize that in doing so, she/he becomes trapped in the position of the "beautiful soul," that is, the soul that is not touched by the disorder and disunity that surround it, by the conditions that create the difference, by the divide between body and soul.

Aristotle himself does not fall into this trap, and it is precisely in this sense that he manages to leave the paradoxicality of the soul – that which is not a body but which actualizes the living body – unresolved, and therefore productive for understanding the psychic element.

While psychology takes on the role of turning the psyche into an object (and as such, the psyche of psychology is a mirage), Aristotle captured the soul by recognizing its reality in the body itself, and we might say that in doing so, he relinquished the possibility of producing knowledge about the psyche as such. The ramifications of this Aristotelian insight, which enable us to identify the affinity between the Aristotelian soul and the psychoanalytic psyche, are numerous. Here we will address two of them: the way in which this affinity is revealed through the myth about the birth of the soul, and the way in which the Aristotelian soul allows us to decipher the question of feminine sexuality – two contexts in which Lacan referred to the concept of the soul in general and the Aristotelian soul in particular.

E. The Birth of the Soul

In Seminar VIII, Lacan refers to the painting "Psyche Surprises Amore," by the sixteenth-century Italian painter Jacopo Zucchi, which depicts a myth about the god of love, Eros, and his lover, Psyche.[28] After obeying for a time the condition that they must leave their love life in the dark (i.e., both in darkness and in secret), Psyche reveals the identity of her lover. The painting shows Psyche surrendering to the temptation to uncover the identity of the one who has been giving her pleasure, holding a lamp in one hand and a knife in the other and illuminating Eros, who is lying at her feet, his body lit and a beautiful bouquet of flowers standing in the foreground and hiding his sex organ. In Zucchi's painting, Lacan notes, Psyche is depicted without wings, in contrast to the way this mythical story is represented in other artistic contexts. The wings that usually signify the soul's immortality are missing here. We should not, however, err in concluding that the story about Eros and Psyche is a story about the love of a man (albeit a divine man) and a woman. Rather, the myth tells us something about the birth of the soul (psyche) from desire (Eros). By analysing this painting in a seminar concerned with transference, Lacan clarifies the place of the soul in relation to the economy of the body, in that the painting shows the moment of Psyche's appearance as a moment of abstention that is identified with castration itself. The birth of the soul, Lacan says, takes place when man's demand for absolute pleasure is actualized in a desire that is only partially satisfied. Lacan uses these terms to describe the link between the myth about the birth of the soul and the psyche born with psychoanalysis, thus also clarifying something about the contribution of the Aristotelian soul to this latter birth.

This is Lacan's reading of the painting: rather than dealing with the love life of Psyche and Amore, the myth concerns the birth of the soul at the moment in which love fails, at the moment in which love threatens to slip away, never to return again. Zucchi's painting depicts the myth about perfect desire at the moment it is turned into human sexual desire – that is, subject to castration. The painting depicts the place of sexual desire without displacement, condensation, or metaphor. That is, this is desire pure and simple, without embellishment, the desire for the divine organ that is replaced by a sign, a bouquet of flowers that denotes castration. The myth of Psyche (like the myth of Oedipus, for example) does not rely on symbols or substitutes, and the birth of the soul takes place at the moment in which Eros is lost as the possibility of a natural, uninterrupted satisfaction of desire, a desire here replaced by the actual subtraction from the body (hiding the organ).

What does the soul signify in this scenario? Zucchi presents Psyche as a spurned, suffering soul; she appears as a subject of pathos both because of what the painting shows and because of what is known about the myth. Psyche is on the brink of making desire elude her forever, because she has been unable to resist her curiosity and has thrown light on the place that cannot be exposed, the place of the cause of desire. This violation of her vow to Eros seals her fate. That is, in Lacan's reading of the painting, Zucchi ties the birth of the soul to the moment in which the cause of desire in its full perfection no longer resides in the pleasured body but eludes it, and what earlier was natural and therefore invisible now becomes visible and therefore non-existent. In the spirit of the terms quoted above, that is, the soul is born at the moment in which the body "snivels," when something is precluded, deprived of the subject, thus producing an inevitable change in the life of the body. And at that moment, when the corporeal reality of desire is lost and becomes a representation, a sign, Psyche is born as a well-equipped agent (equipped with a lamp and a knife). The birth of Psyche is identified with a moment of loss, when a sign replaces the fact of castration (in the painting it is the flower vase). The vase causes something of the body to be subtracted, but as Lacan says, the flowers are not abundant enough to really hide anything. That is, the bouquet signifies something for someone, but it is impossible to say what this thing is, because behind the bouquet there is no one from whom the organ has been removed. We can say that the birth of Psyche is identified with the appearance of the sign of castration (rather than with castration itself).

Psyche herself is however identified with the subtraction from the body of the other. Thus the depiction of castration does not rely on an imaginary possibility (of removing the organ) or a symbolic possibility (of replacing what has been subtracted with what appears to make up for the lack). Castration is the moment in which the reality of *the body appears before the soul as unattainable.* Facing the body, the soul is split between being identified with this body and its organ of pleasure, and being deprived of it.

It is no coincidence that the slipping away of the object of satisfaction and the birth of the soul is related to genital sexuality, as the myth emphasizes. In Caravaggio's sacrifice of Isaac, the viewer is faced with the moment that a sign of the pact between Abraham and his god replaces the actual shedding of blood;[29] here, in Zucchi's painting, in just the same way, we face the moment where an object of desire (the bouquet) indicates that the body organ has slipped away. The hidden divine organ is not replaced but only represented by what appears to occupy its place. The bouquet hence signifies what animates desire by pointing at the real thing as being subtracted. In this sense the birth of the soul is related to genital desire, when the organ is no longer there. When Psyche appears in the light that infuses the painting, she faces the sign of the receding presence of the sexual organ (rather than the phallic signifier that would replace it). As already mentioned, Lacan says that the demand made of the organ is a demand made of the divine, which means that it is a demand made of that which excludes the subject from the order of sexuality – see, on this matter, the debates about the sexuality of the angels, debates that merely indicate that sexual acts do not belong in the heavens or in the lives of the angels. However, the disappearance of natural desire – a desire under which there is neither soul nor subject – enables the constitution of a sexual desire and a different position in relation to sexuality, which Lacan associates with the appearance of Psyche.

The soul is related to the moment in which one faces one's body as alienated, and this moment gives rise to two possibilities. One possibility includes all the forms of denying the alienation from the body, the loss of the body as a natural part of one's being. Denial can also take the form of erasing the corporeal reality of being. The other possibility is that of Psyche, the subject of pathos who snivels at the loss while being identified with this very moment of alienation. Is this not why the myth depicts the historically singular moment of Psyche's birth as a moment of separation and loss? (For each person the soul is born at a singular moment, in contrast to Eros or Venus, who are born every day and every hour anew.) It is the moment in which the universal soul is born in man, which is not a moment that erases the subject, but one in which the subject is born, born with a phallus that signifies the desire lost, the body of pleasure that has slipped away. Here it is the soul/psyche that appears as the pathos-filled carrier of this moment of split and loss.

Lacan proposes we understand the birth of Psyche thus:

> If the phallus as signifier has a place, it is very precisely that of supplying the point where significance disappears in the Other, where the Other is

constituted by the fact that there is somewhere a signifier lacking. Hence the privileged value of this signifier which one can of course write, but which one can only write in parenthesis, by saying indeed precisely the following: that it is the signifier of the point where the signifier is lacking. And it is for this reason that it can become identical to the subject himself to the point that we can write him as barred subject, namely at the only point where we analysts can place a subject as such ... We are linked to the effects which result from the coherence of the signifier as such when a living being makes itself the agent and support of this signifier.[30]

If the place where the soul merged with the thinking body is one from which the subject took off, then here the subject of desire is present, and the birth of the soul marks that the subject is present as the one who knows that the sign of desire in the body of the other is a sign for him alone. This turns subtraction – not in the sense of removing an organ but in the sense of subtracting the possibility of knowing the body of the other – into a constitutive element of being itself.

In this analysis of the painting, Lacan suggests that Psyche's adventures start not because of her beauty, which is at least as great as Venus's, or because of the amazingly perfect love life she has been blessed with, but precisely at the moment in which she is separated from Eros. The soul is identified with the split between natural desire and castrated desire, a split that appears pictorially through a signifier of castration and mythically as the event of Psyche's birth. Psyche signifies the recognition of the unavoidable distance rather than the subduing of this distance. The painting shows the relationship between Eros and Psyche to be one that constitutes the soul at a moment of subtraction from the other's body, a subtraction that is only present through a sign without a signifier, a sign of what is unattainable. The birth of the soul is therefore merely what comes about because the signifier of the other's desire is not given, and in this sense the soul is left to affirm its desire without such a signifier, which it does by making the loss present.

If the birth of the soul posits a moment of divide in corporeal being, then Aristotle's relevance to this analysis lies not only in the way he lays the foundations for understanding the soul as a moment of divide, of separation from the body, but also in another aspect, which lies at the heart of Lacan's allusion to Aristotle. On the Soul is a treatise in search of the lost soul, a soul that has its basis in the body and gradually loosen its grip on this body (in the transition from the psychic faculty responsible for nutrition to the intellectual faculty, whose clear connection to the body can no longer be grasped or distinctly known). If Lacan describes the soul as a moment of snivelling at the loss of natural control over the body, then for Aristotle this snivelling manifests itself in the general course of his treatise, as the soul loses its clear grip on the affections that sustain the body.

F. The Soul as Form and Feminine Sexuality

Aristotle sees the soul as the cause of something being alive, the essence of the living body: "The soul is the cause or source of the living body. The terms cause and source have many senses. But the soul is the cause of its body alike in all three senses which we explicitly recognize. It is (a) the source or origin of movement, it is (b) the end, it is (c) the essence of the whole living body."[31]

For Aristotle it is the form that determines the thing, but even when Aristotle refers to the soul as "the place of forms," form is an inextricable part of the particular thing and does not exist in a separate realm. The necessary connection between the form and the particular case manifests itself for instance in the Aristotelian logic in which every deduction from a universal premise is based on the supposition that the set is not void (i.e., that if we say "all ravens are black," at least one black raven necessarily exists), and therefore the thing's type, the dog's dogness, for example, is what the dog really is. When Aristotle, as quoted above, discusses the status of the soul as a cause, he ascribes to it three dimensions of causality (the soul is *an efficient cause* that creates change in the body, it is a *final cause* in that it determines the finality/purpose of the change, and it is a *formal cause* in that it determines the thing's essence). We can see that each of these dimensions of causality determines an aspect of movement that occurs in the body itself – that is, the soul as cause is not disconnected from the actual existence of the material body: the soul is the first grade of actuality of "that which is 'potentially capable of living'"; the soul is the actuality, what is present in the living body mode of being. We can say that the Aristotelian soul uses the entire body as its body part, and in this sense the body is animated, is guided and moves by virtue of being be-souled. The soul is not a mystical element "behind things," or an attribution of psychic powers to the material body, but rather an occurrence *in* the body that defines its natural movement. Aristotle calls this structure of causality between the soul and the body "*entelecheia*," which refers to the soul as the body's actuality according to the body's mode and direction of movement. The soul is the organization thanks to which a thing can function in ways that are typical of the kind of living activity that is unique to it, can actualize its *modus operandi*, its purpose. Aristotle says that if the axe had a soul, this soul would be to cut; that is, the object's essence, its function, its purpose, are inscribed in the singular thing, in its form and organization, which allow it to fulfil its roles – here, those of an axe. On the other hand, there are contexts in which it is possible to sense form without matter (e.g., the wax takes on the impress of a signet-ring without the iron or gold that make this impression possible). The fact that the soul is the actuality of the body does not mean that the soul is made of physical matter. The soul is *not a material cause*, since it is the first grade of actuality *in matter*.

Further to the question of the relationship that Aristotle posits between form and cause with regard to the soul, there is a debate, as mentioned earlier, regarding the extent to which Aristotle is willing to recognize the existence of a mental faculty that is not dependent on the body. That is, the question that arises is to what extent the fact that the soul is defined through non-material causes allows us to know what the soul is when it only exists as a mode of actuality of a body. The soul, as we have seen, can only be described or characterized in the actuality of the body, which raises the various modes in which sensation, imagination, and thought correspond to a body part. When, however, Aristotle characterizes the soul as potentiality before it thinks, he is asserting that the soul has no nature of its own. Thus by wavering on the question of the relationship between the psychic faculties ("thinking, discriminating and perceiving"[32]), Aristotle shows that the soul differs in essence from the objects in which it is actualized, and also, that the way the soul is actualized comes to resemble the nature of the things in which it is actualized.

As we have shown above, in the final part of *On the Soul* Aristotle claims that it is a mistake to think that the soul shares a similarity with its object, but he also says that the mind and the object of thought are identical. That is, the mind does not resemble sensation and can be actualized independently of its object (the mind can think just as successfully about something that causes much thinking as about something that requires less thinking, about something false as about something true), but because of the identity between the mind and its object, there can be no error in the mind.[33] He further claims that the part of the soul through which the soul knows and understands things is both separate from the body and not separate from it. The mind has no corporeal nature, but it also has no nature of its own; however, if we ask what there is in the soul, we can say that it is a place of forms and that these forms exist in their actuality when the mind thinks.

Aristotle's attempt to describe the soul through the array of Aristotelian causes makes it clear that for him, not only is the soul *an instrument for thinking* about a body that is other to it (a kind of extension of thought in the body), but the soul itself is also *an object of thought* – or, more precisely, a thing that struggles to be an object of thought. That is, if up till now we have seen how the soul, insofar as it is an instrument for thinking *about the body*, is on the winning side of thought, we can now realize that Aristotle *thinks about the soul*. Aristotle thinks about the soul when he locates it in the body as that which is responsible for its movement and affection (change), that is, when he shows the limit of thinking about the soul. Lacan claims in this regard that thinking about the Aristotelian soul is a means to "befriend" what is incomprehensible, but it is a befriending that always fails, and no one illustrates this inherent failure of thought's attempt to befriend the body through the soul better than Aristotle. That is, if thinking about the body through the soul has left the body incomprehensible precisely where the body is corporeal, then thinking about the soul leaves the soul incomprehensible precisely where Aristotle tries, at least to some extent, to rescue it from its submission to the body.

The soul is the body's movement and affection (change), the body's power to move, sense, and imagine, a kind of non-material organ that bears the signs the body makes. The soul is the driving force, the cause of bodily regularity that is not in itself material. The description of the soul as present in the body relies on using the soul as an instrument for thinking about the body, but in the process, the possibility of saying what the soul is as an object of that thought is lost. We will now see the implications of these two aspects of the soul – the soul as an instrument for thinking about the body and the soul as an object of thought – by examining Lacan's discussion of Aristotle with regard to feminine sexuality.

As we have seen, the most distinct expression of the Aristotelian soul is the attempt to use the psychic instrument to turn the Other into something familiar. Aristotle, however, turned speaking about the soul not into a theory, but rather into a discourse of love. Indeed, Lacan says, the only way to speak about the soul is in a love letter, and not just any love letter but *une lettre d'âmour*, a soulover's letter. He even proposes a verb – *âimer* – with grammatical conjugations that would allow anyone to venture and practise a different way to speak about the soul: I soulove, you soulove, and so on. In Zucchi's painting, Lacan relates the birth of the soul to the moment in which the desire of the Other (Eros) is separated from the subject, but leaves a mark or a sign. Faced with this sign, which in itself has no signifying value, one can ask what the Other wants, that is, try to decipher what the Other's desire is, and the soul is intended to enable such deciphering. Aristotle, Lacan will say, offers us the soul as that which loves the Other and by virtue of this soulove manages to cut the Other to its own measure:

> I'm one of those people who doesn't give the psychological presupposi-
> tions, thanks to which all of that lasted so long, a good reputation. Still,
> it is hard to see why the fact of having a soul should be a scandal for
> thought – if it were true. If it were true, the soul could not be spoken except
> on the basis of what allows a being – speaking being, to call it by its name –
> to bear what is intolerable in its world, which assumes that the soul is
> foreign to it, in other words, phantasmatic. Which considers the soul to be
> here – in other words, in this world – owing only to its patience and cour-
> age in confronting it. That is confirmed by the fact that, up until our time,
> the soul has never had any other meaning.[34]

With these words Lacan touches on the heart of the role he ascribes to the soul in Seminar XX, which concerns feminine sexuality. We will have to examine what the characterization of the Aristotelian soul, as we have seen it thus far, can contribute to the examination of feminine sexuality in this seminar. "Isn't it plain to see," Lacan asks, "that the soul is nothing other than the supposed identicalness of this body to everything people think in order to explain it?"[35] In short, the role of the soul, and of the Aristotelian soul as representative of the soul in general, is to pave the way for the speaking being to its body. The soul paves the way for thought to its most obstinate companion – the body, just as it paves the way for the subject to its most indispensable other – his sexual partner. It is the soul that draws the speaking being closer to what is foreign and incomprehensible, what is a scandal for thought and is also its complement, and inseparable partner.

The soul that allows thought to come to terms with the body, serves the important interest of philosophy of *reconciling the scandal of the body with the rule of thought*. The soul appears as a way to resolve this scan-dal, by carrying all that is foreign to us in our body's movement and in the body's effects on us, and that thought has difficulty explaining. The soul, the Aristotelian soul, appears in this context as the repository of signs provided by the body, and through it, it becomes possible to decipher "what the body wants from us." The soul is a kind of phantasmatic adjunct that injects meaning into what cannot be explained. In Aristotle the soul appears as that which bears the life that animates the body, while in psychology, for example, it serves as a general heading for emotions or the effects of worldly suffering, appearing as a different, sensitive, raw aspect of human existence; thus the psychological soul also carries what is a scandal for thought.

It therefore means that for Lacan, the soul is necessary where being is posited from the outset as *speaking being*, that is, as a thought for whom the body is a scandal. Therefore, for the soul to fulfil its role for thought, one must suppose from the outset that the soul is a scandal for thought, that is, that it represents what is foreign to thought. It is precisely this dialectic, Lacan shows, that Aristotle captured with his soul: the place of the soul is the result of removing what is foreign on the one hand, while on the other hand turning this foreign element into a phantasmatic reality and into an object suitable for thought. In order to think about the soul – that is, in order for thought to be assured a place on the winning side of being – it is necessary to invent a soul as a container for all that is insupportable for thought. This is the Aristotelian soul that Lacan utilizes in order to decipher the relation between feminine sexuality (a sexuality defined as other sexuality) and the subject of language. For feminine sexuality is a kind of scandal for the sexuality of the speaking being, which is defined in psychoanalysis as a phallic sexuality.

The soul, then, appears most emblematically as a symptom of what is removed from a certain discursive field. In contrast to the spirit, for example, the soul appears in philosophy in order to allow room for the body while also relieving philosophy of the need to deal with the body in itself. By contrast, "spirit" is the element that lies outside all corporeality, completely unchallenged by bodily matter; the soul is a way of making the body present in thought so that the body remains a distinct and excluded object. Looked at from the other direction, the soul can be seen as a symptom of exclusion. When psychology deals with the psyche or soul, it is driven by an interest that complements the philosophical one: it wishes to explore the soul so that it, the soul, takes upon itself all that is unbearable in the world of the speaking being, leaving this place outside thought and thus allowing thought to think about the soul without being "infected" with soulness. Does this not encapsulate the strange relationship between philosophy and psychology, which play into each other's hands and out of ostensible mutual respect leave thought to philosophy and the soul to psychology?

Lacan believes that through the soul, psychology plants an imaginary other – that is, an other that seems close to being, an intimate part of it – in the place occupied in practice by what is absolutely other to the speaking being – an other that appears in the Lacanian economy under the symbol S(Ø). The Other – the body, for example – is barred in the sense that it is foreign to being, that it is only partially expressible. But through the soul, psychology wishes to mask this lack, to befriend what is foreign, and refuses articulation by interpreting it in terms of soulness. Aristotle's soul, unlike the psychological soul, is a way of saying that there is something unknown in the body and that it is the soul which testifies to this foreignness. The soul is a way of making what is incomprehensible present without making this otherness comprehensible, let alone an object of knowledge. But this soul nevertheless enables us to address the Other as something that provides signs, just as it is the soul that enables us to come to terms with feminine sexuality, an other sexuality that provides signs. It is a way of making what is absolutely other a little closer to being, closer to the speaking being, that is, which is subject to the phallic law. When one throws a stone, one has no idea where it might land; if we posit a soul for the stone, it means that we posit the possibility of knowing what the object's movement is, even if the movement is not knowable. The body is set up for action as woman is set up for sexuality, and the actualization of woman, like the actualization of the body, even if neither depends on the substance we call soul, this soul assumes knowledge of their modes of actualization. The soul is the testimony and the carrier of signs of undecipherable otherness. The soul, in other words, is not a way of interpreting the Other, but a carrier of the sign of its otherness – within one's grasp.

The invention of the soul, Lacan says, is the invention of that which exists in the world and is identified with all that is insufferable, that causes suffering. Whether the suffering is physical or imaginary or symbolic, at the place where something affects or hurts us, the subject – the subject of thought and of the signifier – disappears, and what appears in its place and allows the snivelling body to remerge with the subject, is the soul. The soul is necessary, then, precisely because man is identified with thought. But the soul is not simply the site where we place what is foreign, incomprehensible, or unbearable for the thinking being ("a scandal for thought"); the soul does not occur as a form of exclusion but as a phantasmatic place that allows the speaking being "to befriend" this incomprehensible part that is hard for thought to bear – a befriending that is merely the conquest of the body through the psychic instrument.

To speak about the soul means to tell a story about what is absolutely other by turning it into an organ of desire, which is brought into being's range of vision by a phantasmatic story. In Aristotle's *De Anima* we find the most emblematic example of this strain of thought: in order for us to think about the causes of being alive, that is, possessing a body that has life in it, the soul appears so that it can serve as such a cause, so that instead of speaking about the body through thought, which constitutes an external, separate authority from the body (which in the course of history will become Descartes's solution), it becomes possible for us to use *the soul as the organ of thought in the body*. This is a way of making what is foreign to thought in its organic, real existence attainable and describable, since from the outset, by virtue of its very being, the soul carries a corporeal trait. The psychic instrument enables us to speak in the body on the side of thought.

Thus, if there is a critical importance to Lacan's use of Aristotle, it is that the soul is not only an imaginary container in which we put all that is incomprehensible in the body's snivelling. Even if he did not have all the correct terms, Aristotle understood that being is founded in the body and that the soul is needed in order to grasp something of what is real in the body, of what connects the body to being, of what enables being to possess a body.

Aristotle posited the possibility of knowing the desire of the other through the soul. Is it not, for example, a phantasm to impute a soul to animals and thus assume knowledge about the causes of their actions (for instance, by granting them a soul that has human traits)? This is not that far from positing universal laws that enable knowing what causes the trajectory of a thrown stone. Aristotle posits knowledge at the origin, knowledge of causes, and he was not completely out of bounds in doing so, says Lacan, "except that the body is made of an activity, and that somewhere the entelechy [= complete realization] of this body is based on the substance he calls the soul."[36] It is not just that the place of the Aristotelian soul is phantasmatic, but that through the phantasm the soul mediates the relationship between thought and body, between knowledge and complete otherness. Likewise, the thought of woman as a sexual partner and as an object that powers desire is a phantasmatic mediation of the relationship between the subject – which is subject to the phallic function – and what is completely other from it, that is, woman. The soul, which is the imaginary embodiment of what we do not know and do not understand about the body's snivelling, is also the brave embodiment of a wish to speak about the body, a wish that can only be realized by *violating the total separation between thought and body*. The speaking being considers what it has that can make the body accessible, and answers this question with the soul. To think about the body, even if it is on the winning side of thought, requires something to intermingle with the body on the side of thought, and such is the Aristotelian soul.

Woman herself, then, is souloving (*âmoureuse*). Woman, who is herself a scandal to phallic sexuality, souloves, that is, she posits herself in the Other, cut to its measure. "What can that soul be that they [women] soulove in their partner, who is nevertheless homo to the hilt, from which they cannot get away? That can only, in effect, lead them to … hysteria, namely, to play the part of the man [*faire l'homme*], as I have said, being thus *hommosexual* or *beyondsex* themselves … they love each other as the same [*ells se mêment*] in the Other."[37] Woman is the soul of sexuality: she leaves the otherness of feminine sexuality outside in order to "come to terms" with phallic sexuality.

The conquest of the body with the instrument of the soul, soulove, comes with a price. The price is that soulove, love of the soul, is necessarily a love that is beyond sex (*horsexe*). When the soul is summoned so that what is foreign in the other is loved, this love leaves no residue: love where there is no sex. The soul allows woman to appear as the object of desire of *hommo*, that is, man, but had she remained only in that function of soulover, she would have disappeared under the phallic sexuality. This is why Lacan will say in this seminar that the object we call soul, the object that receives the symbol *a*, is the perverse object in any love, including neurotic love. That is, it is the object that makes the big Other accessible and it is perverse because the one who is perverse identifies with this object as an object that holds the condition for the other's livingness, in other words, for his *jouissance*. It is the soul that allows woman to love man as a woman like all women, because woman uses the soul in order to appear as the object that supports man's desire. That is, in appearing as a woman for man, woman severs herself from the absolute otherness of woman and becomes a woman who is a derivative of man's desire, who is identical with the object that is man's desire. She becomes part of the *hommo*-sexual economy, of the economy determined by man's (*homme*) desire.

It is when woman differentiates herself from the soul (from the same-as-her that exists in other women and men) – that is, from the *hommo*-sexuality that is beyond sexuality – that she is called a woman (rather than a woman who identifies with man's object of *jouissance*) and is defamed (and in French: *diffâme, dit-femme*), that is, placed as a woman, and therefore other.

We can thus see how the soul, in its mediating role, takes us closer to the psychoanalytic thinking that refuses an easy separation between thought and body. Lacan's return to the Aristotelian soul is hence focused on where Aristotle has difficulty positing the soul as a separate authority, identifying a purely mental faculty since this difficulty precludes a separation between thought and body. That is, we can think of thought in the soul, and of the soul as a real presence in the body, as analogous to the way in which the psychoanalytic psyche animates the body, turning the body into a site of psychic economy. This place of the soul is necessary for psychoanalytic thought for exactly the same reason that it forms a cornerstone of Aristotle's philosophy.

How do we account for these two manifestations of the soul, from Aristotle to the gateways of feminine sexuality? We can say that Freud, searching for a way to think about the psyche, found it in the framework of meta-psychology – that is, in order for us to speak of the psyche, it must be turned into an object for thought. We can say that meta-psychology is an Aristotelian endeavour that, by describing the structure and various parts of the psyche, aims to allow us to come to terms with the places where the drive is inscribed in the body and makes the body incomprehensible, unknowable.

To sum up, the practice of soulove encapsulates a possible way to read the connection between Lacan and Aristotle, a connection we have traced in three steps.

The first step is related to the way in which Aristotle establishes the difference between body and soul by bringing them together, a move characterized by Lacan as speaking about the body on the winning side of thought. The soul appears where the body is no longer for itself, but is animated, moved and changed by faculties of the soul.

The second step is related to the way in which Aristotle shows how the soul is connected to some bodily remainder (incomprehensible in itself), a moment Lacan associates with the birth of psyche. Lacan claims the soul refers to the moment in which something incomprehensible is differentiated from the body, and the soul appears as an agent of pathos facing this incomprehensibility.

The third step is related to the way in which Aristotle refers to the soul as having form and purpose; this produces an intricate picture of the soul as actuality and as potentiality. Where the soul eludes decisive characterization in any of these orders, the difficulty of thinking of or about the soul is demonstrated. The soul is on the winning side of thought but is not an object of knowledge.

We can say that Lacan reads Aristotle in order to clarify two ways of thinking and speaking about what is foreign to us and is nonetheless constitutive of the speaking being. One way is that of thinking *with* the soul, in order to eliminate the other's otherness, to turn this otherness into something that is cut to our measure. This is the option of using the soul to eliminate otherness, to sidestep it and its incomprehensible signs. The other option is that of soulove where the soul supports the befriending of the body. Soulove consigns speaking about the soul to failure, to missing its object, but at the same time it grasps something that is essential to the soul. Loving the soul allows thought to say something about it, but this speech, as it turns out, remains equally partial and thwarted: in itself, the fact that something's foreignness is eliminated, that it is loved as if it were an intimate part of us, promises nothing. Aristotle is a soulover because, by means of the psychic instrument, he proposes a move that makes it possible to befriend corporeality. *On the Soul* is the love letter of a true soulover, since through the soul Aristotle breathes movement, animation, and life into what is fundamentally a scandal for thought. Soulove is therefore a way to make use of the soul to befriend, rather than exclude or suppress the reality of the body.

Aristotle dedicates an entire treatise to the soul that moves the body, a soul that he regards as breathing life, as being the first grade of actuality of being-human. Aristotle is a soulover, and "women too are in soulove [*âmoureuses*], in other words … they soulove the soul,"[38] as Lacan says. It is precisely woman, who is radically other from man, who souloves (and not: loves the soul): this is because woman, in order to be other, does not need to know this otherness.

Chapter 4

To Think or Not to Be:
Lacan with Descartes

[Thought] is without cause, but not without object.
                           – Lacan, *L'angoisse*, 26.6.63, 360[311][1]

Descartes's "I think therefore I am" marked a moment in the history of thought in which a new relation was established between the subject and knowledge, a relation that marked the emergence of modern science. This moment, Lacan claims, was essential for psychoanalysis, in that the reason the Cogito marked the appearance of the subject of science was also fundamental for psychoanalysis. With the Cogito, a distinction was made between knowledge and truth, even if ostensibly Descartes believed that the Cogito was the moment of their convergence. Lacan's claim that Descartes inaugurated the distinction between knowledge and truth – a distinction that constitutes a condition for science – may therefore seem like one more instance in which Lacan uses philosophy for his own purposes in a way that does not correspond to the words and professed intentions of the philosophers themselves. This book sets out, among other things, to examine those moments in which Lacan seems to bend the philosophers' words to his own needs, and to understand whether Lacan is mistaken or offering a wrong interpretation, or whether he is pointing to the presence of a distinction, a divide, an awareness, in the writing of the philosopher himself, even if this distinction or awareness remains hidden, suppressed, or half-said.

In Descartes's case, the possibility of a distorted reading may appear even more pertinent, since Descartes himself seems to argue decisively *against* the possibility of separating knowledge from truth. In the preface to the *Meditations*, Descartes refers to two objections raised against his previous writings, and his reply to these objections suggests that he identifies what his mind can know – that is, what he acquires knowledge about – with truth. For example, one criticism levelled against Descartes was that even if, as he says, the human mind only knows itself as a thinking thing, it does not follow that its nature or essence can be reduced to thinking alone. To this Descartes replies: "I will show hereafter how, from the consciousness that nothing besides thinking belongs to the essence of the mind, it follows that nothing else does in truth belong to it."[2] That is, Descartes believes that the *Meditations* will show that the essence of man is *truly* thought, and not just because this is what the subject can know. In the same vein of faith in the convergence of knowledge with truth, he claims that the things of which we have very clear and distinct perception are completely real, notwithstanding critics' claims that the clear presence of a concept in man does not indicate that the thing really exists. That is, Descartes wishes to show that there is no gap between what the thinking object knows to be present, and the truth of that knowledge.

At times Lacan acknowledges that Descartes's position has to do with the scientific discourse to which he gave rise. In his 1970 seminar, for example, he claims that "when Descartes asserts his 'I am thinking therefore I am,' it's by virtue of having for sometimes sustained his 'I am thinking' by calling into question, putting in doubt, this knowledge that I am saying is 'fiddled with,' which is the knowledge already elaborated at length through the master's intervention."[3] Put another way, without the support of an already elaborated knowledge – knowledge that is prior to this "fiddling" through doubt – Descartes would not have been able to insist so strongly that "I think therefore I am." That is, Descartes's radical moves (casting doubt, fiddling with, calling into question) rely on the premise of a prior master's knowledge (call this master "God" or any other guarantor of truth) that would serve as a kind of shield against the possibility of knowledge losing its hold on truth.

What does Lacan mean, then, when he credits Descartes with the distinction between knowledge and truth, a distinction that is so central to psychoanalysis but that can only doubtfully be attributed to Descartes himself? As we will see shortly, Lacan uses a series of arguments to justify his claim that the Cogito implies the separation of knowledge from truth; but the question then arises whether and in what way this distinction is present for Descartes himself. Is this distinction attributed to Descartes because it is implicit in his words, even if not explicitly formulated? Is it a distinction that Descartes knows anything about (however strongly it denies and even contradicts his explicit aim to suture knowledge with truth) and that forms a kind of unconscious of the Cartesian text? Lacan does not answer this question directly, perhaps wishing to avoid deciding what the "real truth" about Descartes is.

Generally speaking, we can say the following: the way in which Lacan refers to the Cogito in the context of psychoanalysis suggests that he does not see himself as an interpreter of Descartes, but as someone who knows how to read Descartes's writings. That is, Lacan is not concerned with examining the range of justified interpretations of the Cartesian writings, since the psychoanalytical reading is never subject to criteria of justification and correctness. The psychoanalytical yardstick for a reading is *the measure of its effectiveness*: Will this reading of Descartes advance/change anything in the way we approach the question of the subject's relationship with knowledge? Knowing how to read the Cogito does not necessarily mean making justified claims, but rather making claims that would be effective in using Descartes's thought.

In what way is the distinction between truth and knowledge present in Descartes? The first and obvious thing that can be said about the Cogito is that it distinguishes between existence and thought; the Cogito argument connects the "I am" to the "I think" by means of an invalid logical inference, claims Lacan. That is, Lacan's reading is based on the fact that the Cogito posits an "I think" that is ascribed to *something else* that does not overlap with thought. The non-equivalence between the two parts of the Cogito argument compels us to examine what distinguishes the thinking thing from its existence, as well as why the I's certainty of thinking does not overlap with the truth of its being. Lacan is concerned with this question in various ways, and it will also be the concern of this chapter. Note that Lacan sometimes emphasizes that Descartes tries to suture and disguise this non-equivalence, and criticizes him for it; whereas at other times Lacan emphasizes precisely the disruption that is obstinately present whenever Descartes tries to transition from "I think" to "I am." In any event, the issue of the relationship between the two parts of the Cogito, between thought and being, is the kernel around which Descartes's *Meditations* revolve. Says Lacan.

How does Lacan read the relationship between thought (knowledge) and existence (the truth of being) in Descartes? We can say that in general, Descartes's Cogito enforces the distinction between truth and knowledge because Descartes does not strive for truth but rather for certainty (of knowledge), while imputing truth to the other – to the one who guarantees, beyond Descartes himself, that what can be known with certainty is true. In Descartes's move to attain certainty there is no internal necessity for truth to exist; and even the necessity for the big Other – that is, for Descartes's God – to exist is the necessity of *knowing* the concept of God as a concept of perfection, infinity, and so on. The truth that is ascribed to the other is beyond the I's grasp ("I possess no other faculty whereby to distinguish truth from error").[4] That is, Descartes distinguishes between the certainty that is established for the thinking I, and the truth that is established in the field of God (who governs and ensures the correspondence between truth and knowledge).

Lacan formulates the distinction between truth and knowledge in Descartes in yet another way by claiming that what enables the thinking I to attain certainty is the fact that this certainty already *presupposes* the existence of true knowledge and the relevant criteria that attest to it (i.e., the clarity and distinctiveness of the attained knowledge). It is "a knowledge always linked, still caught up until then, like a string on its paw [*par un fil à la patte*], on the critical fact that the beginning of this knowledge is linked to the possibility of constituting the truth."[5] That is, in positing the thinking I, Descartes does not claim something about the Cogito's essence; rather, "I think" is an agency (*instance*)[6] that relies on the knowledge already posited along with it, like a string that is tied to a bird's claw and determines the direction of its flight. This postulation that knowledge is something that underpins thinking being even before knowledge is acquired is also the condition for the existence of a scientific discourse. Lacan, in other words, asserts that "the one who thinks" is the one who does not have knowledge but who assumes knowledge, and as the one who does not hold the truth but who supposes the other to be the guarantor of truth.

So for Descartes, "I think" already assumes the real presence of knowledge. It is not that knowledge is *a priori*, or that it is future knowledge; rather, it is present as identical to "the one who knows" (rather than to the sum of the knowledge that the I possesses or will possess). Cartesian being is therefore merely the convergence of the *certainty* that supposes the possibility of knowledge and the *truth* that is posited as supporting this knowledge. Truth is posited by the very existence of certainty as a clear and distinct testimony to the existence of "I think": "From this [from the moment I am thinking] I begin to know what I am with somewhat greater clearness and distinctness than heretofore,"[7] says Descartes, thus indicating that truth is already present when thought substantiates the I, although this truth is not in the possession of the subject of thought. The Cogito does not know why certain things appear before it as clear and distinct, but by ascribing truth to an other who so wishes, the I can see what certainty has led to, to a knowledge that enjoys the status of truth.

But none of this explains what takes place at the moment of the emergence of the certainty that is embodied in "I think" and that produces a necessary split between thought and existence. What is *the reality of thought* that appears at this moment when the Cogito emerges?

> Is there not an absolutely essential element that remains, whatever we do to insert it into this structure, to reduce it? That all the same remains as a final kernel and that is called intuition. Assuredly, it is the question from which Descartes started. I mean, I would point out to you, that mathematical reasoning, as he saw it, extracted nothing efficacious, creative, anything whatsoever that was of the order of reasoning, but simply its start, namely, an original intuition, the one that is posited, established by its original distinction between space and thinking.[8]

The idea that Lacan is expressing in this passage is that Descartes's original drive and his important achievement were related to his *intuition* to distinguish between extension and thought. That is, contrary to the common belief that credits Descartes with inaugurating the subject of thought and reason (as separate from the subject as a body or an extension), Lacan claims that Descartes inaugurated something else: *the kernel from which thought can appear as distinct from extension*. This is the real basis for indicating the *cause of thought* at a moment of intuition (which precedes reasoning and is hence outside the grasp of mathematical thought). Descartes did not inaugurate pure thought as distinct (this was known by the mathematicians of old), but rather the moment of the constitution of thought, the original moment in which thought appears as separate from the order of extension:

> In the next place, I attentively examined what I was and as I observed that I could suppose that I had no body, and that there was no world nor any place in which I might be; but that I could not therefore suppose that I was not; and that, on the contrary … I was a substance whose whole essence or nature consists only in thinking, and which, that it may exist, has need of no place, nor is dependent on any material thing.[9]

The moment of intuition is the moment in which thought appears as separated from the manner of the I's existence in the world. In what follows, we will examine why Lacan sees the kernel of the Cogito as a kernel of intuition. The claim that Descartes is concerned with the *cause* of thought is based on the fact that in the formulation of the Cogito there is no attempt to found the thinking I on its rational qualities, and that no characterization of thought is necessitated by the Cogito argument. The certainty of the Cogito does not depend on the sharpness of thought or on the intellectual powers of the thinker. According to Lacan, the agency (*instance*) of the Cogito is not an agency of cognition, one that is characterized by knowledge. But at the same time, contrary to some interpretations, Lacan is not suggesting that the thinking object is identical with the constitution of a formal agency at a moment where the I has vacated itself from any knowledge, where it encounters the kernel of its existence as a thinking being, a kernel reduced to a kind of empty vessel (which would later become filled with all kinds of thoughts, all clear and distinct, as required in the name of reason). The Cogito argument is not intended to reduce thought to a mere formal instantiation, and just as Descartes does not commit with this argument to the essence of thought, neither does he reduce it to identifying "I think" with a formal and empty label. Rather, the Cogito argument argues that thought exists *as such*, that is, as thought that is real although it is, so to speak, thought that has no character.

The intuition that Lacan ascribes to Descartes is hence not related to the *nature* of thought; rather, it points to the reality of thought as determined at the moment something is inscribed, as "I think." At that moment, intuition separates extension from thought but at the same time serves as the irreducible kernel of the Cogito. It is intuition that makes thought real and distinguishes it from the pure reasoning that is the credo of mathematicians.

For Descartes, "I think" inscribes the kernel of intuition, which is no mean thing. Descartes understood that the inscription of thought is of a different order than thought itself. "I think" is not a symbolic inscription (like a mathematical sign, which includes a mode of reasoning), or an imaginary one (representing an object or a subject of knowledge); rather, intuition is identified with the very act of inscribing thought prior to attributing qualities to thought.

But if "I think" is not equivalent to a mere formal sign, why connect Descartes's Cogito to inscription or writing? Lacan sees the Cogito as a moment of pure writing, the writing of an "I think" that has no reverberations of meaning (such as who is the I who thinks, or what is his thought) and that does not inaugurate a chain of signifiers (nothing stems from the fact that "I think"). It is the writing of a pure trait, neither symbolic nor imaginary, and this trait points to the difference that thought generates from extension; but the trait itself is not a trait of thought but *a trait that inaugurates thought* while separating it from the intuition that allowed thought to appear. For Lacan, this act of writing resembles what he called, following Freud, *the unary trait*. It is the trait that inscribes the subject as different, as separate, without the trait itself containing anything that would define the singularity of the subject, or point to those from whom the subject is separate. That is, the trait has no distinguishing characteristic, but it nevertheless contains the radical difference that establishes the individual case: it is a kind of fingerprint that denotes a difference while resembling any other fingerprint. The unary trait therefore has "depth," a depth that stems from the very act of separation, from the very act of inscription, a depth that is related to the fact that even if the trait resembles any other trait, like a mathematical sign or a groove in a wooden panel, it still constitutes distinctness. In exactly the same way, Descartes's Cogito gives depth to the moment in which thought is constituted, not because thought is essentially different from extending things, and not because thought is unique to the category of thinking objects, but precisely where *thought is inscribed as a trait, a sign that leaves no remainder*.

But how can this relation between the Cogito and the intuition that discerns "the one who thinks" be reconciled with the common claim – which Lacan, as mentioned earlier, does not deny – that the Cogito inaugurates the subject of science, that is, that the subject of the Cogito has an essential connection with knowledge?

> The subject is what is lacking to knowledge. Knowledge in its presence, in its mass, in its own growth regulated by the laws which are different to those of intuition, which are those of the symbolic operation and of a close copulation of number with a real which is above all the real of a knowledge, this is what it is a matter of analyzing in order to give the status, the true status of what is meant by a subject at the historical moment of science.[10]

The Cartesian subject, says Lacan, is concerned with knowledge and in this sense conditions the constitution of science. But the subject of the Cogito does not disappear in knowledge or become assimilated into the relationship between the signs of knowledge and the objects of knowledge. Since the establishment of the subject as a subject of knowledge takes place at a moment of doubt – that is, when the subject is still without knowledge – when knowledge does appear, the subject is what will be subtracted from knowledge in order to enable the constitution of knowledge. The Cogito is therefore the moment of the foundation of a subject of knowledge, but that knowledge is separate from the being of the subject itself. This is the point of departure for understanding the Cartesian subject's connection to science. In order for the thinking subject to be able to construct knowledge, the point of departure must be one in which knowledge does not coincide with this subject, and is not present or included in advance in it, and this is exactly the meaning of intuition at the moment of the Cogito's constitution. *Intuition as the cause of thought is what is excluded*, what is subtracted once thought begins to formulate propositions that carry knowledge.

But the essential moment for science that Descartes delineates has more to it than this. Descartes not only outlines the basic idea that leads to the thinking I as intuition, but also suggests that at the moment of establishing the Cogito, the clarity and distinctness are already present. This is why Descartes marks a revolution in scientific thought, since "from Descartes on, knowledge, that of science, is constituted on the mode of the production of knowledge ... the relationship of the Cartesian subject to that being which is affirmed in it, is founded on the accumulation of knowledge. Knowledge from Descartes on is what can serve to increase knowledge. And this is a completely different question to that of truth."[11] Descartes attributes truth to a different element, to God; he even says that two plus two equals four because this is how God wants it. That is, truth is absolutely handed over to another agency. But because the moment of the subject's constitution as a thinking thing already contains the idea of clear and distinct knowledge, this idea can facilitate the accumulation of knowledge, and *this* is the turning point that Descartes marks with regard to science. The standard for valid knowledge is present even before knowledge itself is created.

Lacan's reading of Descartes's *Meditations* points to the Cogito as the cause of thought, as a moment when under the signifier "I think," thought is distinguished from extension. At this stage something is subtracted from being so that it can appear as an agent of thought and as the cause from which thoughts will ensue. It is this subtraction that is inscribed at the moment the "I think" appears, even before anything can be said about the nature of the thinking thing. In the following sections we look at some of the arguments Lacan develops in order to substantiate this reading.

A. I Think *therefore* I Am

Descartes says: "I think therefore I am"; these words affirm thought plus something else that can be deduced from thought – existence. How should we understand the relation that Descartes establishes between these two affirmative sentences?

The Cogito connects being with thought around an intuitive moment that establishes the possibility of knowledge but is still devoid of knowledge. This connection is signified through the "therefore" (ergo) of the Cogito: think therefore exist. This "therefore," Lacan claims, does not designate a logical necessity,[12] but a causal relationship. It is a *real causality* that presupposes a link between two separates: existence and thought. Lacan proposes that we understand the Cogito as follows: it is I who cast doubt, think, perceive; therefore, I exist. That is, since a thing appears, whose thought is separate from its extension in its world, it follows that this thing that thinks, casts doubt, and so forth – exists. Positing *it* (*ça*) in the act of thinking posits *it* also as existing, yet existing is possible because of the moment in which the thinking I appeared as separate. The something that exists is the very separateness of thought, at the moment of the thinker's distinction as such: as an I think.

Descartes's Cogito, like other Cartesian concepts, is mentioned count-less times in Lacan's teaching, and in general we will see in this chapter that doubt, certainty, thought, the I – all of Descartes's basic concepts – serve Lacan for the same purpose: *to point to what is real in thought.* Descartes's moves are not intended to isolate thought and designate it as the most essential thing for the I's determination; nor are these moves intended to reduce thought to mere formality. Rather, according to Lacan, thought is the element that constitutes the separate existence of a subject. Thought for Descartes is not the essence of the subject, nor does it necessitate the existence of a subject who carries thought or rep-resents it; rather, thought is the very cause of our being.

Thought, Lacan says in Seminar XVII, "is not a category. I would almost say it is an affect."[13] Lacan's claim that thought is an affect creates a shift in the relation between Lacan and Descartes. For the affective dimension of thought can only be seen from the standpoint of psychoanalysis, since thought is merely the moment in which *the speaking being is caught in the discourse*, where the discourse determines the status of this being as what is caught in it. In other words, according to Lacan, Descartes's Cogito received its exemplary value in the history of thought because it revealed precisely this: the way in which the place of

"I think," still without knowledge, is the place where language acquires its realness, where speech constitutes *who* speaks as *what* speaks.

"I think therefore I am" because thought is that moment in which what thinks appears as a thinking *thing*, as a discursive instance. Thought is therefore almost an affect, because it points to a primal moment in which thought appears and creates movement in language, movement that also disrupts the operation of language. Since psychoanalysis sees certain affects (such as anxiety, or shame) as connected to a primordial moment in which a sign, a word, a trait become connected to being, it follows that to say that the thinker is affected by thought, means that the moment of being caught in thought is a moment in which what *thinks* also *is*.

Thought is almost an affect, Lacan says, but it is not a category. To say that thought is not a category means that thought does not define or identify the thinking thing; thought is not a function that singles out a set (the set of "all the thinking things"), but thought is an affect, that is, it qualifies the subject's way of being, of being determined by thought. "All determination of the subject, and therefore of thought, depends on discourse,"[14] claims Lacan, and at this point we can see the kinship between Descartes's thinking I and the Hegelian master. Both appear as "I-am" – *m'être*[15] – that is, with a signifier that appears as the effect of the presence of a thinking thing, a presence of what does not necessarily think but is *what* thinks; to begin with, thought is suspended, is deferred in relation to the possibility of saying "I *think*." The Hegelian master, just like the Cogito, thinks without knowing what he thinks, without knowing (since the slave thinks and knows in his stead).

The question thus arises: if thought is not a category and if existence is only a sign that inscribes the I in discourse, "I think therefore I am" may be comprised of two clauses that merely repeat the same thing; it is difficult to see what interval there is between the two. However, Lacan, although turning to the Cogito in different places for different purposes, sticks to his position that "I am" *adds something* to "I think." In Seminar IX he calls the "I think therefore I am" *an impossibility*; that is, he suggests that it is impossible to formulate the connection between the two parts of the Cogito (i.e., they do not state the same or compose one whole). But it is this impossibility that gives Descartes's subject, the subject of philosophizing for hundreds of years, its special *weight*. Lacan says that what weighs (*peser*) in the Cogito stems from the weightiness of thought (*penser*).[16] If the thinking being has weight, we can understand why even if "I am" adds nothing to "I think," they are not equivalent or overlapping. Something else than thought weighs on the subject in thinking, and this something that gives weight to thought is indicated by the causal connection.

To understand what *weighs* in thought, let us recall that the analyst knows that when the subject says "*this* is what I'm thinking of," "this" refers back to "the place from which I'm thinking," rather than necessarily to the content of what one is thinking about. This is because for psychoanalysis, this place from which one is thinking is the place of the fundamental split between *what* one is thinking and the *it* that is thinking – that is, the place where the subject of the unconscious is constituted. From this place one can return to the Cogito and examine what is the weight of thought in Descartes; this will reveal the privileged presence of a pure "I think" that promises that in each and every moment the subject's existence will be ensured due to the very fact that he thinks: "I am conscious that I exist, and I who know that I exist inquire into what I am."[17]

Does Descartes's formula imply, then, that in order to ensure his existence (*s'assurer d'être*) the subject must *rethink* again and again his thinking being? Is it enough for him to think about his being in order to touch his existence, that is, his thinking *being*? This possibility we have arrived at – that the weight of thought is related to the fact that whenever an I thinks about his being, he ensures the existence of a thinking being – is one that seems different from Descartes's assertions in the two first meditations, where the certainty of the "I think" seems to almost spontaneously erupt by virtue of the very fact that I is thinking, but also feeling, sensing, or imagining. But the difference between these two possibilities (between being as a consequence of the reflexivity of the fact of thinking, and being as a spontaneous consequence of there being a thing that thinks) are two different ways of understanding the "something else" that is added to thought as part of the Cogito. Note that Lacan certainly does not read Descartes as someone who relies on a facile philosophical correlation between the fact of thought and the fact of existence. For Descartes, there is nothing self-evident in the appearance of being by virtue of thought; so rather than go beyond the philosopher in order to highlight his mistake or myopia, we should examine what, for Descartes, is that thinking being (*être pensant*) without which the "I think" would have no weight.

The certainty of the Cogito is not self-evident, claims Lacan. When the "I" thinks, it already outlines the presence of something to which thought is ascribed. That is, thought appears to necessitate the presence of a thinking thing even before anything is said about the *nature* of thought and even when the *existence* of a thinking being is denied. In other words, the certainty of the Cogito appears to camouflage the causal gap that opens up between "I think" and the thing that thinks.

In his seminar on "Identification" Lacan seems to suggest that "I think" is the sign of an act of intervention, in the course of which a place is assigned to the thinking being. This intervention testifies to the gap between thinking and being, and that gap is sustained by the Cogito without the Cogito clarifying either the category of thought or the determination of thought by existence. The Cogito, in other words, attests to the weight of thought on the signifier of the I, as revealed in a number of grammatical "symptoms" that accompany the thinking being. Lacan points, for example, to the possibility of constructing verbs in which thought is prefixed by something else – *recompenser, décompenser, surcompenser* – these composite verbs generate equally legitimate constructions and produce the same effect (of certainty in the existence of the thinking I). This is a sign of what Descartes himself attests to: the thinking thing does not necessarily think – that is, thought is not a necessary qualification of the *res cogitans*.[18]

A second grammatical sign Lacan refers to is the impossibility of identifying the "I think" with a thinking being (an I who both thinks and exists). Try, for example, to turn the thinking being into a composite noun – *êtrepensant*; since only the I can say "I think," and even then, this I think does not turn the I into a thinking being. The thinking I has to overcome an irreducible gap between thinking and being (in order to say about himself with exemplary evidentiality that he is a thing that thinks). Thus, even the "I" cannot appear as the one who thinks, but only as "I think," that is, only as the one who says "I think."

There is another possibility for addressing the being of the thinking I through the conjugation of a verb – *pensêtre*: "je pensêtre," "tu pensêtres," "il pensêtre," and so on.[19] We can ask whether *pensêtre* turns the thinking I into a thinking being/thing. *Pensêtre* leaves no gap in which to know what it means to attribute thought to being; any possible reflexivity of thought about the nature of the thinking being has been eliminated. Lacan claims that *pensêtre* is a way of rejecting the knowledge of the "I think" about the nature of thought as the essence of being. In other words, we again come full circle to face the same conclusion: *the Cogito is a moment devoid of knowledge about thought and the being on whom thought weighs.*

Being, then, cannot simultaneously be *êtrepensant* and think, and when I thinks it cannot be certain of its thoughts. As was indicated earlier, a thinking being can be reduced to the following formulation: "I think: 'I am a thinking being'" (i.e., the thinking being is merely the content of thought rather than a possible declension of "I think"). Now if it is a matter of a thing whose being lies in its very thinking, then being determines only the register of thought, while thinking does not determine much and can be either thought, sensation, dream, or hallucination. When being knows in advance in what register it operates – that is, in what register of thought – it means it has knowledge about the fact that it is thinking even when it is a thinking being that is dreaming, for example. That is, here the thinking being is assigned the position of god.

From the grammatical analysis and from Lacan's other arguments it emerges that the Cogito creates an impossible link between its two clauses, and also that the only way to overcome this, albeit partially, is through the *I*: the *ego cogito*. Indeed, although the I is placed under radical doubt in Descartes's argument, when the body and the senses are thoroughly denied the I nevertheless survives the sceptical move and remains beyond doubt: "But when I *see* or *think I see* … it is simply not possible that I who am now thinking am not *something*."[20] Why is it that *doubt stops at the I*? Why does the hyperbolic doubt protect the I, leaving it in its vacillation (between thought and existence) beyond doubt? If the I is necessarily something, then it cannot exist only as either thinking or being, or only as thought *per se* (for thought as such does not guarantee certainty). That is, the certainty that the Cartesian method presents us with in relation to the I is the certainty of the I's presence as a *vanishing presence*, says Lacan. "I think and I am not," that is, I waste all my being in thinking, and only when I stop thinking for a moment can I glimpse the fact that I am. Yet the I is certain, it perseveres despite the split between thinking and being.

Lacan stresses that the I does not necessarily think and does not necessarily exist, and he again offers grammatical signs of this fact. The I is often repressed, even suppressed, in speech or in thought. Therefore, when one asks in French, "Who did this?," the answer cannot be *je*, only *moi*. Or when one pronounces the sentence "I don't know" (Je *ne* sais pas), it will appear in speech as "ch'sais pas," that is, the negation entails the *suppression of the I* (the e of the ego). This is not anecdotal information on the part of Lacan: the way language is used exhibits the presence of the subject involved in speaking and thinking. Lacan claims that the French exposes the fact that while the I can be subject to all kinds of negation, when one says "I don't know" the negation "ne" applies to the knowing rather than to the I. The I is the only component that is revealed as the irreducible element of the Cogito; the I is what the Cogito affirms beyond all negation, even if the I knows nothing and even if its existence is repressed.

In our examination of the Cogito argument we have found that *it is impossible to affirm either of the two clauses of the Cogito and that the only thing that has weight in the Cogito is the vanishing presence of the I.* This presence is affirmed only under the sign of negation: the I has no thoughts, nor does it exist as a thinking substance. Lacan shows that the formula of the Cogito ties together two propositions that not only are unaffirmable but are not of the same order. Hence, the only way to understand the statement is as follows: I think about myself that I am a thinking being, a formulation whose importance does not lie in the affirmation of thought. Rather, it shows the impossibility of simultaneously ascribing thought and existence to the one who thinks and to the one who exists as a thinking being. There is no way to substantiate the Cogito argument with all its parts, or to substantiate it as one (i.e., as *pensêtre*). Lacan therefore proposes approaching the Cogito argument by negating the elements of the formula, a move that is necessitated by the Cogito argument in its original form, in which the possibility of a thinking being is validated by the negation of (knowledge about) being in the form of doubt.

In this section we have seen how Lacan arrives at the conclusion that the original Cogito should be replaced with a negation of one of the argument's clauses (or both, as we will see below). Negation is necessitated by an analysis of the Cartesian Cogito itself: an I that thinks does not necessarily exist as a thinking thing, and an I that exists is not necessarily thinking. This is why stating the cogito argument affirmatively must take the following formulation: "I am the one who thinks: 'therefore I am.'"[21] The only part of the cogito argument that remains beyond doubt and cannot be negated is the I – it is what flickers into being by virtue of the very movement between thought and existence.

Let us turn, now, to examine further the place of negation in Lacan's interpretation of the Cogito.

B. Either I Do Not Think or I Am Not

In psychoanalysis, negation points to what cannot be thought and is therefore denied existence. When Freud's patient is asked about the identity of a figure that appeared in his dream, he answers: "It is not my mother." The negation of the mother's existence in the dream is not just another case of repression, because rather than offering a substitute formation in place of what has been rejected, it opens up a vacant space (i.e., the negated thing is not there). Here, the negation of existence points to a psychic cause in relation to which thinking about the mother is unbearable.[22] That is, where the ego does not wish to think about the mother and therefore negates her existence, there appears the cause responsible for negating the object.

Freud shows in this context that the dreamer denies the mother existence in his dream because of the dictates of the pleasure principle: thinking about the mother is undesirable and unenjoyable and therefore she is deprived of existence in the dream. That is, the negation is dictated by considerations of pleasure, and the thing whose existence is negated because it disrupts pleasure, in fact affirms the presence of pleasure for the subject. "This is not what I was thinking about," says the subject, thus negating something's existence out of libidinal considerations, since the negation means pushing the negated thing to the place where the ego is not. We can say that through the negation the I empties its arena of undesirable things, thus confirming the pleasure principle, which according to psychoanalysis is the fundamental principle of organizing psychic reality.

Negation for Freud thus has two affirmative effects. Negating the existence of what is not pleasurable for the I requires that this thing exist, but elsewhere. Furthermore, this negation indicates the presence of the pleasure principle, that is, it requires the existence of the subject of the unconscious whose psychic economy is determined by the pleasure principle.

The proximity between the Freudian negation and the radical doubt that enables the Cogito's certainty was not lost on Lacan, who in Seminar XI (1963–64) approached Descartes's Cogito through operations of negation. As mentioned earlier, the presence of negation in Descartes is already evident in the act of doubting. Descartes's doubt is what is called methodical doubt – that is, doubt that is distinguished from scepticism. Scepticism concerns the nature of reality (i.e., it negates existence without remainder); however, Descartes does not doubt reality, but rather one's ability to know its true nature, and therefore, although his doubting is sweeping (radical), the reality of things and bodies will return to substantiate the I's knowledge further down the line. In other words, Descartes's doubt is not an absolute negation (the rejection and complete non-acknowledgment of what has been negated), but rather a temporary denial or repression. Negation in the form of doubt is necessary, because the basis for bringing back reality is the I affirmed by way of doubt as the irreducible weight of the Cogito. That is, the Cogito will reconstitute knowledge following and subject to a procedure of negation from which the I will re-emerge triumphant.

The subject of psychoanalysis also doubts. She does not know the source of her suffering or the cause of her actions and does not recognize herself in them. Faced with the formations of the unconscious, the subject is in the sceptical position of "it is not me" (who is responsible for the slip of the tongue, the suffering in the symptom, the illogic of the dream, the badly taken decisions), although all of these formations are the subject's own invention. The unconscious entails a necessary split between *thinking* (saying or doing) and *being*, as the unconscious formation is detached from the thinking I. The formation of the unconscious is like saying: "this [the symptom, the slip of the tongue] is where the not-I thinks" (or where I do not think). In any case, psychoanalysis forces us to acknowledge that negating the I or negating thought in the I is not nothing.

Just as the certainty of the Cartesian subject requires the negation of all that is usually connected to his existence (his body, his knowledge, his beliefs), so the subject of the unconscious must negate her thinking in order to find her being. The Cartesian subject thinks where he is not, while the subject of the unconscious exists where she does not think, and these two possibilities are equally conditioned on doubt imposed on one of the elements in the form of negation.

Just as the I does not think where the slip of the tongue is made, so the Cartesian I does not think where his thought led him to a series of unfounded or faulty beliefs. "I do not think where I believed I was, and therefore I think where I am not" is a formulation that may express what the Cogito's formula reveals, a formulation that emphasizes that Descartes's doubting resembles the psychoanalytical split between thought and existence. Where I exist (in the world of bodies, sensations, and beliefs), I do not think, and in order to think, the subject must empty the field of the I of everything that accompanies its existence. When Descartes pinpointed the I as the place from which thoughts have been banished, he left us no choice but to regard the I as not thinking, says Lacan.[23] That is, Descartes's Cogito is suffused with the logic of negation, because the place of the thinking I is determined by a negation of what the I is when he is not thinking. The result of the negation is not the negation of the agent himself (i.e., the I); rather, the I maintains itself as thinking by saying "I am not" (i.e., by negating its existence rather than itself). Where I am I do not think, and in order to appear as a thinking I, I must negate all that is included in my existence. The sphere in which the I is located is therefore not a sphere identified with any thought about the I; rather, the I is affirmed by way of negation. The I recognizes itself in what is located outside the place in which it thinks; that is, what exists under negation outside the place of "I think" is exactly what maintains the I itself as thinking.

More than they are intended to logically prove the possible inferences from the Cogito argument, these intricacies – which Lacan traces in various ways and versions throughout his teaching – are meant to show how, *in the Lacanian usage, the Cogito appears both as the subject of the unconscious (whose being depends on what he does not know) and as the subject of science (whose thought depends on obliterating his being).* That is, the Cogito is the vehicle of an inevitable vacillation and split between thought and being. Owing to the presence of this unavoidable split in the Cartesian argument, the attempt to grapple with the certainty that grips the Cogito does not point to a mistake on Descartes's part, but rather reveals that through the Cogito, Descartes says more than his system of thought seems to say explicitly.

For Descartes, the certainty of "I think" empties the subject of both body and thoughts, leaving behind only the fact of thinking itself. We can thus see the mechanism of negation as the mechanism that supports the radical dualism of body and soul in Descartes. Likewise, since "I think" lacks a body and lacks a trait of singular existence, the Cogito could give birth to the subject of science as a universal subject rather than a singular/particular subject. "I think" does not signify anything singular in the thinking subject. But psychoanalysis, in the trajectory it traces in relation to the Cogito, ends up with an "I think" that is not devoid of singular reality, and this therefore demands a formulation of the body-and-mind relations in Descartes in different terms than are usually understood. In the wake of psychoanalysis, singularity returns in the shape of a signifier or a trait that receives affirmation precisely by virtue of the negation of existence. Due to the negation of existence, *"I think" appears as a singular site* that is signified through a trait of *jouissance.* The signifier that represents me, be it a symptom or any other singular trait, is a trait of *jouissance* that signifies the "don't exist" in the arena of thought.

In order to explain these assertions, we will return to Descartes and see that just as in the Freudian negation, doubt (or negation) enables the affirmation of what has been negated. It is the realm of the things that are cast out by doubt that defines and necessitates the boundaries of the I, whose reality is redetermined through the don't-think or don't-exist. The negation of thought and the doubt concerning existence have the essential effect of affirming the place of "not I." Lacan explains the logic that allows the affirmation of the I as a result of doubt/negation through the example of "I do not desire," which demonstrates how the consequences of negation do not concern the existence of what has been negated. Faced with the assertion "I do not desire X," the subject will respond with the question, "What is it that you do not desire?" The negation of desire does not simply mean the affirmation of the object of desire (as in the case of Freud's patient's dream, which is accompanied by the negation of the object of the dream: the mother); rather than negating the subject's desire, it actually constitutes the subject of desire somewhere else. The negation of desire is the I's denial of the fact that she desires, and thus the constitution of a different agency, not-I, to which desire is attributed. Rather than making desire disappear, the erasure of I-as-desiring constitutes the reality of desire somewhere else, where the subject of the unconscious is located.

Descartes's methodical doubt unfolds as the gradual reduction of consciousness, vacating it of any support, of any objective correlation. The subject that remains after the methodical doubt is a vanishing point preserved only by the act of saying "I think." Lacan describes this movement from existence without thought to the certainty of thought as a moment in which the subject wagers on the signifier where the signifier has nothing yet of the subject. The subject does not have a signifier to represent him, to embody any dimension of his existence. What is left in the wake of doubt is therefore an empty point, which is filled by the subject of the saying with a strictly formal subjectivity, cleansed of any content or substance. Kant, Hegel, Husserl, and Lacan agree that Descartes's mistake is that he substantiates the empty place of the Cogito by turning it into a thing that thinks and therefore exists, for in contrast to what Descartes ostensibly claims, the Cogito is not a sphere of existence.

But in a statement that comes very close to positing psychoanalysis as a philosophy, Lacan refrains from joining those who claim that Descartes naively fell into the trap of existence. Lacan states that Descartes knew very well that in exploring the relation between being and thought, what was at stake was the question of Being (être) and not of being (étant). "Being" is what the Greek word einai indicates (which can be equated with the French "ce que c'était être"): what was there before we spoke about it; what *is* as being about to disappear. Everyone knows, claims Lacan, that the philosophical tradition gradually distanced itself from this original discovery, from this primary invention of Greek thought. Relative to this distancing, Descartes had a place of honour. With the Cogito, Descartes "purely and simply substitutes the relation of thinking to being with the instauration of the being of the I."[24] Scientific thought was born with Descartes because he refused to treat the I of thought as Being. It would be Freud who, with psychoanalysis, marked the *return to the question of Being* as it occupied the Greek philosophers.

Lacan's point is that the philosopher, Descartes, was not blind to the cause of the I's thought, to the fact that the relation between thought and being – that is, between thought and the thinking I – implies the question of Being rather than the question of being as such. Descartes decided philosophically to refuse the question of Being, and in this way also decided the history of philosophy (clearly, given that the Cogito has been constantly discussed in philosophical discourse ever since).

This is what stands behind Lacan's assertion that the Cogito is concerned with the cause of thought, a cause that Descartes subtracts from the Cogito rather than assimilates as something that "has just disappeared." This is why "I think" appears as an empty place, a pure and minimal sign that cannot be ascribed any content. The subject cannot be attributed with any uniqueness or character, because it is inscribed as I, a place from which something has been subtracted. "I think" is the place from which the cause of thought, which connects the thought with the thinking being, has been subtracted. Just as "I think" supposes what has been subtracted from it, so the signifier always already supposes another signifier that differs from it ("I" necessarily supposes "not I"). We can say that one signifier is already counted as two, because it includes what is missing from it, and this lack in the order of the signifier, that is, in the symbolic order, is not innocent: where something has been subtracted in order to inscribe the I as thinking, the subtracted signifier is also presentified. The subject is signified by a barred S ($), that is, the subject appears as crossed out. What is deprived of existence cannot appear on the plane of the I, but it returns in other ways, through the power of negation to affirm the real weight of thought.

But remember that while Lacan proposes a way to read Descartes through the mechanism of negation, Descartes himself, once he had created the vanishing point of the subject, chose to ensure that this point did not disappear, and did not rely on what was affirmed by the negation. Descartes insures himself against the possible disappearance of the I by attaching it to the Other, to God. He turns the certainty of the I into a certainty of knowledge, although once the point of certainty of the "I think" is posited, there is no guidance as to the nature of the knowledge it holds. The certainty, described as a flash of clarity and distinctness, is supported by God, to whom this criterion of certainty is ascribed. Through God, the split of the Cartesian subject is eventually undone and the I who was barred from knowledge reacquires it.

But Lacan tries to show that although Descartes draws back from the split revealed in the Cogito, his subject cannot be so easily sutured, not even by God. The weight that the I carries and prevents a suture is examined by Lacan through the concept of alienation.

Alienation is the name given by Lacan to the unavoidable subtraction of being that accompanies the *ego cogito*. As we will see, in the spirit of the assertions examined thus far, alienation indicates the reduction of the subject to a *vanishing point*, while also exposing the *centre of gravity* of the I thereby produced. Alienation is neither an affect nor an effect, but is identical with the very instituting of the Cartesian ego under a signifier, a signifier that embodies the enforced choice of thought over existence. The I-Cogito is the result of a choice that is neither free nor autonomous, although ostensibly it is always possible to choose between one signifier and another. This paradox can be found, for example, in the first law of psychoanalysis, that of free association, where the subject is asked to speak spontaneously while being totally free to choose to say (to the analyst) whatever comes to her mind. It is precisely in this place of ostensible freedom that the subject is revealed as trapped and that the free choice turns out to be an enforced one.

It is not simply that the enforced choice is accompanied by the loss of what was not chosen; the option that *was* chosen is itself charged with loss. To demonstrate this, Lacan uses the example of someone who is asked at gunpoint to make a free choice: "Your money or your life." If he chooses the money he will lose his life, and if he chooses life then without money it will be a life not worth living. That is, the loss entailed in what is not chosen nullifies the choice that *is* made. The Cogito is an identical case in which one stands with one's back against the wall obliged to choose between thought and being. As long as you think about what to choose, you let existence slip away, whereas the moment you stop thinking, the choice has already been made. The subject of the Cogito is forced to choose thought rather than being, and give up his existence. The Cogito shows that it is impossible to choose being without thought, because without thinking, existence does not appear to be an option.

This, then, is Lacan's proposal for reading Descartes through negation: the Cogito inscribes the subject's being as dependent on thought. Choosing thought does not make the resurrection of being possible, and what will return is the "don't exist." How should we understand this affirmative effect of negation, the affirmation of the "don't exist"?

Lacan demonstrates what the negation of existence means through fantasy, since the latter affirms the presence of the I as am-not.[25] Fantasy requires the presence of an I as the one who relates the fantasy, who reflects about it.[26] But while the fantasy is recounted by an I-think, the I is not present in the fantasy itself. Thus in the recurring fantasy among Freud's patients relating that "a child is being beaten," the interpretation of the fantasy over the course of the analysis will at no stage lead to the patient identifying with the fantasy's content or attributing what is included in it to himself. Following the analysis, the fantasy will change: from "a child is being beaten" – a general and *impersonal* formulation – the patient will arrive at other formulations, such as "my father is beating my brother" or "the teacher is beating another child"; but the subject will never be able to say "my father is beating me," although this is in fact the only version through which the role of fantasy in psychic life is revealed. In other words, the I does not exist in the fantasy; its existence is negated and is thus determined as not-I (through a brother or another child). The presence of the I as a speaker is accompanied by the negation of being, a negation that manifests itself in the simple grammatical fact that the fantasy is not narrated in the first person, that is, the I as a being has been removed from it. The emergence of being in relation to fantasy is therefore through "I am-not."

This is the meaning of the enforced choice in the drama unfolded by Descartes, which shows how choosing thought confirms the existence of the thinking subject as not-I. The subject who necessarily chooses thought is represented by a signifier that locates him as an agent of speech and enunciation and is thereby subtracted from the field of existence. It is this subtraction of the I that allows the I to be resurrected as something. If it is possible to condition existence on thought, it is because what will be affirmed by the negation is not the existence of the subject, but that thing in the subject that was subtracted in combining the I with the signifier "think."

How does this subtraction occur? If the subject chooses thought, he himself is made present in it through a signifier or a meaning that is of the Other. However, that part in being that is not represented is necessarily subtracted from thought, and it slips under the signifier[27] as what cannot be represented or made present in thought. The subtraction is what psychoanalysis calls the unconscious. In other words, the unconscious is not thoughtless or meaningless but what appears as subtracted from the domain of thought in the field of the Other. The enforced choice in thought is in this sense a choice of a necessarily trimmed-off meaning, thought from which a part has been subtracted, and this part triggers formations of the unconscious. The unconscious resides in the negation of being in the domain of meaning, which means that the subject appears on the side of thought as an empty set, as a negation of being.

In this empty place, the subject of meaning and thought appears. If the I had chosen being, it would have lost the connection with its being as I think, with what allows it, for example, to desire to know something about the place in which it does not think. This is why choosing thought and meaning is a negation of being, a negation that affirms the existence of a thinking I. This is because the absence of being that stems from the subject choosing thought is also an encounter with what is subtracted from the place of thought, the being of the one who thinks.

Thus, the subject's only possibility of existing is in thought, by clinging to a positive element of meaning, the I, which paradoxically brings with it the effacement and disappearance of its own being. It is the vacillation between meaning and erasure that constitutes the subject of the unconscious, who is none other than the subject of thought. The choice of the meaningful signifier is a choice to disconnect from what refuses meaning, and the message from being will return as the message from the unconscious. It is not I. It is not I who was there.

The Cogito in Lacan is not the Cogito that philosophers are likely to talk about, since it is caught in the structure of alienation and therefore cannot substantiate being through thought. On the contrary, the repressed part of thought constantly returns to haunt and disrupt thought. But Lacan shows that only due to the inability to integrate the two parts, in the place where being intersects with meaning, is a weight created for the subject of thought. The result of the Cogito, of placing oneself under the certainty of "I think," is the subject of the unconscious, that is, the necessary inverse of "I think" which is – not-I am.

To sum up this section, it is through alienation – that is, the enforced choice that reduces the subject to the emptiness of thought – that Lacan shows what it means for Descartes to affirm existence on the basis of affirming thought, and he does this in two ways. First, choosing "I think" is paid for by the loss of access to an essential signifier, which remains structurally inaccessible. This dimension is identical to Freud's primary repression, to the identification of the subject with the repression of what is irretrievable. Without an enforced choice, meaning and existence would have converged at a mythical point of correspondence and transparency that Descartes necessarily postulates. The subtraction posited as the Cogito's point of departure therefore acts as an affirmation of being, which is not retrieved as such but is identified with the moment of subtraction itself, with the cause of thought.

Second, as Lacan showed, Descartes achieves the certainty of the Cogito by "resurrecting" the I, by positing the I as what is irreducible. By denying any knowledge through which the I could have accrued content to support its being, the thinking I receives the weight of being, that is, it appears as the thing that thinks. The Cogito is hence the split presence of an I on the one hand and the subject reduced to an instance of thought on the other hand.

C. I Don't Think and I Am Not

Cogito ergo sum is structured like an implication. In philosophical logic, an implication means that in the relation between the *protasis* (condition) and the *apodosis* (consequence), both clauses partake in the same discursive world, and the relationship between the truth or falsity of the condition and the truth or falsity of the consequence will determine the truth or falsity of the implication. Psychoanalysis rejects the possibility of situating the cause and the consequence in the same discursive world, and as we have seen, Lacan's interpretation of the Cogito precludes seeing the relation between the argument's condition and its consequence as a simple, complementary one. For Lacan, the separation between the two parts of the Cogito stems from the fact that positing one clause of the argument requires negating the other – that is, that the affirmation of one side be the negation of the other. Although the negation is implied in the Cogito argument, Lacan recognizes that Descartes wishes not to surrender to the resulting implications. According to Lacan, Descartes's "therefore" embodies precisely the force of the negation, because it ascribes being to the I under whom nothing exists, since all we have is the fact that this I – thinks. In this sense, "therefore" is a way of going beyond the refusal of being embodied in the very positing of "I think," for the comprehensive negation of any knowledge (through radical doubt) supports and affirms the resurrection of being on another level.

Descartes, Lacan claims, uses the Cogito's "therefore" to refuse the difficult path that leads from thought to being, the path that has occupied philosophy since antiquity. Descartes takes "the shortcut of being the one who thinks ... because already the question of its own existence is, for its part, assured."[28] He avoids this question by determining that "I am" does not include any aspect of being beyond the being of I – as thinking.

It is a short step from the negation of one clause in the Cogito argument to the negation of both clauses. The double-negation is like saying that only in the negation of existence, which constitutes the I as am-not, will the I-think necessarily appear as an I from whose field of thought something has been subtracted – that is, as don't-think. In this sense, the double-negation reformulates the Cogito in a way that confirms the I's existence as a necessary product of the negation of existence and of the subtraction from thought.

The double-negation, Lacan claims, is not meant to effect a maximum reduction of the thinking thing – on the contrary. The shortcut that Descartes took by using the "therefore" does not necessarily stem from a blindness to the implications of the Cogito argument; the shortcut can also be the product of two negations that the Cogito is based on, two negations that affirm the existence of a One. The Cogito created a relation between two negations, one of which results in "not I" (thinks) and the other in "I (am) not." According to Lacan, Descartes, motivated by his wish for certainty, emptied the Cogito of both thought and existence, thus creating an encounter between the two sides of the Cogito, an encounter that is marked as necessary because the "I think" has already been vacated of any element that could have disrupted the truth of the implication. The structure of negation, which first stems from emptying the sphere of thought by virtue of doubt, creates zero distance between the two clauses of the implication.

The point is that for Descartes, reducing the distance between thought and existence through double-negation is supported by the certain presence of God. For Lacan, reducing the distance between thought and existence through double-negation designates the distance between them as the only reality left. In Seminar XIV, Lacan claims that the role of analysis is to reopen this distance and offer an interpretation, uniquely for each subject, of the way that "not I" means "I (am) not." Freud's general interpretation of this gap, and of the ontological weight it entails, is this sentence: "Where It was, there must I be" – *Wo Es war soll Ich werden* – which means that the "not I" (Id, in Freudian terms) will occupy the place of the "I (am) not," which is the unconscious. Rather than dwelling on the intricacies of Lacan's reading, we will merely emphasize here that under this reading, reducing the distance between the parts of the Cogito is revealed as entailed by the negation of the Cogito's two parts, and that the aim of analysis is to make this distance a real and decisive one for the subject.

If the Cogito offers a way to focus on the rupture between two negations, it is because this rupture clarifies the difference between attempting to suture it through God, and attempting to maintain it. The reality of thought is the reality of one subject, not of a specific subject but of any one whose desire can endow the distance between "I do not think" and "I am not" with meaning.

D. I Think therefore I Am One

In Seminar XVII, Lacan returns to Descartes's Cogito in order to "examine it and revise it." The main basis for Lacan's reading here is the claim that *"the cause, the 'ergo,' is thought."*[29] *Ergo* is the cause and the condition for the effect of a language on thought, and Lacan momentarily replaces the *ergo* with ego – that is, the *ergo* already supposes "I think," because in order to deduce "I am" from "I think," the *ergo* must suppose an ego *in action*, something that acts in the name of "one." *Ergo* is the ego in action. It indicates the movement and the transition from the moment of the emergence of the sign called the *unary trait* to the effect of this inscription – a network of signifiers in which the subject is caught (which is how the subject resides in language, according to Lacan). Let us examine the development of Lacan's argument more closely.

First, in order for us to think about thought as a cause, we must detach it from its conception as a *category*, as a homogeneous space that can, for example, classify certain people as belonging to the history of thought (under the heading "thinkers," for example), or categorize certain entities as belonging to the category of thought (e.g., the species called *"Homo sapiens"*). The philosophical tradition has blurred the preliminary presence and traces of knowledge by treating thought as a category. Extracting oneself from this tradition therefore requires an act, and Descartes's act is to doubt the knowledge on which the "master of thought" has long speculated ("thought" is a master signifier in the hands of whoever claims to control the limits of the category

of thought). Through the Cogito, Lacan claims, Descartes manages to
extricate thought from the control of the master and of "the history of
thought," to detach it from its status as a category; he situates thought
as (almost) an affect rather than a category.[30] Thought is almost an affect,
says Lacan (although affectivity does not capture the most fundamental
thing about thought, for reasons we will see presently), in the sense that
the affect is the only testimony to the speaking being's entrapment in
discourse. Descartes's Cogito received its exemplary value in the history of thought precisely because it uncovered this fact: that the place of
the subject who thinks without knowledge is the place where language
acquires its reality, where speech constitutes the one *who* speaks as *what*
speaks, as the thinking thing.

The claim that thought is an affect brings Lacan's readings of Descartes
full circle, with a move intended to reveal another aspect of the Cartesian attempt to constitute the reality of thought. The current link in this
chain suggests that although "I think" is neither identical to "I am" nor
a logical deduction from it, the moment of positing "I think" is, in fact,
not foreign to being but touches upon it. "I think" is a primal inscription
of "I am." The present discussion thus implies that we must distinguish
between two dimensions of thought. One is the affective dimension,
where the subject is inscribed through the mark "I think." The other is
the dimension of knowledge, where the subject is already woven into a
network of signifiers. In the second dimension of thought, the subject is
already caught as an object of the discourse, which according to the psychoanalytical conception determines, for instance, his being castrated,
his being-towards-death, his being a man or a woman, and so on.

The Cogito, then, is the moment that *precedes* the appearance of the
subject under a signifier, or the moment in which the subject *extricates
herself* from the already woven knowledge, through a sign that inscribes
her as *one*. Although the *one* is not characterized, is not a unity, and does
not mark a singularity, without this sign the assertion that any "I think"
is *one* would not be possible. That is, the possibility of marking any "I
think" with the seal of *one* would not be created otherwise. Once the
subject appears, for example as a woman, it will already be one subject
among others, conditioned on the signifier of the Other, rather than the
"I think" as *one*.

In relation to thought as an effect of inscription, it is important to note
that Lacan emphasizes *the aspect of writing* in the Cogito, because only
writing, the inscription of a trait, has the effect of one. While speech
has an effect of subtracting the object (in speech the word replaces the

thing), *writing captures the object*. Therefore, for example, the writing of Euclidean geometry captures something real about the logic of space, that is, it captures the birth of the space of extension (though on another level, geometrical language loses its object because it presents a space with ideal characteristics).

Incidentally, the topic of writing was crucial to the seminar on which the current discussion is based, Seminar XVII. That seminar took place in a turbulent year (1969), and in his lectures Lacan mentioned remarks from his listeners, who contended that the real things were happening outside rather than on the blackboard in the lecture room. Lacan replied that they were in error: if there was any chance of capturing something of the reality of revolution, it was only through what was written on the blackboard. And he further emphasized that only from the perspective of the psychoanalytical discourse was it possible to see that the effect of written discourse is to capture the object-dimension in the revolutionizing-I (a dimension that cannot be otherwise articulated nor represented). We can see why, against this backdrop, "I think" is understood as writing rather than saying. The moment of the inscription of "I think" is a moment in which a trait of thought is inscribed in being. "I think" serves as a trait, and consequently it becomes possible to say "therefore I am" as an identical clause to the proposition "I am signified as one."

Thought, then, is an affect, that is, a product of the inscription of a nameless thing through a sign. The inscription through a sign has an effect, which is that of creating a one, a one that is neither a unity (of the two) nor a one and only. "By virtue of a singular *one*, of what bears the mark from this moment forward, the effect of language arises, as does the first affect."[31] The first affect is the "oneness" that inscribes being.

$$\frac{\text{I am one}}{\text{I think} = \text{therefore I am one}}$$

Here the effect of division is already marked by an "I am" which elides the "I am marked by the one"... It is as a function of this initial position of the "I am" that the "I am thinking" can be even so much as written. You will recall how I have been writing it for a long time now – "I am thinking: 'therefore I am.'" This "therefore I am" is thought.

Lacan inverts the order of things here, so as to indicate the weight of thought as a trait of the existence-of-one. It is not thought that sustains me; rather, there is an existence that precedes the "therefore I am." It is the existence of the one. "Therefore I am" is already the thought of one. Put differently, "I think" is a function of "I am marked as one," which is the initial position of the one as existing. "I am" is therefore an initial position of "I am marked as one," a kind of central function of identification that marks being as one. When the Cogito appears based on the existence of the one, it inscribes what is already entrapped there in saying "I think," that is, a *unarity* that grounds the "I think."

So *ergo* is the only thought that appears in the formulation of the Cogito, because it links the trait of thought (rather than thought itself) to being. The movement in the Cogito between "I think" and "I am," is the movement that registers this trait of thought, and this trait is represented in the Cogito formulation with *ergo*.

Chapter 5

Lacan Wagers with Pascal

We do not require great education of the mind to understand that here is no real and lasting satisfaction; that our pleasures are only vanity; that our evils are infinite; and, lastly, that death, which threatens us every moment, must infallibly place us within a few years under the dreadful necessity of being forever either annihilated or unhappy … All I know is that I must soon die, but what I know least is this very death which I cannot escape.

– Pascal, *Pensées*, §194[67–8]

Every man's career is committed to something that has death as its limit.

– Lacan, *Seminar XVI*

In a book written by Georges Brunet on Pascal's wager, one finds a reproduction of two folded pieces of paper found in Pascal's pocket, on which he described his wager. These papers, densely covered by Pascal's handwriting, are commonly seen as the manuscript of "Pascal's Wager." The pieces of paper whose facsimile is appended to Brunet's book show how Pascal mulled over the formulation of his wager, the wager designed to prove to every person that faith is preferable to denial. Since these pieces of paper include things that Pascal wrote horizontally, vertically, at the top, the bottom, and the margins, and everywhere there was a gap, the words cannot be read in one direction but only by turning the paper in different directions according to the direction of the writing. The work of deciphering "the wager" is therefore far from simple, even on this technical level. In his book Brunet is concerned with reconstructing the text from the manuscript (since there are several edited versions of Pascal's "Pensées"),[1] and with attempting to reconstruct, like other commentators, the wager's logic.

"Pascal's Wager," which over the years has gained a certain conceptual independence, has generated numerous debates among philosophers about the wager's probabilistic basis and about whether Pascal actually succeeded in rationally proving that it is more beneficial to postulate the existence of God than to deny His existence. Naturally, however, the folded papers raise not only the question of the mental logic and the persuasiveness of the wager, but also that of their signifying function, or, in other words, the relation between the wager and the signifying form it takes. Pascal's wager, deciphered from these pieces of paper covered with handwriting from end to end, imposes on the reader a signifying presence that exceeds its philosophical validity, raising the question of what is actually being calculated by Pascal when he formulates the wager on religious belief.

But first, let us unpack this notion of "signifying presence." Let us recall Little Hans's dream that "in the night there was a big giraffe in the room and a crumpled one: and the big one called out because I took the crumpled one away from it. Then it stopped calling out: and I sat down on top of the crumpled one."[2]

Instead of analysing this dream as the dream of a child embroiled in a family drama between his two parents – the father who is a big giraffe and the mother who is a giraffe made of crumpled paper – Lacan focuses on the difference between a real giraffe and a paper giraffe as the decisive difference in illuminating the child's desire.[3] The giraffe as a pure signifier (made of wrinkled paper) determines the way in which we should approach the boy's fantasy as presented in the dream. The crumpled giraffe, Lacan says, is the metonymy for the way in which the boy perceives his place in relation to the mother (rather than a representation of one of the actors in the drama). The boy sits on top of the crumpled giraffe and causes the big giraffe to scream, that is, the crumpled giraffe is not a representation of what is desired but a mode of demonstrating the status of the desired object. The object of desire can only appear as crumpled paper that can be rolled into a ball, a formless shape that is no longer a giraffe and carries no other clear sense. Hans's dream becomes a testimony to his vacillation between himself being the mother's phallus (according to his own perception, as reflected in the dream), an imaginary presentation of what the mother wants, and himself being separate from the phallus, distinct from the mother's object of desire. The giraffe made of crumpled paper signifies this psychic movement of Hans's between these two dimensions of the mother's desire: as its object on the one hand, and as excess in relation to the mother's desire on the other hand. The paper giraffe can no longer be sat on or hugged – at the most, it can be crushed and rolled into a ball. This is the transition from the imaginary object that is desired as it "really" is and that appears in the dream as a real giraffe (an object of exchange – one that is assigned "objective" value or sense), and the symbolic object of desire, an object turned into a two-dimensional signifier, into pure form (an object that has been rejected as an object of simple exchange according to its imaginary value).[4]

This movement in relation to the object is realized through Little Hans's "artistic" gesture, of adding a "willy" to the giraffe drawn by his father as a kind of symbolic supplement. The willy is entirely graphic, like an organ or an attribute that is separate from the giraffe's body. The willy is evidence that the object "giraffe" has turned into a signifier of desire, for it can no longer be integrated as a real object of material presence. The distance between the subject and his object of desire has thus been exposed in the dream.

Hans's dream exemplifies how the object of desire loses its material and meaningful qualities for which it is desired and is turned into a signifier. This transition occurs through the excess of formal traits in the object – traits that change its status and function. If in Hans's case this excess is exemplified through the graphic sign of a phallus being added to the paper giraffe, in Pascal the folded paper that has to be constantly turned around in order to read the different parts is the embodiment of the wager, of the inexhaustible desire for grace[5] when grace is not there to validate the wager. The scribbled-on paper that requires tireless and diligent deciphering points to what the desire for grace produces, rather than to the existence of grace itself. Thus, what Lacan claims regarding Pascal is that the wager does not produce certainty with regard to God, but does produce certainty with regard to the existence of an object that is being desired through the postulation of grace. An object that appears as a kind of leftover, an excess of the act of wagering itself.

Returning to the piece of paper, this signifier also embodies the fact that there is no point of view from which the wager can be seen in full. Although Pascal presents the wager as subject to principles of rationality, probability, and usefulness, we can say that the wager is a calculated move that fails with respect to these criteria. Lacan will show in relation to Pascal's wager that wherever we posit a certain principle of calculation (of maximum benefit, of probability, and so on), this principle will become radically external to the wager itself. Which means that if, for example, we think that probability is a principle that lends a definite

Figure 1 Pascal's wager. Blaise Pascal, *Pensées et opuscules* (Thoughts and Minor Works), ed. Léon Brunschvicg. Paris: Hachette, 1922, III §233, 436.

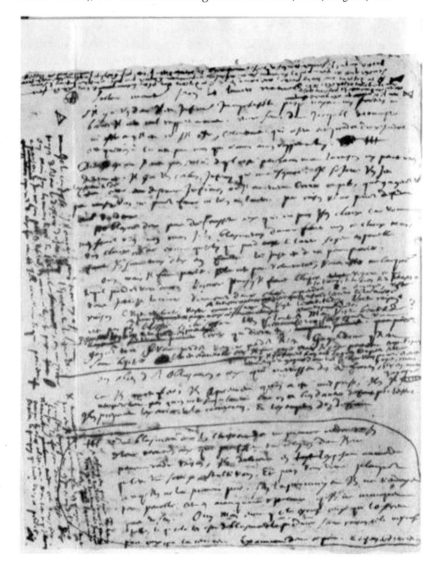

Figure 2 Giraffe with willy.

widdler

value to the possibility of belief in God's existence, we will see that probability reveals to us a completely different truth about the thing that is actually at stake. We can say that the radical alienation that exists between man and god creates a difficulty in turning the uncertainty about God's existence into the certainty of a belief. Lacan will claim that Pascal does not solve the question of God's existence or of the motive for faith, but manages to extricate a fixed relation between the two, and that this relation is the true object of the wager.

The handwritten pages therefore divert us from the question of what it is justified to wager on and whether the wager is worthwhile, to the question of how one wagers and on what. In shifting our interest from the imaginary question "Does God exist?" to the symbolic question regarding the effect of what we do not know (God's existence) on our earthly life, we encounter an obscure scribble on a piece of paper that embodies the wager as an impossible movement between a senseless gain (signified in the wager as eternity or infinity) and a weightless loss (signified in the wager as zero): the pair infinity/nothing lies at the basis of Pascal's wager.[6] Thus, the paper covered with Pascal's handwriting illustrates the meaning of Pascal's wager better than any interpretation given to it, be it moral, religious, or rational, because it shows that Pascal's wager is not concerned with renouncing pleasures for a Christian life of faith, but is rather positioned at the very heart of modern morality: How does one live in the shadow of the not-knowing, in the absence of any correlations between values and faith, between investment and enjoyment, between work and gain? From this position, the desire to decipher what is written on the paper is metonymic of the wager itself.

Pascal's pieces of paper appear as a kind of topological form, in which what is represented through them – that is, the question whether there is a God (if so, the believer is promised the immortality of his soul in the next life; if not, the soul is subject to the distress of a human life in this world without redemption – is not embodied in the content of the pieces of paper but rather in the actual movement they produce, this way and that way. The pieces of paper are the signifier of the impossibility of knowing, for the question as to whether there is an infinity and what its nature is, is a question we cannot answer. But within this unknowing there is a certainty that Pascal sees as the certainty of wagering on a God. Lacan will formulate this as *the certainty of the absolute wager*, which appears within the impossibility of knowing the Other or ascribing any regularity to the Other's domain.

The quotes at the beginning of this chapter signify that Lacan's interest in Pascal is related to the question of death, or rather, to the way in which the limit postulated for life has a far-reaching effect on life. We can say that Lacan's interest in Pascal is related to Pascal's interest in death, which, being a limit, is present in life itself; the presence of death as a limit or as a constant threat turns life itself into hell. It is death that for Pascal produces a radical change in the possibilities of placing oneself within life itself: Should we ignore the fact of death and live a life of blindness and stupidity, or confront this fact with full responsibility? Contrary to received opinion, Lacan claims that Pascal is not dealing with the existence of an eternal hell or heaven outside life itself or beyond it, but rather with its existence, as a limit with a moral significance, here, in the place where man's life is lived in practice. Hell is not identified with eternity but is here, in life itself. Pascal, in other words, is not occupied with trying to solve the question of eternity and the afterlife, but rather with the question of the moral responsibility of those whose lives are lived in the hell of an existence in the shadow of death, where what there is at the beginning of life and what there is at the end of it is unknowable.

A. The Necessity of the Wager

Pascal is a philosopher whose *Pensées* are familiar to every high school pupil in France and who is studied alongside Descartes, Rousseau, Spinoza, and others. Lacan refers to Pascal as "a man of his time,[7] which highlights the fact that Lacan tries to decipher Pascal's thought inside rather than outside the context in which Pascal is registered in the history of philosophy. But Pascal is engraved in the canonical historical memory of every French person according to a specific schema, just as Descartes is engraved in the historical memory around the Cogito. Pascal is remembered as a brilliant mathematician and inventor[8] who following a mystical revelation became a philosopher of the Christian faith. His principal work, composed of fragments of thoughts and published under the title *Pensées*, is commonly seen as the text that represents Pascal's conversion into a religious thinker. *Pensées* is a work centred on establishing the Christian faith as a moral and intellectual necessity. But even if Lacan reads Pascal as a man of his time, considering that the affinity of Pascal's philosophy with religion has a similar status (of common knowledge) in French culture as the affinity of Descartes's philosophy with modern science, Lacan's reading of Pascal is surprising and can be viewed as verging on heresy. Lacan sees Pascal as someone who is not concerned at all with the question of God's existence, as someone for whom the Father–God is already dead. For Lacan, Pascal's conception of God goes against the entire tradition of Western philosophical thought about God, while at the same time revealing its closeness to the Freudian thinking about the father: it is the dead father who determines the life of the drive, that is, whose presence is real.

This use of Pascal is typical of Lacan in the sense that it is impossible to say unequivocally if it is a use for the ends of psychoanalysis or for those of philosophy. Pascal was part of a war between religion and reason that was waged during his lifetime, but in addition, he draws Lacan's attention because through his wager he formulates an ethical position that is related to the positing of belief in God as a necessity. The wager on God is merely a recognition of the reality of the Father (the Other) in human experience despite his being a dead father and even though the question of his existence is not subject to human judgment. The ethics that postulates an absolute and real element which is unknowable but which must be wagered on (for reasons yet to be formulated) is a crucial ethics for philosophy but also for psychoanalysis.

Lacan mentioned Pascal on numerous occasions throughout his teaching years. We will focus here mainly on a concentrated analysis of Pascal's wager that spreads over several lessons of the seminar Lacan gave in the years 1968–69 titled "From an Other to the other." The wager itself, in its original form, appears in the following famous paragraph in *Pensées*:

> Let us weigh the gain and the loss in wagering that God is. Let us estimate these two chances. If you gain, you gain all; if you lose, you lose nothing. Wager, then, without hesitation that He is.[9]

From Pascal's formulation of the wager we can see that he measures the necessity of the wager on God in terms of gain and loss, where both gain and loss alternate between all and nothing, or eternity versus nothingness. When we present the meaning of Pascal's wager in its canonical form, it appears thus:

	S believes	S does not believe
God exists	∞	$-\infty$
God does not exist	nothing	x

Pascal's wager, as quoted above, refers to the left-hand side of the table and is formulated in terms of gain and loss. If we bet that God exists, and we turn out to be wrong, we lose nothing; but if we turn out to be right, we gain everything. The difficulty with this interpretation of the wager is that its two main terms are undeciphered. On the one hand, how can we measure the infinity we have gained when we know nothing about what is beyond life's limit? Pascal himself says: "For after all what is man in nature? A nothing in relation to infinity, all in relation to nothing, a central point between nothing and all and infinitely far from understanding either. The ends of things and their beginnings are impregnably concealed from him in an impenetrable secret. He is equally incapable of seeing the nothingness out of which he was drawn and the infinite in which he is engulfed."[10] The possible gain remains unknown, undecipherable.

On the other hand, what does it mean to lose nothing? If our life is worth nothing, then in what sense does a wager take place at all if the thing we are wagering on is worthless? Pascal says a little later that the wagerer wagers on something certain in order to gain or lose for certain, whereas here it seems that this condition for the wager does not hold, or at least, that the question of what is being wagered becomes blurred in Pascal. How then can a wager be posited on the basis of two values – nothingness and infinity – when there is no way of knowing what these values are? The gain on the side of belief and the loss on the side of non-belief turn out to be unknowns.

While the values determining the wager are unknown, the wager itself, independently of whether the terms it is based on are deciphered, is presented by Pascal as necessary. The wager is necessary in the sense that without it, without a decision one way or the other (there is eternal life or there is not), what is left is doubt, which causes the greatest misery. It is better to wager than to suffer this doubt. But Pascal assumes that the wager is necessary in another sense: human existence is such that even if man is busy with countless forms of distraction or avoidance, he is faced with the wager. Precisely because reason is incapable of deciding on the question of the soul's immortality, precisely because it is impossible to know through rational means whether God exists, it is necessary to wager on eternity.

Let us turn to the right-hand side of the wager's structure as it is represented in the table. This side concerns the question of our gain and loss in the event that we have chosen not to place our bet on God and it turns out we were right or wrong. Here the question of the wager becomes more complicated, since in this part of the table there are two terms representing gain and loss about which it is difficult to say what they relate to: What is the loss we suffer if we choose not to believe and God does exist? In one of the chapters of *Pensées* ("The Misery of Man without God"), Pascal describes the miserable lives of those who do not wager on belief. But what is this deprivation of happiness, posited here as the negation of infinity, in relation to the unavoidable misery that characterizes our life on earth in any case ("nature makes us always unhappy in every state ...")?[11] What is the difference between the nothing we have lost if God does not exist and the misery we have "gained" if God exists and we have no faith?

The final term, on the lower right-hand side, raises the question of what we risk in the act of wagering – that is, What precisely are the stakes here? – when the wager has in fact not taken place, when we have not lost or gained anything. This fourth option, which concerns the rejection of faith when God does not exist, clarifies and isolates *the object of the wager itself*: What is it that we wagered on, separately from the compensation or the punishment imposed on us? At this stage, the object of the wager is a complete unknown (here represented by X).

As we will see, Lacan uses these terms employed in Pascal's wager (infinity, zero, minus-infinity, and unknown) to point out that Pascal's wager deals with gain and loss not in order to assess the worthwhileness of the wager on God, but because the considerations of gain and loss reveal that something else is at stake in the wager. Since it is hard to find a standard of measurement or of counting that would decipher Pascal's wager in terms of definite gain and loss (eternity, in both its positive and negative aspects, being beyond the scope of our understanding), it follows that Pascal's wager applies to man's life in *this* world rather than the next. Thus Lacan will show that Pascal does not seek to decide through the wager or even to contribute to the debate about the existence or non-existence of God. Pascal is concerned with the question about that thing in the subject itself in whose name both the believer and the denier wager. That is, *Pascal is concerned with the object of belief in the subject, the thing that is put at stake in the act of the wager.* Lacan will show that the logic of the wager, which is built on the principles of the mathematical series and of probability, is calculated in such a way that it leaves one term – a term that influences the values of all the other terms – uncountable. This logic will stem from the seeming calculability that the wager postulates, and through that calculability will reach the non-calculative basis of the wager, which produces real value in the life of the subject (and does not determine a transcendent value beyond this life). At the end of the chapter we will see how Pascal's philosophical courage serves Lacan when he comes to reposit the concept of the Other in the seminar in question, Seminar XVI, "From an Other to the other."

But before we break down the wager into its components and examine its implications, let us return to Lacan's claim that Pascal was "a man of his time" ("un homme en son temps"), for Lacan goes to a lot of trouble to point out the philosophical, or rather the anti-philosophical, implications to be drawn from Pascal's way of building the logic that necessitates faith. Lacan places Pascal in a kind of opposition to the Western philosophical tradition, which is mainly concerned with wrangling with the ontological proof of God's existence. Pascal, who was a contemporary of Descartes,[12] outlined a program that does not overlap with or even follow the philosophical one.

The philosophical tradition relies on the ontological argument posited by Descartes in order to prove God's existence, and on its refutation by Kant. Descartes postulated God's existence from man's concept of infinity, which is foreign to man's own finiteness and therefore testifies to the existence of a being that is more complete and perfect than he is. Thus, according to Descartes, with regard to attributes of corporeal things (extension, shape, position, motion), even if these attributes are not in me since I am a thinking thing, these concepts still exist in me because I have a notion of myself as extended substance. Only the concept of God – that is, of an infinite, eternal, immutable, omniscient, and omnipotent substance – is a concept that cannot be derived from myself. "So, from what has been said it must be concluded that God necessarily exists," since the concept of the infinite has been placed in me by a substance that is truly infinite.[13] Kant sets out to refute these proofs of God's existence as an infinite entity whose cause cannot be found in man himself. Kant creates a God that is only an idea, albeit a very useful one: "The concept of a supreme being is in many respects a very useful idea. But this idea, precisely because it is merely that, is quite incapable of allowing us to expand, by means of it alone, our cognition regarding what exists."[14] The idea of infinity cannot in itself point to the existence of something infinite in the world.

The philosophical tradition relies on Kant's refutation of the ontological argument (regarding the necessary existence of God); that is, it approaches the question of God's existence with a basic suspicion that the question conceals a move that lends reality to what is produced by human cognition alone. Lacan also notes that from Descartes on, the entire philosophical tradition is located on this axis, which ends with the refutation of the ontological argument for the existence of God; the opposition to Pascal's wager is also raised in the name of this opposition. This opposition, however, as well as the argument that had provoked it, takes the same imaginary position towards the (ideal or real) substance that constitutes the object of belief. Who is the Other about whom we can ask whether its existence is necessary, and what is the status of this existence? This question regarding the existence of God, in all its versions, Lacan will say, is an imaginary question and is not the one that Pascal is concerned with.[15]

The imaginary God that philosophy postulates fulfils the same function whether the philosopher ascribes a real or an ideal existence to this God. Let us note in this context that Pascal claims with regard to Descartes that the latter sought to dispense with God but could not refrain from postulating his existence "in order to set the world in motion."[16] Pascal's opposition stems from the fact that in his eyes, the Cartesian God is a God of whose existence there are rational proofs, but who is foreign to man and external to his daily practice. This God plugs a gap in Descartes's method, but there is no real necessity for Him. In the spirit of Pascal, we can say that in Kant, God plays a similar role – God completes a lack in the method without being truly necessary. In this sense, the commitment to God's real existence is identical to the commitment to his ideal existence. Pascal, Lacan claims, diverges from this axis, for it is utterly impossible to ask about the existence of Pascal's God on the imaginary plane. This is not the God of the philosophers, for the wager assumes that the minute we place God in the equation, we have already renounced the possibility of answering the question regarding God's existence. Pascal's God, Lacan says, "is not the God of the philosophers."[17] What concerns Pascal is not God's actual existence, but the stakes involved in postulating his existence. What is the reality of what is present for us as infinity from the moment we realize that we do not know if God exists, nor what she is?

If Pascal's wager is not a wager on the existence of God, what is it on? We can begin by saying that Pascal wagers on his being and on truth. Pascal is willing to offer these as a guarantee for what is unknowable, not in order to acquire knowledge about them, but because through the wager he gains something of his being and of truth that is not attainable otherwise. The wager, to use Alain Badiou's language, is a form of betting without which the truth about being would not be revealed. The question of God's existence as an unanswerable question is a stage in examining the nature of the thing in man that serves as a guarantee in the wager on infinity.[18] In this sense, in psychoanalytical terms, we can say that Pascal is neurotic: he is willing to recognize his inability to know the essence of his being (eternal or finite) and the limits of his existence because the two are beyond his cognition. The neurotic knows that she does not know, but she also insists on knowing the truth and does not renounce it, even if she lives in constant doubt as to the possibility of positing truth in the realm of the Other. Pascal, since he wagers on truth but does not believe in its attainability, is not a typical philosopher, and therefore he can say: "To make light of philosophy is to be a true philosopher."[19] The typical philosopher believes that truth lies within thought's reach. The philosopher's doubt is the temporary doubt of reason that is yet to attain the truth. The doubt of the anti-philosopher is a doubt about the existence of truth, a doubt that can be replaced by the certainty of the wager.

The willingness to wager provokes philosophical opposition, Lacan says, not because Pascal does not meet some definite standard of logical rigour, but because the philosopher is not willing to wager on truth as being outside the reach of reason. The philosopher will tend to produce an attainable image of truth and of the Supreme Being that controls his existence.[20]

But Pascal's diversion from philosophy is connected to something else as well. In his wager on God, Pascal assumes the presence of a certainty of a kind that has led many commentators to see his philosophy as based on intuition more than on a rational move. Pascal pins his hopes on providence more than on reason. Some proof of that can be found in the two types of mind that Pascal postulated and through which he challenged the Cartesian notion of the unity of the mind. Pascal claims that there is a *mathematical mind* and an *intuitive mind*. The disadvantage of the first mind is that it is abstract and removed from man's ordinary use and field of vision; the disadvantage of the second mind is that it is close to common use and therefore requires effort in order to see the principles of geometry. "There are then two kinds of intellect: the one able to penetrate acutely and deeply into the conclusions of given premises, and this is the precise intellect; the other able to comprehend a great number of premises without confusing them, and this is the mathematical intellect. The one has force and exactness, the other comprehension."[21] Pascal also believes that judgment in general and moral judgment in particular are a matter not of intellect but of intuition.

It is evident that for Pascal there is no correspondence between the types of mind and the types of sciences; both types of mind provide us with modes of certainty, and both are equally lacking before infinity or before the attempt to formulate a final principle. In other words, our senses cannot grasp an excessive abundance, while our mathematical mind fails to attain the basic principle that grounds all other principles. "The ends of things and their beginnings are impregnably concealed from him in an impenetrable secret."[22] Pascal does not believe in the supremacy of reason; nor does he believe in its precedence or in its separability from sensible intuition or from affections. "We know truth, not only by the reason, but also by the heart, and it is in this last way that we know first principles; and reason, which has no part in it, tries in vain to impugn them ... Principles are intuited, propositions are inferred, all with certainty, though in different ways."[23]

The struggle between reason and affection or intuition, however, does not produce a person with two souls; rather, "man knows that he is wretched. He is therefore wretched, because he is so; but he is really great because he knows it."[24] Pascal does not see the two types of mind as complementing each other, but neither does he perceive man as a split subject, home to two contrasting forces. Pascal does not posit a dualism of the mathematical mind and the intuitive mind – that is, he posits neither a total split between reason and affection nor the possibility of a combination between them.

Pascal does, however, break Descartes's unity of consciousness, and he also points out that the mathematical, abstract mind is not the only source of *certain* knowledge. The Cartesian I abandoned truth in favour of clear and distinct knowledge, whereas Pascal inverts this relation and points to truth as the reality that determines most of all the accessibility of knowledge. We know something about the presence of truth even if we have no way of knowing how to give shape to this truth, since we pray, Pascal says, to the infinite and unified being. In order for this inversion between truth and knowledge to work, Pascal enables the intuitive mind to be present within scientific thought itself as its necessary foundation. We should not understand from this that Pascal gives precedence to affection or sensory cognition over the mind, but rather that he points to the way in which the "other" cognition is necessary, since it knows something about what derives from the principles, as opposed to rational cognition, which knows something only about the principles, disconnectedly from their material embodiment.

But what is the relevance of the two types of mind to the wager? Since judgment requires sensory cognition, without it man would not have strived for an unknowable truth. Conversely, without the ability to reason, it would not have been possible to convince anyone of the worthwhileness of the wager:

> You will be faithful, honest, humble, grateful, generous, a sincere friend, truthful. Certainly you will not have those poisonous pleasures, glory and luxury ... I will tell you that you will thereby gain in this life, and that, at each step you take on this road, you will see so great certainty of gain, so much nothingness in what you risk, that you will at last recognize that you have wagered for something certain and infinite, for which you have given nothing.[25]

Rational cognition offers reasons relating to gain and loss here and in the next life. But in order to justify the wager, we require a judgment of a different order. For Pascal, as opposed to Descartes, the rational mind does not serve as a preferred or primary authority. At the basis of the judgment that concerns choosing faith, we will find the other cognition, which frees man from subjugation to affections and from striving for enjoyment, although it does not promise him anything with a known value in return. It is the necessity of the wager that enables the mind to recognize the impossibility of eradicating the question of the infinite through the blindness of denial or by diverting the mind from it. We will also see in Pascal's words that the wager itself makes man's miserable life worthwhile and turns the loss of pleasures into nothing. That is, the wager as a movement from nothing to infinity (everything) already suggests an escape from the calculation of gain and loss.

According to Lacan, the entanglements of rational reasons formulated in terms of gain and loss hide behind them other reasons, which are the real reasons for the wager. In another discussion of Pascal's wager – in a seminar from 1965–66 dealing with the object of psychoanalysis – Lacan suggests that the reason for Pascal's wager cannot be rational, for such a reason depends on knowledge, and as we have seen, we have no knowledge about the existence and infiniteness of God. The moment we decide that "God exists" or "God does not exist" we have already identified with one side of the wager: with faith or denial; but by doing so we have lost the connection of our choice with the object of the wager prior to that decision. The wager is on something that is not to be identified with gaining or losing.[26]

In order to preserve this object that is prior to any moment of decision – that is, in order *to preserve the object of the wager rather than the object of choice* – we have to postulate what Lacan calls "absolute chance." This chance, unlike that chance posited by Einstein through the image of God playing dice, is not defined through rules of probability. The wager is on an object that has been lost and that it is impossible to reconstitute – an object that is not subject to any regularity but that is nevertheless present as a reason to wager. Lacan claims that the wager, the choice between heads or tails (*croix ou pile*), is the absolute real – that is, it is the point at which every knowledge and science arrives. At this point we are obliged to decide either this way or the other way, because up to this point nothing has obliged us to decide whether all our calculations and measurements had not been for naught. The wager is the moment in which we run up against the limit, rather than a point of decision. It is a point in which we run up against the real status of chance, against the place where in a real sense there is the certainty of "either this or that." We will have to return to the question of what is the object we run up against at this point, since Lacan's analysis implies that Pascal's wager brings us as close as possible to this unrepresented object that is in the field of the Other. At this stage we should merely note that Lacan sees the wagerer as someone who dares to postulate absolute chance, that is, to postulate chance with no commitment to a future decision on definite grounds.

It seems, then, that according to Lacan, Pascal postulates a principle that lies outside rational cognition – that is, outside what knowledge can attain – but this principle is the reason for the mind's operation. That it is impossible to turn this reason for wagering into an object of knowledge does not mean that this reason lies in the field of the intuitive mind. Nor can we say that it is the misery or distress of the human fate that is the reason for the wager. It seems that for Pascal, man's trouble and misery are structural, and therefore he does not at all consider the exchange between misery and happiness as a yardstick for assessing the human situation. He therefore suggests a wager that is not purely intellectual but neither does it stem from desires or sensory inclinations. The wager follows the principle of absolute chance and hence the object of the wager cannot be identified by either the rational mind or by the intuitive mind.

Pascal binds the necessity of the wager with the moment of the renunciation of knowledge. We renounce knowledge – that is, the existence of a regularity, even a probabilistic one, and even a regularity that is currently unknown to us but that might become clear somewhere down the line and give sense to the chance occurrence. This renunciation of knowledge implies that the possibility of affirming the existence of a supreme Other is also renounced. It is this renunciation that lies at the basis of Pascal's wager. Pascal establishes the position of the true wagerer, who is willing to pin his hopes on God from this position of renunciation. Pascal does not justify the wager with any other capacity (beyond the mind of the principles and the mind of intuition) that would establish faith and moral judgment. Instead he suggests a mechanism of wagering as the ultimate act that produces certainty where the promise of knowledge has ceased to exist. This wager is far-reaching not in the sense that it points to the complexity of the human subject, who moves between several different qualities (of reason on the one hand and of the heart's intuition on the other), but in the sense that the human subject must wager, and in relation to the wager both the heart's distractions just as much as the mind's distanciations are equally futile and pointless. Human being is to be found in none of them. From the moment we recognize that we do not know whether there is a God or what this God is, the matter of God becomes "a matter of discourse." That is, once we accept the basis of the wager, Lacan claims, the question ceases to be: "Does God exist or not?" and starts to be: "Do I exist or not?" That is, the question is where the subject stands in relation to the not-knowing; the question becomes a question of the I's standing in relation to the wager on God, a question of discourse.[27]

When we look briefly at another text by Pascal, "Preface to the Treatise on Vacuum," we see the import of placing the wager in relation to knowledge in the scientific context. In this text, in which Pascal sets out to prove the existence of a vacuum, he deals with the relationship between the respect we should have for the ancients and the myopia that led them to believe that nature does not suffer a vacuum. But we too, Pascal says, "say that the diamond is the hardest of all bodies," because generally speaking the truth we wager on is always subordinate to our knowledge at the time. It is true that truth is always preferable, "since she is always older than all the opinions that we have had of her,"[28] but truth is always wagered on out of partial knowledge or partial blindness. The ancients as well as later natural scientists should be seen as a single man who subsists forever and learns continually, and therefore "it is in ourselves that we should find this antiquity that we revere in others."[29] Pascal points to truth as a definite presence in every knowledge; this truth is subtracted in various ways at every stage of the inquiry. Antiquity, as well as later inquiry, is a way of wagering on a certain segment that that particular time allows to be seen. The wager, in other words, is necessary for the postulation of a vacuum just as much as it is necessary for the negation of vacuum.

So what is at stake in "Pascal's wager"? "That the duration of this life is but a moment; that the state of death is eternal, whatever may be its nature; and that thus all our actions and thoughts must take such different directions, according to the state of that eternity."[30] Pascal is a philosopher who postulates death as the thing that determines in an absolute way the status of life and its meaning. To live means to already, and from the outset, take into account life's loss. And Pascal not only posits the fact of death as the most relevant fact for philosophy, but also sees the fact of death as a matter of crucial moral importance: "It is certain that the mortality or immortality of the soul must make an entire difference to morality. And yet philosophers have constructed their ethics independently of this."[31] Pascal not only posits death as the only subject worth philosophizing on, but also posits the question of death as that which is not included and which *cannot* be included in the realm of knowledge; therefore, it is useless to attempt to further clarify its nature. Death here serves as a kind of general name for anything that is beyond human cognition or attainability: eternity, nothingness, infinity. It is "impregnably concealed from him in an impenetrable secret."[32]

Pascal distinguishes between finite things, whose existence and nature we know, and things like infinity, whose existence we know but not their nature (because they have no limits). But there are also things such as God, of which we know neither the existence nor the nature, because God has neither extension nor limits: "He has no affinity to us."[33] Pascal, Lacan will claim, locates the heart of human morality where concepts such as the good, God, and eternity are outside the reach of knowledge but nevertheless accrue real presence by virtue of the wager, and thus Pascal formulates a philosophy of morality that is inherently different from anything that preceded it and from anything that will follow it. "The immortality of the soul is a matter which is of so great consequence to us and which touches us so profoundly that we must have lost all feeling to be indifferent as to knowing what it is."[34] The wager is the only way to deal with what is outside human comprehension in a way that is not philosophical or metaphysical – that is, not part of dealing with the nature of infinity, the existence of God, or the existence of man in relation to eternity. The wager is a way to deal with what is outside human comprehension as the principle of a moral life.

Pascal, often negatively, signifies the interest in the eternal element that is hidden from our understanding through human desire: "There are two kinds of people one can call reasonable; those who serve God with all their heart because they know Him, and those who seek Him with all their heart because they do not know Him."[35] As opposed to them, many people have thrown off the yoke of faith, do not believe in the existence of a God who watches their actions, and see themselves as masters of their own conduct and accountable to no one. These people, Pascal says, have no reason to be self-satisfied but on the contrary should go about sad because "if they thought of it seriously, they would see that this is so bad a mistake, so contrary to good sense, so opposed to decency."[36] What is the relationship between the wager and the different forms of faith or the refusal of faith that characterize human beings with their various proclivities?

It seems that for Pascal the wager creates a necessary rift between the act of the wager and the forms of faith. The wager on faith does not equal a state of faith. Why? Since at the basis of human existence lies an incomparably distressing and sad thing – that is, the finiteness of existence – and since this thing is present as incomprehensible and unthinkable, the wager on the existence of God becomes unavoidable. The wager is an act that derives from the absence of knowledge and from the inevitable failure of reason. Faith is an insistence on a moral commitment, but not because faith enables us to know what it is impossible to know otherwise. Faith is a commitment that exists no matter what, and it derives from the recognition that this faith does not and will not have any reinforcement or support of any kind. In other words, for Pascal it is the wager and not faith that lends a moral status to man's position. The wager is necessary not because morally we are required to decide whether a supreme being exists. The question about the existence of a supreme being is exactly the question of the philosopher, but not of Pascal. The wager is necessary precisely because the reason for faith cannot be reduced to the question of the existence or non-existence of an Other, and because faith derives from a wager on truth but not from a knowledge of truth.

As mentioned earlier, however, Pascal recognizes that human beings may serve God while thinking that they know him (e.g., as a concerned father, as Providence) and thus avoid the necessity of the wager no less than those who reject any thought of the soul's immortality. In the chapter that deals with the necessity of the wager, Pascal is also occupied with all those who, more or less condemnably, use different ways to avoid facing up to this necessity to wager. For all of these, the wager is necessary because it attests to the fundamental human ethics: the wager is a necessity in the sense that every human being is trapped in it, even if she imagines that she has distanced herself from the position from which the wager is made. The wager is a necessity in the sense that one cannot be other to oneself, and therefore whether she has chosen the path of faith or the path of denial, "not only the zeal of those who seek Him proves God, but also the blindness of those who seek Him not."[37]

Pascal's wager is a wager on faith. Faith in what? It cannot be faith in God, because the question of whether God exists cannot be answered. It cannot be faith in pure logic, free of practical inferences and affections, because human faith cannot be free of human nature. The wager, then, *is the most human act possible, because it points to a commitment to our being nothing.* Pascal's wager, Lacan says, allows us to affirm what being is without naming it or articulating its nature.[38]

B. A Nothing That Is Not Zero and an Infinity That Can Be Calculated

"The finite is annihilated in the presence of the infinite, and becomes a pure nothing."[39] Pascal bases the wager on the concepts of nothing and infinity, but since we are ignorant of the nature of infinity, since man, Pascal says, understands neither the ends of things nor their beginnings, and since the seals on these extremities cannot be broken, the question that arises is how this pole of the wager can be described. It seems that according to Pascal, the promise held by an eternal God, if such a God indeed exists, is a multiplication of life itself. When Pascal presents his wager and recommends taking the position of faith in God, he establishes the wager on a numerical proliferation of life, that is, on the multiplication of that which is deficient, rather than on something that is from an order different from that of finite life: "You would be imprudent, when you are forced to play, not to chance your life to gain three at a game where there is an equal risk of loss and gain ... But there is here an infinity of an infinitely happy life to gain ... and what you stake is finite ... there is no time to hesitate."[40] But does Pascal mean that we can calculate infinity by multiplying what we do know about life itself?

If in facing infinity what is finite is nothing, and if what stands vis-à-vis eternity is a finite life, then the possible loss from the game is zero. But the last quote from Pascal shows that infinity is not measured in relation to zero, but in relation to one life. That is, Pascal says that life is nothing in relation to infinity, but he immediately also claims that the distance between life and infinity is the distance between one life and an infinity of happy lives. The wager zeroes life and turns it into nothing, but at the same time also turns life into something, thus allowing the unknown term of infinity to gain meaning. This is indeed Lacan's suggestion: the wager is not a wager on what is beyond life and in relation to which life itself is nothing. Rather, the wager on eternity becomes possible because in the wager itself life receives value in relation to eternity. How does Lacan reach this conclusion?

First, in order to examine this conclusion, we should note that considering the loss of life according to Christian morality as nothing, requires faith. A belief in eternity is required in order to turn life into a pure nothing, the nothing that is being risked by wagering. Does this mean that the wager can only take place where faith has already been established? But we claimed that the wager precedes the possibility of faith. Entering the wager is therefore entering the wager on faith. To enter the wager is to already have traversed calculations of gain and loss, since the risk is set at zero. But this traversing itself entails a loss, since the loss cannot be nothing. There is no wager if nothing is at stake. A loss, albeit minimal, must be posited in order for the wager to work. It seems that the necessary relation between the wager and faith makes the basis of the wager fictional, since although logically the wager precedes faith, in practice the wager is already a wager on faith. Thus it is impossible to determine the moment in which the wager is made.

Lacan's reading of Pascal accounts for what seems to be *Pascal's zigzagging between mathematical considerations and ethical ones*. Lacan's claim is that Pascal distinguishes between the wager that involves the subject and the wager as a game conducted according to certain rules. For the game to work it has to refer to some numerically defined gain/loss, or at least some defined principles from which probabilities for the realization of the wager's promise can be derived. That is, as long as we are treating the wager as a game with certain rules, we have to measure the probability of gain/loss and compare the two in order to justify the wager. It is in this context that we should understand Pascal's claim that "the uncertainty of the gain is proportioned to the certainty of the stake according to the proportion of the chances of gain and loss. Hence it comes that, if there are as many risks on one side as on the other, the course is to play even."[41] But the minute we begin dealing with the subject involved in the wager, it is no longer possible to measure the chances of gain and loss as even. Here it is no longer about calculating the chances for gain or loss. Rather, for the wagering subject it is about one life that is lost the moment the wager is made, because life is staked as a guarantee. Pascal's wager, which posits what is at stake, life and its pleasures, as what is annihilated in the presence of the infinite, must posit a renunciation of something for the wager to take place. The game will not take place if there is nothing at stake, and the only thing that can be at stake is the life given as a guarantee in a real way rather than as an optional possibility. *The minute a subject is involved, the thing that is at stake is no longer of the order of counting or of calculation.*

On the other hand, the partner in the game offers "an infinity of an infinitely happy life." Pascal illustrates the wagerer's situation vis-à-vis the promise with the case of an imprisoned man who knows that his sentence has been decided. He can learn what his sentence is within an hour, and within this hour obtain its repeal. It would be unnatural for this man to spend his time playing cards instead of trying to ascertain his sentence.[42] As long as he does not know what his sentence is, his chances of gaining:losing are 50:50, but from the moment he tries to ascertain his sentence, there is a chance that he would succeed in repealing it if pronounced guilty. This example thus illustrates the difference between the position prior to the wager (the effort to find out what the sentence is) and the moment of the wager itself, in which the prisoner takes his life in his hands, in both senses: he is facing the real possibility of losing his life, but he is also renouncing his life's pleasures (playing cards) for this end. Here the wager can no longer be measured by mathematical means; it can only be measured through a logic of a different status, a logic that already involves moral considerations.

What seems like a lack of consistency on Pascal's part is related therefore to the *distinction between the game and the wager*. In the game one risks a miserable and finite life for an equal chance of gaining or losing; in the wager one risks one's life for the chance to win an infinity of an infinitely happy life (or an infinity of misery). In both cases we are dealing with a calculation, but of a different order. In the game the relation between the risk and the possible gain is unknown (it is an undefined relation), whereas in the wager the risk and the chance accrue a real value because *here the subject of the wager is a function in the game.*

Despite the difference, Lacan says, the game and the wager are interwoven. One can extricate from the wager a game theory in which it is possible to formulate a structure of decision making without involving a wagerer and his partner. This is true as long as we recognize that the moment the I appears in the game, the difference becomes more acute. When the I appears in the game, he wagers on the immortality of his own soul, that is, he pins his hopes on the Other in order for the latter to appear as a place for his wager. The crucial question asked in Pascal's wager therefore is not whether God exists, but whether the subject can appear as "the I who wagers" on God. In this context of wagering on the Other in order for the subject to be able to appear as an "I" in the game, we can no longer say that nothing is at stake, for the subject is wagering on his very being by projecting it on the unknowable infinity. The thing with which one wagers, Lacan says, forms a yardstick in relation to the thing which is at stake; the life with which one wagers is a yardstick that cannot be measured, and is nonetheless something *in relation to which* the wager accrues its value: "a relation is designated then between the effect of loss, that is to say the object lost as much as we indicate it with an *a*, and this place called the Other, without which it [the *a*] would not have been produced, a place yet unknown and unmeasurable."[43] Lacan's claim is that the role of the wager is to carry the renunciation of something that has no name or measure (*a*) to the place of the unknown Other in order to enable the Other to appear as real. That is, the nothing that was reset to zero at the moment of the wager becomes the fixed proportion between the moment of entering the wager and a purpose (a recognition of eternity) that lies at the end of the move. It is hence the *object a* that allows the pairing of nothing/infinity, because the *a* is what they have in common. Note that for psychoanalysis, as we will see towards the end of this chapter, at the end of the move we do not arrive at a recognition of eternity; rather, *the question of the existence of eternity loses its relevance.*

Pascal calls the thing one wagers with "zero," but Lacan claims that *Pascal ascribes zero value to the something with which we wager because this something has no exchange value*, and not because it is nothing. The wager has meaning only if we wager with something that cannot be exchanged for something else, that cannot be measured in units of gain. Even if the subject wagers with something that has no exchange value, this something is what allows the subject to occupy a place in the wager, to accept rather than reject the value to be gained by wagering. That is, what suggests that the subject's place is not zero is the fact that Pascal signifies this place through the one of "one life" (with which the I wagers).

How should we understand the positing of the one? A one that is not a numerical identity but an identification of something as one?

At the end of Seminar XVI, when Lacan is free to say what he calls "the important things," he claims that the *one* is the place of the master, but a master who miraculously does not take the place of the subject but rather that of the object. The real master, Lacan says, is the one who takes the place of the object. In this context Pascal can be seen as a real master, a capitalist one (remember that Pascal invented the calculating machine). In contrast to the masochist who also takes the place of the object, the real master takes the place of the object independent of the presence of a big Other. The master, says Lacan, *fait le maître*, in both senses: he creates a master and is himself a master. In other words, the master does not look for an Other he can depend on, but on the contrary, vacates the domain of the Other, cleanses it of everything and leaves it as an empty set. The master, as opposed to the slave, sees himself in everything he encounters, that is, he has a tendency to replicate himself and to find himself everywhere. This vacancy is necessary in order for the *object a* – which represents what the subject wagers with – to appear in this place of the Other. The subject who wagers is someone who does not rely on there being established rules to the game; he does not count on an Other who knows and ensures the rules. The wagerer puts his own being at stake, by allowing his own being to appear in the field of the Other, which has been vacated of everything else. This is the reason, we should add, that Lacan uses Pascal extensively in his seminar: to build the domain of the Other around an object rather than around pre-given principles.

This point of entering the wager where the subject appears as a *one* is connected, in Lacan's thought, with the concept of the *unary trait*. This trait distinguishes a singular subject although, when examined, it does not seem to hold any special meaning. The uniqueness of the unary trait is not to be found in the character or personal value that the trait indicates; rather, the trait comes in place of something. It is like a hunter who cuts a notch on the butt of his gun for every animal he manages to capture.[44] In principle, the trait that appears on the butt for the animal captured today is no different from any previous trait. Also, from the moment the first notch had been cut, the next notches will testify to the following captures. Because there is no difference between the lines notched on the butt, we end up with a repetitive series that reproduces the same trait over and over again. But in practice each trait bears in a real way the existence of a specific animal and of specific hunting circumstances that the trait, in the moment of its appearance, both erased on the one hand and preserved on the other. The unary trait is, in principle, a (less bloody) instantiation of this very idea, as it distinguishes the subject in its singular occurrence.

Such a relation between subject and a sign is created in Pascal's wager: in order to "calculate" the wager, the subject appears through one, the trait that marks her as the one who wagers but that carries no distinct value of this singular subject. The one is totally arbitrary but carries with it something that is not arbitrary, which is what there is in the wagerer's being and that she stakes in the wager. That is, in the first appearance of the one we have already created $1 + a$, where the a marks the excess but also the subtraction created in the moment the wager took place. The a is the effect of positing the trait as unary: 1.

This is how Lacan explains the entry into the wager: since the Other is an empty set, the Other assimilates the unary trait so that the subject can be represented, under a kind of signifier. Where does this signifier come from? From nowhere – it appears in this place only thanks to the retroactive effectiveness of repetition.[45]

Philosophical commentators see the zeroing of the risk in the wager as a mistake on Pascal's part (since the loss cannot be nothing even in the limited sense that the loss indicates the mistaken move connected to the loss of faith), or they ascribe to this zero the meaning of a status quo – that is, they view it as pointing to a state that remains unchanged.[46] In relation to these interpretations, Lacan extracts from Pascal *the replacement of the zero with something*, and shows that Pascal answers the question of how to "count" the loss, which calculation-wise is worthless. Contrary to common opinion, Lacan believes that this loss is not zero, because it is a loss of being that regains its value through the wager.

In other words, according to Lacan, Pascal affirms the nothingness as the thing one wagers with in order to stress that there is no exchange value for the object of the wager in relation to the infinity that is at stake. Man's distress on earth no longer counts once faith promises eternity. One life has no exchange value when measured against eternal life. It follows that in Lacan's interpretation, zero means nothingness – that is, something undefined that creates the movement of the wager (between zero and infinity) and that represents a fixed relation between them (a finite distance) all through the move of the wager. This thing with which one wagers cannot be given a price tag. In order to prove that Pascal himself points in this direction, Lacan claims that Pascal "suspects that nothing is not nothing, that it is something that [we] can put on the scales, especially at the level at which we must put it within the wager,"[47] for the nothing appears in a pairing with infinity and with a one. *The nothing weighs.* Pascal calls "nothing" the point, any point from which one departs. In the one direction, in the direction of the decrease, this point runs up against a limit (where 1 is posited), and in the other direction, the direction of the increase, it does not run up against anything (this is the pole of infinity). The zero is Pascal's departure point, and through it, because it is the worthless thing that is appended to the one, the series is created: "without infinity, there is no zero that must be taken into account. Because the zero was there in the first place in order to produce it."[48] That is, it is necessary to determine a departure point (zero point) through the act of the wager, without which it will not be possible to posit infinity at the other end.

What also testifies to the way Pascal understands the zero is his claim that "unity joined to infinity adds nothing to it, no more than one foot to an infinite measure."[49] Again we see that the one does not appear as a numerical value but as the element that produces a series, and the series is described by Pascal himself: "If there were an infinity of chances, of which one only would be for you, you would still be right in wagering one to win two, and you would act stupidly, being obliged to play, by refusing to stake one against three at a game in which out of an infinity of chances there is one for you."[50] If we add one to infinity, nothing will change, but the positing of one produces a series of exponents: life raised to the power of two, life raised to the power of three, and so on. Thus without positing the one we would not have reached the infinite number of happy lives. *Why is the positing of the one capable of producing a series?* Because the moment the one – that is, the wager on life – appears, that which is included in life and which we have renounced is dropped from the calculation, is nullified and kept outside the exchange relations. This something that is nullified in the presence of the one is the cause for the formation of a series, without serving as an element in it.

That is, Lacan deciphers what Pascal says in the terms of a mathematical series as attesting to the presence of the object of wager in each and every stage. The series, Lacan says, does not represent steadily increasing values, but rather creates a fixed relation between the one life and the exponents of the ever-proliferating lives. We see that at the foundation of the wager there forms a relation between quasi-zero and infinity (a in relation to A), and this relation produces a series. If we look for where the series starts, we find, Pascal tells us, that the series starts with the positing of the 1 and that this positing of the 1 gives rise to a series that includes what had been there, unsignified, before we posited the 1; this something now appears as a fixed value throughout the series.

$$\frac{1}{A+1} \cdot \frac{a}{1} \rightarrow \frac{A}{a+A} \cdot \frac{a}{A}$$

We know nothing about the nature of what the one replaces (the thing through which we enter the wager), but the renunciation that takes place through the positing of the one enables the something we will call "a chance" to replace what we have renounced. Therefore, in this place of the chance against the loss, a proportion is created between the one and the thing we have renounced, and this proportion can be expressed thus: $a/1$. But this proportion equals the relation between 1 and $a + 1$, because the loss is *appended* to the positing of the one; the proportion of $a/1$ also equals the relation between 1 and $a - 1$, because the renunciation is *subtracted* from the signifier (1). In both cases a series is formed that preserves the same proportion (the a is the fixed value in the series). The moment the one appears, it is replicated, it repeats itself because it registers in its repetition something that was not registered before: "that which, at the origin, was not marked, the first One, is inscribed in order to be found again, already altered, as at the origin it was not marked."[51]

The question is what limits the repetition: Does it have a limit? That thing that was not signified originally becomes the fixed proportion in a series whose limit is in infinity. At any point we reach we will find the infinity from which something has been subtracted, even if arithmetically this subtraction is totally insignificant, is "zeroed." This mathematical expression exposes the nature of Pascal's wager: a wager on something unknown that is included in life against an infinite number of happy lives. That is, the renunciation of what is called "life" will appear in the infinity (of happy lives) and will now "deduct" something from this infinity. By virtue of the initial loss, the value of life has been regained through the repetition of the a.

This relation of proportion does not express luck, the lucky encounter between the loss and something that will make up for it; rather, it is a mathematical relation that enables the creation of a series. When Pascal says that "there is not an infinite distance between the certainty staked and the uncertainty of the gain,"[52] he is actually saying that it is possible to measure the relation between the risk (the wager = $a - 1$ or $a + 1$) and the gain (= an infinite series). This claim about the measurable distance contradicts what is implied by the canonical formulation of the wager. Usually it seems that the wager points to an infinite distance between nothingness and infinity (in that, for example, life's pleasures lose any value in relation to infinity; that is, nothingness and infinity are incommensurable). In contrast to this implication, in creating a series Pascal's wager produces a relation between the two terms.

In this way, as Lacan suggests, it is Pascal's mathematical analysis that causes what veils the renunciation *to move a little*. Under the veil there appears an unmeasurable object that embodies the promise implied in the renunciation. Positing the wager through a mathematical discourse that produces a series reveals what Pascal's wager is actually about, which is the object (that is outside any calculation) staked in the wager.

Pascal's mathematical analysis of the wager enables us to demonstrate that the series that stems from renunciation simultaneously produces a fixed value that is not nothing. For this reason, however far we progress in the series, even to infinity, "the I of knowledge will never attain its sufficiency, the one that is being articulated in the Hegelian theme of *Selbstbewusstsein*. In fact, in the very measure of its perfection, the I of jouissance remains entirely excluded."[53] In contrast to Hegel's self-consciousness, a consciousness that knows itself, for Pascal the wager is irreducible and accompanies the I in its transition from the moment of the renunciation of a happy life to the moment of gaining an infinitely infinite happy life. Even at the moment of realizing the gain, the unknown value of the wager is present. For Pascal the positing of the wager creates the *a* as a fixed offset that accompanies the series and that never disappears. For this reason, self-consciousness, knowing oneself in infinity, is impossible, and the wagerer is destined not to reach self-knowledge.

We can sum up by reformulating the wager table, remembering that the consequences of the mathematically formulated wager are connected to the extrication of the I as someone who appears as committed to the wager. As Lacan says, the unity of any pair is a thought that can only be thought from the point of view of one of the two. That is, the asymmetry of probability is necessary since Pascal's wager is made from the point of view that establishes a positive probability of the existence of God; that is, the I places himself from the point of view of someone who is willing to wager.

The I therefore appears committed to the wager; he wagers on "heads," that is, on faith in the Father-God (in French, between "heads or tails," *croix ou pile*, the wager is on the cross – *croix*).

Against	For
$a, -\infty$	zero, ∞
a, zero	$-a$, zero

Given a subject who wagers on faith, what are his considerations for (on the right-hand side of the table) and against (on the left-hand side of the table) the wager?

Arguments for the wager: I can lose nothing but gain infinity (upper right); I can gain nothing but I will also lose nothing (lower right).

Arguments against the wager: I will not lose the a and will get ("gain") eternal hell ($-\infty$); or I will neither lose the a nor gain anything.

According to Lacan, Pascal wagers in order to isolate what is at stake – the a that is revealed in all the forms of the wager – and thus he gets to the heart of Pascal's moral theory. For, Lacan says, it took a long time and an entire philosophical tradition (the tradition called "idealism") to consolidate a way of making the effects of representation on the represented disappear. While for Aristotle what is being represented (*upokeimenon*) is connected to the logic of its representation, for Kant the represented, the *noumenon*, is suspended behind what appears as phenomenon. In other words, the unknown thing, the thing-in-itself, had to be excluded for the subject to know something, to be able to formulate the principles *a priori*.[54] Pascal's achievement can be understood in this context: he postulates the wager in order to isolate what cannot be attained as a real presence in representation itself, while renouncing any postulation of objective knowledge. When approached in these terms, Pascal's project is intimately close to that of Freud, it amounts to the recognition of a knowledge that says: "there is somewhere a truth that does not know itself ... and it is there that we must find the truth about the knowledge."[55]

C. From an Other to the Other – the Wager on the Object

Pascal presents a relevant case for Lacan's thinking in the late 1960s. On the one hand, Pascal's wager is a *typical act*, dealt with by Lacan in the year prior to the seminar on which we have been focusing here, Seminar XV on the psychoanalytic act. As an act, the wager is not located in a defined temporal moment, it does not bear a meaning or a sense, it is not judged according to its outcome, it requires the subject to risk his being, and it is not the result of definite knowledge. In all of these senses Pascal illustrates the meaning of the concept of the *act*. On the other hand, Pascal's wager embodies the way in which logic changes according to the different modes of articulating or formulating a discourse. Thus the discourse that describes the wager through the agency of the subject whose certainty does not depend on knowledge, follows a different structural logic than the discourse examined from the place of the master who controls the rules of the game. In this sense the discussion of Pascal prefigures the seminar of the following year, Seminar XVII, in which Lacan would describe four structures of social discourse.

Lacan connects Pascal with modern morality because Pascal embodies the break that was later formulated in Kant's theory of morality: the break that separates happiness and well-being from the moral good. The moment that pleasure and happiness do not serve as guides for establishing morality, we can no longer find a seemingly natural correspondence between pleasure and man's moral tendency. Once such a correspondence has been subverted, once the worthy deed does not promise pleasure or well-being for the subject, the pleasure principle becomes subordinate to ideologies and moral dicta that distinguish proper from improper pleasures. In this context Pascal serves as a relatively early example in the history of moral thought of the absence of a correspondence between the moral good and well-being, because the wager on eternity does not promise anything that entails pleasure or gain in any evident way.

The affinity between Pascal and what Lacan calls "modern morality" can explain the context in which the discussion of Pascal appears in Lacan: capitalism. For there is no more obvious place than capitalism to embody the ideologization of pleasure, precisely because capitalism assumes a relation between control over the means of production and pleasurable practices. But the attempt to indicate a correlation between the principle of pleasure and capitalist success, fails. To illustrate this, we can compare a leaflet recommending an annual holiday on Switzerland's snowy peaks with the actual running around with heavy equipment between ski lifts and busy crowds. A "good life" has become something that is only loosely linked with pleasurable practices. Is it connected to the fact that contrary to the *ethos* that accompanies capitalism explicitly (that capital will buy any pleasure under the sun), it is based on an ideology that sees too much pleasure as something dangerous? Something that must be tamed?

For capitalism illustrates the most flagrant breach of any correspondence between well-being and pleasure: the means of production are not put at the service of pleasure, gain does not promise pleasure, and the wasting of resources – the goal of every capitalist – contradicts any economical calculation. In this context, Lacan says, we live in an era that complicates the relationship between knowledge and pleasure, at least as far as stopping pleasure in its pure sense is concerned. "What is called exploitation of the worker consists very precisely in this, that jouissance, being excluded from work, grants it right away, in the same manner that we have evoked, the effect of a point in infinity, all its reality, and this is what provokes this kind of aporia which suggest the new meaning, absent from the context of antiquity, without precedent, which takes on, with regard to the empire of society, the word *revolution*."[56] Capitalism assumes work to be a practice necessary for the production of benefit and pleasure. Yet the work of the worker yields little pleasure. Capitalism grounds the benefit of work at a point on the horizon, outside the real value that work had (in times of antiquity, for instance). In order to gain the infinity of promised pleasure, we have to clear the field of labour of any pleasure, so that a series that ends with infinity can be created. That is, we have to clear labour of any pleasurable episodes in order for infinite pleasure to appear at the limit of the series. In this context, revolution is the struggle to regain lost pleasures, but is in practice a struggle for infinite (utopian) pleasure whose distance from the practice of renunciation has long been unmeasurable. In light of this, Pascal's wager seems to present a clear case in the history of thought in which calculations of gain and loss serve at most as a mask for the loss of being.

Lacan lists a series of examples that suggest that pleasure is mediated by an Other who nullifies whatever can please in practice in the name of proper enjoyment. Horace perceives leisure as *otium cum dignitate* (leisure with dignity), and submitting enjoyment to this dictum produces a concept of proper enjoyment that ascribes moral value to non-work. Hedonism is an ideology of minimum work for increasing enjoyment; asceticism is minimum work in order to leave enjoyment's dominion; and for the capitalist, non-work entails guilt. Thus the capitalist will find himself carrying ski equipment to the lifts as part of the work involved in a holiday from work. These examples indicate that the relation of work (or leisure) to pleasure and benefit creates an equation whose elements collapse into one another. The practice required to attain pleasure is already tainted with the ideologization of pleasure. Complicating the relation between knowledge and pleasure means that only revolution – that is, a wager – may enable the reorganization of the field of pleasure.

In order to rediscover something about the possibility of experiencing pleasure from work or from leisure, we have to empty the field of the Other, and this is what we see in Pascal. Pascal empties the field of the Other of knowledge and principles in order that the postulation of infinity can subsist. The wager is vital if one is to be able to place one-self in the world and say that this world is "an infinite sphere, the centre of which is everywhere, the circumference nowhere."[57] From the point of view of the metaphysician, Lacan says, Pascal is wrong, because for the metaphysician the centre is nowhere, whereas the circumference, the infinity of the sphere's surface, is everywhere. But Pascal does not see the transcendent element, which is beyond life itself, as the deter-mining factor; on the contrary, he sees man, the reality of his nullity and of his renunciation, as the world's kernel. From the metaphysical point of view, man is lost in relation to the world because the world's eternal-ness is beyond his understanding.

But how do we turn eternity into a real part of life itself? Pascal is wrong from the metaphysical point of view, but this mistake attests to the place the wager holds for him. Eternity is nowhere, but man's life is everywhere, and therefore man must take his life in his hands, and the only wager that is possible for him is the wager on life. From Hegel we know that only the master wagers on his life (the slave, Lacan will claim, does not wager on his life because if he loses it he cannot work), and therefore it is Pascal who wagers on what the metaphysician, the master of the meaning of life, wishes to avoid, and he also wagers on what the slave seeks to disregard: the value of life *per se*.

In relation to the world relative to which man is lost, in relation to the Other, who lacks identity and form, man appears with the object he has, the one of his life. One life that will necessarily produce a series of lives. "Pascal's wager assumes the possibility, which is not only fundamen-tal but also essential and that is structurally present in every subject, according to which the domain in relation to which the demand of *a*, the object of desire is created, is the domain of the Other split in rela-tion to its own Being."[58] That is, the subject who appears with one life in the field of the Other, in this infinite and limitless sphere, can create a trait, can leave a mark through which nothingness turns out to weigh something.

Instead of assuming to the Other knowledge about man and his fate, instead of seeing the Other as the one who is responsible for the rules of the game, and whose results are subject to the laws of probability, the wager postulates the Other on different grounds. For according to Lacan's interpretation, Pascal understood that the Other counts only on condition that the I is ready to wager.

In the place where the I wagers on the Other, knowledge is postu-lated (that an infinite and happy life awaits him), knowledge that is not the knowledge concerning the existence or inexistence of God. It is the knowledge of the subject and not a knowledge about or of the Other, and it is knowledge that is created with the wager (and that does not pre-exist the wager). In turning to God as someone who promises man the benefits of eternal existence in the afterlife, Pascal enables us to approach the unknown not through an orderly discourse of probabilistic principles, but through a wager that is unsupported by knowledge. Subject to the described conditions, Pascal shows us what there is in the Other that pertains to one's morality.

Pascal is a master, Lacan says, and as a master he has no knowledge. Later in history we will find masters who are conscious of their being masters and who possess knowledge. These will be absolute masters, the greatest masters since the dawn of history. But as long as the master holds no knowledge, he serves as the cause for the formation of knowledge, without himself being an element in the series. The master is the reason for the desire for knowledge (the slave will find himself improving his knowledge in order to serve the master properly). Pascal is the reason for the believer's desire for knowledge, and therefore Pascal advises those who cannot find faith in their hearts to improve their knowledge of the religious practice until faith appears by virtue of the ritualistic act.

The Jewish God, unlike the Christian one, is a God of the word, a God who speaks, but who speaks not only in words but also through a burning bush, in sounds and visions. The God of the Christians is a God who does not speak.[59] In this sense, in the inquiry into the field of the Other, that is God, we encounter the God of the philosophers, whose presence requires proof. It is one God as opposed to the Jewish God that is not one, that does not demand or claim oneness: the God of the burning bush and of Mount Sinai does not claim to be the only God. "I am what I am," he says. Pascal wagers on this God in order to make him his, that is, in order for him – like the God of the Jews, the God of Abraham, Isaac, and Jacob – to become the God who guarantees the believer's, Pascal's, life.

The answer to the question whether God exists is not found in deciding either way, but rather in understanding that the question is inevitable, that it relates to the fundamental concern of every subject (What is going to happen once death is there?), and that it cannot be posed without taking a risk, without wagering. The only zero in this system is that of the subject who quits the game or decides not to enter it. *Within the game the zero merely veils something that cannot be formulated or*

known but whose reality is never in doubt. Through the wager, therefore, it is not the question whether God exists, but the question whether
I exist that is being formulated. The wager refers to the subject's placement as an I from which a piece of pleasure has been taken in the name
of eternity, since, for Pascal, "there is no good in this life but in the hope
of another."[60]

True knowledge, Lacan says, is a discourse without words, not a
knowledge under the patronage of the Other. This is indeed the knowledge promised by psychoanalysis, and this is what psychoanalysis has
learned from Pascal, since from God no answer can be expected. If Pascal remained in the position of the anti-philosopher, then in the act of
his wager he renounced the possibility of encountering eternity at the
end of life. If Pascal traversed the position of the anti-philosopher, then
perhaps he directed the whole wager towards the possibility that one
day he would meet his God and the promised immortality of his soul.
Psychoanalysis, unlike philosophy, does not believe in a chance of this
kind. In the place where the subject has found something of her Being,
it no longer matters whether God exists or not. The analytical wager
aims at the effect of the subject's encounter with what does not depend
on the analyst to sustain it, at the place where the analyst stops being
relevant. At the endpoint of the analysis the subject receives something
from the object that up till that point had been supported and sustained
by the analyst, and at that moment the analyst becomes inexistent. The
subject takes the position of *en-soi*, that is, for himself.

Pascal, perhaps, at the end of the road, found his God; but in any
case, through Pascal's wager Lacan manages to formulate not only the
wager to which the philosopher is committed, but also the wager of the
psychoanalysed subject.

Chapter 6

The Erotics of the One:
Lacan with Kant

It is absolutely not unthinkable to say that from a certain angle [*The Critique of Pure Reason*] can be read as an erotic book ... I had always allowed myself to be persuaded that it was badly written in German, because first of all the Germans, with certain exceptions, have the reputation of writing badly. It is not true: *The Critique of Pure Reason* is written as well as Freud's books – and that is no small thing.

– Lacan, L'identification, 21.2.62

Needless to say, Lacan's compliment to Kant's writing is not merely a matter of style or approach, and the analogy between Kant and Freud concerns more than their way of writing in German. In the immediate context of this paragraph, the issue of German is related to the question that Lacan asks himself as a teacher – whether his students read what he advises them to read, and whether they are working on learning German, as he recommends that they do. Lacan compares this situation, in which for most of his listeners the answer is negative – that is, they have not worked on their German in order to read Kant or Freud in the original – to an image that appears in Bunuel's film *Un chien andalou*, of a man who uses two ropes to drag a piano on which lie the bodies of two dead donkeys. But what does it mean to "drag a piano," and what can the strange combination of a piano and a donkey's corpse reveal? The Surrealist metaphor, which Lacan does not bother to interpret, appears here only to emphasize that in order to produce a melody one must do the work of dragging the piano, overcoming its weight and any obstacles that stand in one's way; it is not enough to elegantly step up to the piano and play it. The Surrealist metaphor may also teach us that just like the juxtaposition of Kant and Freudian sexuality, the seemingly absurd juxtaposition of a piano and a dead donkey, just like the juxtaposition of Kant with Freudian eroticism, can be extremely revealing. We can say that in order to get anything out of Kant, one must drag him on one's back and feel his full weight, and Lacan calls on his students to rediscover Kant just as he called on them to rediscover Freud, by being fully committed to taking him on. In both cases, that of Freud and that of Kant, the call is to read the original. Just as rediscovering Freud means reading him word for word, prior to or beyond the obfuscations caused by his commentators and opponents, so Kant, when he is read in the French translation, turns into something monotonous and dusty; therefore he must be reread *à la lettre*, that is, to the letter. Only then will the monotony make way for the erotics of this text. The eroticism of the Kantian text is therefore not given, but must be discovered by knowing how to read Kant, just as the meaning of Surrealist metaphors is not given to the viewer but requires the work of reading.

For Lacan, returning to the philosophers with whom he is concerned means returning to the original texts verbatim, but in such a way that the *return* this reading enacts must be qualified. Just as after Lacan one cannot return to Freud without taking into account the way in which Lacan reads him,[1] so Lacan's return to Kant changes something in the way we read Kant. We may say that reading Kant word for word in order to discover his affinity with psychoanalysis walks a thin line with respect to the limits of valid reading. Not because such a reading does injustice to the *correctness* of the philosophical text, but because it can seem as if Lacan's reading claims something about Kant that in Kant's own terms goes beyond the principles that are immanent to thought – something that Kant himself cannot take into account without betraying his method, without falling into an illusion. In a similar way we can see that Lacan's reading of Freud completely changes the balance between the unconscious as inscription and the unconscious as meaning in Freud – this reading's correctness (in the sense that it is based on things that Freud says) thus does not diminish the transformative effect it has on our understanding of Freud.

Back to Kant, we can see that he is often concerned with the subject of illusions; in the introduction to the transcendental dialectic in *The Critique of Pure Reason*, he is engaged with illusions and errors of judgment that reflect the tendency of human cognition to see subjective necessity as objective necessity, or to be carried beyond the empirical use of the categories and the limits of possible experience. That is, error by illusion

flows from an unnoticed influence of sensibility on our pure understanding so that "the subjective bases of the judgment meld with the
objective ones."[2] There is a range of possible errors of judgment: some
result from not paying "enough attention to the boundaries of the terri-
tory on which alone our pure understanding is permitted to engage in
its play."[3] But some are unavoidable and stem, as mentioned just now,
from the illusion that subjective principles that have an objective look
can indeed be taken to denote things in themselves (e.g., the illusion
that the world must have a beginning in time beyond the intuition that
determines a limit on temporal phenomena).

As we will see below, Lacan's main claim regarding Kant is that
illusions, errors of judgment, moves that determine certainty, are all
impossible to eliminate, because in Kant the formal elements that
originate in the pure understanding, are *real*. The *a priori* principles,
those that coordinate and determine the objects of experience, precisely hold an irreducible presence; they constitute the real object that
human cognition encounters.[4] That is, Lacan uses Kant, and especially
the *a priori* formal aspects that determine what can be thought and
under which principles, to explore the *real dimension* in psychic reality and to show that the Kantian method is one that gives place to the
unconscious. The formal principles, Lacan claims, have a real dimension, the real in this context being understood thus: *the real is that which
refuses or opposes the symbolization embodied in the formal principle, or, in
other words, the real is where one encounters the impossible in applying a
formal principle.*

Here, as with regard to other philosophers, Lacan does not merely
say that Kant is wrong or that Kant ignores the fact that human understanding encompasses more than he believes. Rather, Lacan shows that
Kant says more than he knows he says. Thus, for example, in the introduction to the Transcendental Dialectic, dealing with transcendental
illusions, Kant explicitly states that the illusions are not mistakes that
stem from the misapplication of an intellectual principle to experience:
"Transcendental illusion ... does not cease even when we have already
uncovered it and have ... had distinct insight into its nullity ... This is
an illusion that we cannot at all avoid."[5] Lacan when reading Kant presupposes the unconscious – that is, the unconscious serves Lacan as a
kind of reading finger. Thus in the two following chapters that discuss
Kant we will see, among other things, that Lacan's claim about what is
real in the formal rules of the understanding does not deviate from the
Kantian insight, but rather reveals its power.

It is in this sense that, in these chapters, we will be examining the limits of the legitimate reading of Kant, by reading two of his fundamental concepts: one, *the concept of unity*, is at the heart of the first critique (*The Critique of Pure Reason*) and is the subject of the present chapter; the other, *the good*, is at the heart of the second critique (*The Critique of Practical Reason*) and will occupy us in the following chapter. Examining the way Lacan reads these two ideas in Kant – the idea of unity and the idea of the good and the moral law – will enable us to discover something about the limits of Lacan's reading. Later we will return to Lacan in order to understand why, from his point of view, Kantian thought is not only not foreign to the spirit of psychoanalysis but indeed contributes to the conceptual exploration that he carries out.

A. The Unifying Function in Kant

But before we touch on the question of unity, which (along with morality) is the main issue that engages Lacan with regard to Kant, we must clarify in what way returning to Kant "to the letter"– a task that accompanies Lacan throughout much of his teaching – reveals the eroticism in Kant's writing, and whether this revelation inevitably exceeds the limits of any legitimate reading of Kant. To answer these questions, we will have to take a brief detour through Kant's philosophy; this will also acquaint us with the centrality of the synthetic or unifying function in his thought. Lacan used the idea of unity in Kant in relation to the question of identification, with which he was occupied in his seminar of 1961–62, but unity as a Kantian concept occupied him in several other contexts as well, from some of the seminars through the *Écrits* and up to the television interview he gave in 1973.[6]

In *Television*, Lacan refers to the Kantian question: *What can we know?*[7] On the face of it, this question cannot be answered by the analytical discourse, which presupposes a subject of the unconscious; the unconscious shifts the limits of knowledge and obliges the psychoanalyst to answer the Kantian question with the unconscious. Surprisingly, however, Lacan says that answering the question "What can I know?" by referring to the unconscious merely *repeats* what Kant himself says. That is, the supposition of the unconscious adds nothing to what Kant supposes in relation to the limits of knowledge. How can this be? Lacan explains that he can know "nothing in any case that doesn't have the structure of language; whence it follows that the distance I can go *within* this limit is a matter of logic."[8] Lacan's answer does not deviate from

Kant's, because for Kant the possibilities of empirical experience are *a priori* determined based on the rules of the understanding, and these set the limits of knowledge. This means that the foundations of the understanding determine *a priori* what can become a sign in scientific discourse; they decide scientific possibilities – the fact, for instance, that one day science will lead to the event of landing on the moon.

Lacan reads the Kantian logic as creating a structure of signs that can be deciphered and used to create *real possibilities*, which are not known but which are posited within the language that this logic instructs us how to operate in. Lacan derives this conclusion from Kant's logic that allows us to walk in the field of knowledge and determine its possibilities. Logic according to Kant has two aspects. There is general logic, which is abstracted from all the empirical conditions or from objects and the differences between them, and which concerns only the fundamental form of thinking; this, Kant claims, is logic as the science of the rules of the understanding and no more. But in addition to general logic there is transcendental logic, a special logic that adds a further set of rules and concepts to the structure of the rules of pure thinking, and this logic applies to the possibilities of thinking certain objects, not in their practical implementation, but in a completely *a priori* way.[9] What one can know is within the limit set by logic insofar as transcendental logic refers *a priori* to *objects* as the possible content of cognition.[10] This is how Kant describes what he calls transcendental logic: "We shall expect, then, that there may perhaps be concepts referring a priori to objects ... We frame in advance the idea of a science of pure understanding and of rational cognition, whereby we think objects completely a priori."[11]

As we will see, Kant does not entirely explain how the transition between general logic (which posits general principles of understanding that prevent, for instance, the possibility of contradiction) and the empirical objects it leads to (which can show that the contradiction refers to two situations in two different points in time) takes place, or how science deciphers pure logic for its needs – or at least he leaves these questions open to different interpretations. But be that as it may, what Lacan emphasizes with regard to Kant is that according to the structure of Kantian thought, the moon landing was already inscribed in the pure knowledge of the principles and the categories, because the possibility of thinking an object is already present in a certain sense in the way knowledge is formulated *a priori*. The possibilities of cognizing an object are already established.

This explains why Lacan can claim that in his answer to the question of what can be known, he merely echoes Kant, albeit, he adds, with one reservation that stems from the fact that Kant "reveals himself as the plaything of his unconscious."[12] Kant does not think or calculate possible bodies of knowledge that can become actualized by virtue of the principles of the pure understanding I; he does not refer to the real possibility of *a priori* supposing a knowledge that is not yet known. Kant is ignorant, in other words, of the fact that he *includes the unconscious in pure knowledge*. Lacan's claim is that in order to answer the question of what can be known, Kant constructs a system of principles that lays the foundations for an unknown knowledge. Moreover, in order to posit such knowledge one must in the first place ascribe real status to these principles. This real status means that pure principles *include* the possibility of thinking something as an object even though it is impossible to know this object. What can be thought but not known, and is ascribed by Lacan to Kant, is in fact the knowledge that is included in the transition from the pure principles of transcendental logic to the various areas of knowledge, knowledge that must be somehow included in the logical principles themselves. In order to enable such a transition, Lacan claims, the effects of the presence of the object that is not yet thought are in a certain sense already taken into account and present, defining the limits of possible knowledge. What is real in the structure is therefore Kant's unconscious, an unconscious that is needed in order to decipher the Kantian method, which constructs a natural science/pure knowledge that includes all the scientific possibilities for cognizing objects.

"Kant's unconscious" is thus the *real element* that parallels the possible effects of the system, that is, the fact that there must be something in the system itself that creates the possibility of thinking about a yet unknown thing. Kant's unconscious is what causes such effects, what creates the possibilities and limit of cognition.

To further investigate Lacan's reference to Kant and to the pure formalism of his method, we should therefore decipher what is the object that Lacan exposes and whose presence serves to expose Kant's unconscious. For that purpose, we will briefly examine the concepts of cause and causality in Kant, since Kant's discussion of causality seems foundational to what Lacan ascribes to Kant. If we posit Kant's unconscious in relation to the mechanism of pure understanding, then given the effects of the cognitive apparatus – like the effect of establishing causal relations among phenomena – we are obliged to assume a prior cause that allowed this effect to be created. Kant's unconscious is not equal to the objects that can be thought, that can be given to cognition; *Kant's unconscious equals the object-cause that is necessarily present as the basis of the mechanism of understanding and that generates unknown objects of knowledge.* Such an object is described by Kant himself, in his discussion of causality.

Causality is an indispensable principle for creating links between phenomena, because causality (along with the principles of permanence and simultaneity) is an objective (rather than empirical) principle responsible for the very possibility of experience.[13] Kant says that cognizing the objective relation that exists between successive perceptions requires "the conception of 'the relation of cause and effect,' the former of which determines the latter in time, as its necessary consequence, and not as something which might possibly antecede (or which might in some cases not be perceived to follow)."[14] Causal relations first entail an inverted priority, since the causal connection precedes the connection between phenomena, rather than the other way around. Thus the location of a phenomenon in time (e.g., the appearance of smoke) can only take place because a cause is necessarily posited as an *a priori* condition for the possibility of this phenomenon occurring; conversely, in relation to empirical cognition, we perceive the appearance of smoke as a change in relation to what was not there before, and to what cannot be returned to.[15] In the section that deals with the (regulating) principles in accordance with which experience is unified (called *the second analogy*[16]), Kant shows how causality imposes necessity on perceptions that would otherwise maintain accidental, subjective connections. Thus Kant points to causality as determining an objective relation to a necessary cause; only based on this principle will an empirical cognition of phenomena as objects of experience located on a sequential continuum in time become possible.

In this context Kant discusses cause as an object to which the manifold of phenomena are connected. As soon as a relation is perceived between representations, "I cognize an object that I must place in time in a determinate position, which ... cannot be otherwise assigned to it."[17] When we cognize an appearance in accordance with the law of cause and effect, objects of experience are made possible.[18] This object of causal connection raises a special difficulty, because on the one hand it must be seen as an object of cognition (rather than as an object in itself), but on the other hand it cannot be identified with the representation. This object, the transcendental object that necessarily precedes what appears in the order of representations, is not itself given to cognition, but is rather an object of the understanding that remains unknown.[19] Nonetheless, without it the synthesis of the manifold through the relations of cause and effect would not have been possible; indeed, the very possibility of thinking phenomena as located in some order in time would not have existed.

The distance between phenomenon as representation[20] and phenomenon as transcendental object explains why any phenomenon requires its cause, although the cause is not a preceding state complemented by its consequence. The manifold of phenomena appear before us as effects of an *a priori* causal connection, a transcendental object of causal relations. So we also require the difference between the temporal location of phenomena and the time of the causal connection in order to clarify how a successive order of phenomena is the expression of a necessary relation. The principle of causality means that appearances given to perception are not merely representations between which there is an accidental connection, but rather phenomena related necessarily. Causality for Kant is not only a synthetic principle that connects representations, but also an *a priori* principle of the understanding – that is, a principle that precedes intuition but that makes it possible to understand something from the multiplicity of intuitions: "That something happens, therefore, is a perception that belongs to a possible experience, which becomes actual if I regard the position of the appearance as determined in time, thus if I regard it as an object, which can always be found in the connection of perceptions in accordance with a rule."[21] Thus for Kant, the causal association of phenomena is seen as the effect of an *a priori* rule, and given that the order originates in the rule rather than in the phenomena, it points to the presence of a necessary object as the basis of the causal connection in time.

Although it is not mentioned by Lacan specifically, this Kantian discussion emerges as a relevant context when we encounter Lacan's distinction in the seminar on "Anxiety" (1962–63) between "objectivity" and "objectality," a distinction he associates with Kant. "Objectivity," Lacan claims, "is the ultimate term in Western scientific thought, the correlate to a pure reason which, at the end of the day, is translated into – is summed up by, is spelt out in – a logical formalism." The objective object is the complement of pure reason, while the object of "objectality" is something else. Objectality "is the correlate to a pathos of the cut. But, paradoxically, this is where the same formalism, in Kant's sense of the term, meets up with its effect."[22] This effect was misrecognized by Kant. Kant's formalism encounters the *objectal object* as its necessary effect, although Kant mistakenly believes that the object that the formal system he has constructed encounters is *objective*. That is, Kant encounters an object whose effect is "a pathos of the cut," and this encounter, Lacan claims, occurs where Kant, who is absorbed with causality as a necessary principle, leaves out the object-cause, that is, leaves out what justifies the causal principle as, "irrefutable, irreducible and almost ungraspable to critique."[23] By the pathos of the cut Lacan distinguishes the objectal split that Kant's formalism leads to, from the objective continuity that Kant assumes (according to which the manifold in experience is correlated with the unifying principle of pure understanding).

The pathos of the cut created by the mechanism of the understanding is not then Lacan's invention; rather, as we have shown, Kant himself points to a transcendental object assumed in order to connect representations by causality. That object is necessary in that it lies beyond the power of cognition. That is, the Kantian method is based on something that the formal system produces as heterogeneous to it, an object that is not cognizable but that is a precondition for the objects of experience to be cognizable and knowable. As we have seen in the quote from Kant, the order of phenomena does not include the object-cause, and this fact is the driving force behind the Kantian critique. Lacan goes on to say in this context that formalism does not and cannot succeed in eliminating the objectal dimension of the cause, a dimension that remains ungraspable to the critique. In other words, Lacan's claim is that in order to understand how the transition from the *a priori* formal principles of the understanding to the dimension of experience becomes possible, we must see the presence of an *object-cause* that no *a priori* principle can eliminate and that is caught in the transcendental machine of *a priori* principles.

It is this object, caught in the cogs of the machine of pure understanding, that explains why Lacan ascribes *eroticism* to the Kantian text. This object, necessarily caught up in the formal principles and without which the latter would mean absolutely nothing to us, is a *piece of flesh* (*morceau charnel*) – not a piece that is taken from the experiencing cognition, but a piece that is posited in various ways in the very framework of objective understanding:

> This formalism doesn't only summon us and furnish[] us with the frameworks of our thinking and our transcendental aesthetics, it seizes hold of us at a particular place. We give it not only the matter, not only our Being of thought, but the corporeal morsel that is torn from us as such. This

morsel is what circulates in logical formalism such as it has been constituted through our work on the use of the signifier. This portion of ourselves is what is caught in the machine, and it can never be retrieved. As
a lost object, at the different levels of the bodily experience where its cut
occurs, it is the underpinning, the authentic substrate, of any function of
cause.[24]

Lacan formulates here in objectal terms what appears in Kant in
terms of an objective object. The object-cause is actually a piece of being,
a corporeal thing, without which we would not be caught in thought,
in intuition, in understanding. This piece of being is the real cause of
the constitution of cognition with its different parts, and this cause is
therefore tossed about among the parts of the Kantian critique. Without
the erotics of the body, the thought machine would not be able to turn
its wheels. Incidentally, Lacan's claim that Kant's body is caught in his
philosophy is not far from Kant's own claim in "The Conflict of the Faculties" about the relationship of his own body with the philosophical
task he has undertaken.[25]

The objectal cause caught in the wheels of the objective machine is
also the one that Lacan assumes in his interpretation of Kant's concept
of unity. Causality and unity are not far from each other, since causality
as an *a priori* condition for the possibility of conjoining the manifold is
a condition of the understanding that relies on the *unity of apperception*,
that is, on cognition being fundamentally subject to a synthetic principle of unification. The causal relation relies on the unifying power of
apperception that *a priori* posits the manifold's aspiration to the one.

Cognitive action, be it in the field of intuition or of understanding, is
enabled by *a priori* unity assumed for every representation, unity that
allows cognition to connect all phenomena in one internal intuition, to
conjoin the manifold under one "thinking I." For Kant, unity ensures,
first, the limits of cognition – that its borders will not be breached,
that the *a priori* rules of understanding and intuition will only operate in regard to what the limits of cognition can posit as a possibility.
In Kant's words: "that the table of them [of concepts of understand-
ing] be complete, and that they entirely exhaust the entire field of pure
understanding ... Now this completeness is possible only by means of
an idea of the whole of the a priori cognition of the understanding."[26] That
is, unity is a fundamental conception that posits, prior to experience,
the wholeness of the understanding, in the sense that it applies to any
manifold that may appear under it.

But in addition to this intellectual synthesis, another synthesis is required, one that will enable the concepts, which are merely forms of thought, to be applied to objects that can be known by the senses, that is, as phenomena in time and space. Unity of the second kind is a basic assumption of the transcendental deduction, which is the part of *The Critique of Pure Reason* that deals with the ways in which concepts that were not derived from experience can refer *a priori* to objects and apply to them. Here, unity is not simply a preliminary supposition; it also characterizes the way in which the understanding *acts* on representations and objects: "In all subsumptions of an object under a concept, the representations of the former must be **homogeneous** with the latter ... Now pure concepts of understanding, however, in comparison with empirical (indeed, in general sensible) intuitions are entirely unhomogeneous and can never be encountered in any intuition."[27] That is, unity of experience is subsumed under a concept of unity, yet unity, as a pure principle of understanding, is completely foreign to the manifold and cannot be encountered in intuitions.

This is the complex place that unity occupies in Kant: unity embodies the *a priori* conditions of the understanding's striving for the totality that precedes any experience. That is, on the one hand unity is a transcendental object that makes the connecting of the manifold possible. On the other hand, unity is also the striving, which is realized only partially and conditionally in the field of experience, for the co-organization of the elements that validate experience. We can say that unity is present in various orders of cognition that do not necessarily harmonize. Unity is actualized through the synthesis created by applying the categories, yet it is also assumed prior to any representation. Unity is present in each of the orders of cognition: in reason, in the understanding, and in the modes of intuition, according to what distinguishes one order of cognition from the other. Unity is also what creates and makes possible the connections among the different orders of cognition. At this stage we can say that from the point of view of Lacan, Kant maintains the cut between the orders of cognition while embodying the wish for homogeneity in the various aspects of cognition, a formulation that already points to the presence of the "pathos of the cut" that Lacan will emphasize in his reading of Kant (although for Kant, as already mentioned, the pathos of the cut can be sutured, at least partially, by the synthetic power of cognition).

Kant identifies the unity that points to the very possibility of connectivity and that precedes any act of cognition as the "*a priori synthetic unity of the apperception."* Kant refers to the element that unites and mediates between the concepts of the understanding and representations as the *transcendental schema*, that is, as what enables the implementation of understanding on phenomena. Here the emphasis is on the act of unification that takes place by virtue of a unity of cognition at each of its levels of operation.

Schematism is one of the most debated and open-to-interpretation concepts in Kant's philosophy. This is because the schematism that connects the categories (i.e., pure concepts of the understanding that refer, according to a set number of functions, to the objects of intuition[28]) to the manifold of experience assumes a distance that should be bridged. Schematism is described as a third element that enables the *subsumption of the object to the concepts* despite the unbridgeable separation between the sensible and the rational in human cognition, a separation that Kant never tires of emphasizing. As already noted, Kant devotes much of his philosophical energy to distinguishing between the pure elements of the understanding and the possibility of experience, which is not derived from the pure understanding but whose limits and structure are determined by it; he repeatedly warns against empirical entities slipping into rational considerations. By means of this *a priori* dimension in human cognition that furnishes terms of synthesis, Kant establishes the *radical difference* between concept and intuition, between the sphere of pure reason and pure understanding on the one hand,[29] and the sphere of experience on the other. One term that serves this synthesis is presentation,[30] but cognition as a whole is examined as a set of *a priori* conditions that determine not only the way in which beings can become essentially objects of thought, and the conditions under which the world of phenomena can be revealed to us (as subject to forms of space and time, as subsumed under forms of connectivity such as causality, continuity), but also the way in which certain elements that lie outside the world of experience, such as purposefulness or eternal life, can be given to thought (as pure rational elements).

The inherent heterogeneity of the very structure of cognition is emphasized not only through the difference between the empirical presentation and the pure conditions of cognition (that precede experience), but also through the difference between pure concepts that apply to an object, and those that are not bound to an object. There are concepts, says Kant in the introduction to the *Critique*, such as the concepts of cause, that are actualized in objects of the understanding and on which the possibility of experience relies, and there are concepts that have been stripped of any attribute that is learned from experience, such as the concept of causality or spatiality (according to the latter, while an object takes up space, which requires an *a priori* form of intuition, space as a pure form is not dependent on the presence of an object[31]). The objects of experience that have an *a priori* origin must be distinguished from concepts that are located outside the sphere of possible experience and that are connected to the very essence of reason: such are the striving for the unconditioned, the absolute realm, and the striving for unity in any one of its aspects.

It should therefore be remembered that although Kant aspires to a systematic description of the structure of cognition as a whole, the unity of cognition is achieved on top of essential differences between its parts (reason, understanding, and imagination and their further divisions) – essential in the sense that they are to some extent unbridgeable. This is a unity that is fundamentally based on difference. Kant stresses the transcendental dimension, that is, the conditions that predetermine the ways in which the cognitive powers encounter the world; this *a priori* dimension determines all the planes on which the cognitive operation is revealed to us in ways we perceive and understand things. But this should not obscure the incompatibility, the lack of reciprocity, between the empirical order and the *a priori* order, between the necessity that resides in pure thought and the way concept is tied to the sensible object – between, for example, causality as an *a priori* category of relation, and the change we perceive in the empirical object as contingent.

In addition to the rule that is given in the pure concept of the understanding, transcendental philosophy can at the same time indicate *a priori* the case to which the rules ought to be applied, says Kant.[32] Hence, unity as a pure concept of understanding exists side by side with the indispensable function that this unity fulfils in relation to the capabilities of imaging [representing] and understanding an object, and in relation to the manifold ways in which the understanding chooses its objects of thought. In Kant, necessity, separateness and multiplicity both sustain and derive from the unity of consciousness.

Transcendental philosophy must explain the conditions under which perceptions that come together only contingently are in harmony with concepts; hence the *a priori* principles and terms are serving as a kind of lodestone for the array of objects. Our subjective and private judgments must be given to objective principles. For example, it is essential that in the cognition of objects of experience they will be located in one time, but an explanation is needed as to how we get from a representation (of an object located in time) to a temporal form of intuition according to an *a priori* necessary principle. Kant shows how the form of time is an *a priori* condition (in line with a necessity that precedes experience) that has a pure dimension, but also how time determines the possibility that an object will appear as located in time. This difference between the two dimensions of the concept of time is essential for Kant (and he uses the analogies of experience to explain the possibility of moving between these dimensions), since permanence, succession, and simultaneity, which are the principal modes of temporal composition, differ from the way in which empirical things are connected to each other, which can seem merely accidental. Kant goes on to say that

> experience is an empirical cognition, i.e., a cognition that determines an object through perceptions. It is therefore a synthesis of perceptions, which is not itself contained in perception, but contains the synthetic unity of the manifold of perception in one consciousness ... But since experience is a cognition of objects through perception, consequently the relation in the existence of the manifold is to be represented in it not as it is juxtaposed in time but as it is objectively in time, yet since time itself cannot be perceived, the determination of the existence of objects in time can only come about through their combination in time in general, hence only through a priori connecting concepts. Now since these always carry necessity along with them, experience is thus possible only through a representation of the necessary connection of the perceptions.[33]

Time, whether organizing empirical phenomena or as a form that precede experience, is not in itself an object of cognition, but is what determines our ability to perceive objects and connect them in time. This example of temporal intuition shows us that for Kant time determines our modes of experiencing, although time is not identified with any component of experience itself; time is also a pure form of temporal intuition, which precedes any experience, and in relation to which the essential principles of the operation of time are determined and formulated.

What thus comes into focus – against this insistence on the difference between the pure intellectual sphere and the empirical sphere that stems from the pure principles; between concepts that apply to objects and those that do not – is the criticality of the concept of unity to the transcendental philosophy, as well as the question of what enables the subsumption of an object that belongs to one order under a concept that belongs to another. The very insistence on distinguishing between that which is in experience and that which originates spontaneously in understanding prior to experience, gives rise to the crucial need to connect the two. Since we are dealing with different orders of cognition, it is not enough to say that such linking and conjunction stem from the primordial element of unity; rather, unity is also an *act of conjunction*, of a synthesis that is already driven by *a priori* unity.

To use the example that Kant gives at the beginning of the section on schematism (which is the mechanism responsible for clarifying the conditions under which the phenomenon is determined in relation to the pure category or in relation to the pure intellectual concept): "Thus the empirical concept of a *plate* has homogeneity with the pure geometrical concept of a *circle*, for the roundness that is thought in the former can be intuited in the latter."[34] Roundness is a pure geometric concept that does not contain any conceptual attribute prior to experience and that applies to sensible objects such as plates. The examination of the ways in which the pure concept is presented in the sensible object, and the path from the plate to the *a priori* concept of roundness, are central to Kant's project.

Precisely because of the separation between the circle as a sensible representation and the rules of understanding that make that representation possible, the ways to posit the phenomenon under the category are not self-evident. As Allison says, unification poses a problem because "this separation [of the sensible and intellectual conditions of cognition] seems to preclude the possibility of synthetic *a priori* judgements that apply the categories to appearances."[35] That is, while the application of the categories gives necessary validity to experience, this requires an *interpretation* of the connection between representations and concepts. This movement between separation and synthesis is merely a kind of transformation in which an intellectual concept gains a sensible status.

In other words, as with other mediating elements employed by Kant, the linking of object and concept, of intuition to rules, postulates a movement that is not simple, because it feeds on a clearly disharmonic unity. This movement and its disharmony are essential to the Kantian method and, as we will see, may clarify how Kant becomes a central philosopher for Lacan.

The problem of unity is thus twofold. First, it concerns the transition that occurs between the concept and the object. That is, how can we understand the correspondence between phenomena, as representations given in experience, and the pure concepts of the understanding, which are the *a priori* principles that organize thought prior to any possible experience? Second, the question of unity concerns the meta-principle that ties together all the separate parts of cognition, all its perceptions and knowable objects, and this tying together must rely on a formal condition that precedes any experience and in fact neither entails nor is contained in our experience. The difficulty related to the synthesis of objects and concepts seems to originate in the existence of a supreme principle of unity, which is defined at the outset as a principle that neither depends on nor maintains any link with representations of phenomena: "The pure understanding separates itself completely not only from everything empirical, but even from all sensibility. It is therefore a unity that subsists on its own, which is sufficient by itself, and which is not to be supplemented by any external additions."[36]

This passage suggests that, for Kant, unity should be considered separately from principles of synthesis that operate in the different parts of cognition. Yet even if pure understanding ascribes unity to our cognition, unity is required also for the field of sensibility, and rules of conjunction are required for the field of categories, and so on. Every aspect of cognition is subject to its own unification, according to its own principles (even if Kant wishes to prove that all levels of synthesis ultimately converge on one unity). This passage also suggests that the unity of pure understanding does not stem from an external source, but is a fundamental form that stems spontaneously from understanding itself. That is, the meta-unity is the umbrella principle that inspires forms of unity and possibilities of conjunction in the different domains of cognition. Note, however, in this context that although the demand for unity exists everywhere in Kant, there is no unity that generally applies by default (the analogies of experience demonstrate the difficulty in bringing sensible representations under the principles of pure understanding). Unity is not a unity of unification.

"The **I think** must be able to accompany all my representations; for otherwise something would be represented in me that could not be thought at all, which is as much as to say that the representation would either be impossible, or else at least would be nothing for me."[37] The representation of unity under the "I think" accompanies all representations but does not concern the activity of thought or the creation of sensible representations; rather, it is a principle that conditions the possibility of something appearing as representation. The ability to ascribe any representation or intuition to an "I think" is not conditional on the unification of the representations or intuitions themselves, but rather on the presence of an *a priori* unity of consciousness, and from this unity, the synthesis of representations into one structure is derived. The unity of apperception (i.e., the inner sense of a unified mind) is the original principle that determines that everything that appears within the limits of cognition belongs to one consciousness; without this unity, nothing can be thought, perceived, or known. This unity thus has an objective validity (i.e., it does not imply anything about *the way in which* things will be actually thought or known). Likewise, it should not be inferred from the unity of apperception that this unity can be viewed as a kind of primal or immediate inner sense of unity: "In the synthetic original unity of apperception, I am conscious of myself not as I appear to myself, nor **as** I am in myself, but only **that** I am. This **representation** is a thinking, not an intuiting … I therefore have no cognition of myself as I am but only as I appear to myself."[38]

This dimension of unity of self that presides whenever something is thought or perceived is not equivalent to self-consciousness; that is, the unity of apperception does not and cannot determine the specific ways in which thought itself turns outer appearances into representations. *The unity of apperception does not go beyond the preliminary condition that determines consciousness as one.* The synthesis of understanding, considered in itself, "is nothing other than the unity of the action of which it is conscious as such even without sensibility."[39] That is, even if understanding can bring under its unity the manifold of intuitions, this preliminary "unity" is not itself presented in the way things are intuited. Hence, unity, like all the pure *a priori* principles of the intellectual apparatus, is not in itself an object of cognition, nor can it be applied to the way in which representations are synthetized. Unity is not unified consciousness of oneself, nor is it a representation (of a unified object). In general, the way in which apperception is related to the representation of objects is not straightforwardly defined.

Why does Lacan need this principle of a prior inner sense of being one for psychoanalysis? In psychoanalysis the *pathos of the cut* (rather than of unity) is the basis for any conception of subjectivity. Significantly, in several places where Lacan portrays Kant as a typical representative of the philosophical discourse, he describes the tendency towards totality as an expression of philosophical cowardice. Thus, for example, he describes Kantian method as an attempt to organize knowledge in such a way that the structure of cognition remains uninterrupted. In this vein, Kant's transcendental idealism – which introduces the phenomenon as an object of thought through pure conditions of cognition, while leaving out the *noumenon*, the thing in itself – is one that reflects this philosophical interest in keeping the cognitive structure conveniently intact. Kant's idealism (which means that something in the relations of the subject, that is, the *noumenon*, the object in itself, remains suspended) essentially postulates that "the thinking being is only dealing with his own measure, that he poses as a terminal point, the referential point that is in question for him. Now it is from this measure that he believes he is able to state in an *a priori* fashion at least the fundamental laws."[40] Kant is presented here as cutting a circle to the measure of cognition, so that the object of thought and the conditions for its cognition will maximally correspond. At this point Lacan seems to see the Kantian unity as an apex of correspondence between thought and the thinker, between the representation and the principles underlying the mind.

The most extreme expression of this critical position towards Kant is found in an almost parodic description of Kant's project that appears in Seminar XI. Here, referring to the picture, to the field of vision, and to the object of the gaze, Lacan compares the psychoanalytical response to the question "What do you see in the picture?" with the Kantian response to "What can I know?" Lacan sees the pictorial plane as determined by the gaze located in the picture, that is, through what has been subtracted from the subject so that she desires to come and see what is in the picture. Had the picture not allowed room for something that the subject cannot know, and had the picture not failed to make up for this lack, the desire to see would not have arisen. The picture splits the subject (between the subject of the look *at* the picture and the subject of the gaze *looked at* from the picture) and fails to make up for or respond to what the subject demands from it, which is what makes looking at the picture possible. It is desire for a lack that creates a viewer for the picture. Kant solves the problem of representation differently. From a philosophical point of view, when I am presented with a representation "I assure myself that I know quite a lot about it, I assure myself as a consciousness that knows that it is only representation, and that there is, beyond, the thing, the thing itself. Behind the phenomenon, there is the noumenon, for example. I may not be able to do anything about it, because my *transcendental categories*, as Kant would say, do just as they please and force me to take the thing in their way. But, then, that's all right, really – everything works out for the best."[41] In these passages, Lacan sees Kant as someone who applies the philosophical method to ensure that the totality works without residue, remainder, or disruption.

While such references should obviously not be taken lightly or under-estimated, however, the present study suggests that the passages that teach us about the real affinity between Lacan and philosophy are passages in which Lacan refrains from such general "diagnoses."

The main Lacanian text on which the rest of this chapter will focus is a seminar in which Lacan emphasizes the synthetic function of unity in order to point to an object that gains its full presence precisely through Kant. The Kantian movement from the manifold towards unity on the one hand, and Kant's postulation of an all-embracing unity that precedes any cognition of unity on the other, make appear the object that is effectively at stake in the Kantian discourse around the question of unity – an object that only the psychoanalytical reading can reveal.

B. The Erotics of the One

Thus far we have been examining the classic interpretive issues that arise from Kantian philosophy, issues that also guided Lacan as he turned to Kant. We can now clarify how, with this reading, Kant's critique turns into an erotic treatise. The eroticism implied in Kant's critique is found precisely where Kant looks for a relation or a link between elements that maintain an irreducible difference. It is an eroticism that looks for unity among things that have no rapport. As we will see, it is in relation to unity, as that which maintains difference while insisting on the necessity of unicity (and on the striving for such unicity), that Lacan "diagnoses" Kant as an eroticist.

The claim about the erotics of the Kantian text arises where Lacan points to the difference between the object as deriving from a concept, and the object as subject to the logic of the signifier. The logic of the signifier will bring to light a different dimension of the objectality raised by the Kantian text and will lead us to the discussion of unity. In the transcendental deduction, Kant distinguishes between space as an object given in accordance with a form of sensible intuition and space as a formal intuition – that is, as an *a priori* intuition that does not belong to the senses.[42] The correspondence between space as a pure form of intuition and space as a way of comprehending the manifold as a relation in space, seems to point precisely to the difference between signifier and concept to which Lacan is referring.

To illustrate this difference, Lacan refers to the breast,[43] an object-organ that is displaced from the field of anatomy on the one hand, and that of nursing on the other, into the erotic field. There is a moment when the real breast becomes an erotic object, and Lacan claims that it is impossible to understand this change without the logic of the signifier, the signifier of a specific demand whose object appears to be this organ. The ensuing change relies on the fact that the eroticism of the object is made possible only because this object of oral eroticism is totally different from the breast as an organ of feminine anatomy. That is, the object itself is transformed; it no longer corresponds to an (anatomical or developmental) concept and appears as a signifier, that is, as an embodiment of a pure concept.

As it turns into a signifier, the body part already carries a trace of the singularity of a specific subject's desire. In other words, it is the connection between concept and object, which is based on unification by virtue of a pure concept, that is responsible for the object appearing as a signifier of eroticism. To understand this, we need to understand the movement from perceiving the breast as an object that has a certain anatomical function, or as subject to the drive towards the first object (of nursing), to the breast's appearance as a site of a particular desire. Lacan's claim is that this movement occurs by virtue of a unification that cannot be pinpointed as such but whose distinct effect is the emergence of the individual's desire as a particular desire. "The paradox of this One is precisely the following: it is that the more it resembles, I mean the more everything which belongs to the diversity of appearances is effaced from it, the more it supports, the more it incarnates I would say, if you will allow me this word, difference as such."[44] As an erotic body part, the breast is neither a concept nor an object of experience. It is precisely when the empirical phenomenon embodies an intellectual principle that is clearly separate from it, that the phenomenon becomes an erotic object. This is the reasoning that explains why the Kantian method is neither logical in the usual sense nor conceptual, since this logic of the signifier cannot be approached though formal logic, nor through concepts. The signifier presents us with an object that does not comply with logical principles or with conceptual categories, and this reading of Kant in terms of the signifier entitles his writing to be designated as "erotic."

By way of explanation, let us return to Kant's example of the geometrical roundness embodied in the plate: "In all subsumptions of an object under a concept, the representations of the former must be *homogeneous* with the latter ... Thus the empirical concept of a *plate* has homogeneity with the pure geometrical concept of a *circle*, for the roundness that is thought in the former can be intuited in the latter."[45] But getting from the concept of roundness to the representation of a round object is not that simple; the homogeneity that pairs a concept with an object does not exist of its own accord, since the concepts of the understanding, like the concept of roundness, are completely heterogeneous to empirical and sensible objects. How then is the homogeneity between the two elements ensured? By virtue of a third element, Kant says – specifically, by virtue of a mediating representation or a schema that enables the manifold to be synthesized under a concept. For Lacan, this "third element" signifies the transformation the object undergoes under the concept "round." The roundness of the plate is neither formal nor conceptual, but belongs to the logic of the signifier. Why? Because the plate exhibits pure roundness, which cannot in fact be demonstrated. This exhibition in the object fully exposes the fact that the manifold cannot be found in the pure concept and that the concept cannot be demonstrated in the manifold of representations. The plate becomes an impossible site of encounter between the pure formal element, the concept of roundness, and the sensible element that is the object; this is because the plate is not an actualization of the concept of roundness, nor is it possible to completely strip the plate of its roundness in such a way that it remains an object. This is why the plate's roundness is not merely formal, but neither is it an embodiment of a concept. Consequently, we can say that the signifier "roundness" is the signifier of the one within the manifold, and the more we try to eliminate the differences between the various round sensible objects, so that they correspond to the concept "round," the more the differences will become apparent between the roundness of each object and the pure concept, which knows nothing about the manifold, but which the round objects signify. This is how Kant generates a relation between the concept and the object – it is a relation between two entities that maintain an irreducible difference by means of the conceptual element that charges the object with the logic of the signifier.

Thus the desire for unity, for the (third) unifying element, demonstrates the absolute difference between the object that carries the signs of generality, and the object that signifies the singularity of the occurrence. The relevant object belongs neither to the two (or manifold) nor to the one.

Hence, it is precisely through the most acute formulation of the supreme unity of the pure understanding – the unity of apperception responsible for the emergence of a signifying dimension in every part of the *Critique* – that we can begin to see why the synthetic-unifying mechanism that organizes and threads together the parts of Kant's text is relevant for Lacan. Lacan uses Kant's synthetic function under the principle of unity precisely in order to expose the remainders that this unifying function leaves behind, to point to the object that is caught up in the synthetic mechanism.

The tendency towards the one of unity, the postulation of unity as an *a priori* necessity for the operation of cognition, which always remains heterogeneous and foreign to the unifying operation per se, is common to both psychoanalysis and Kant. While the pure concepts of the understanding fulfil this unifying function for Kant, a similar function can be attributed to Freud's unconscious and to the unary trait in Lacan:

> But in addition to the concept of the manifold and of its synthesis, the concept of combination also carries with it the concept of the unity of the manifold. Combination is the representation of the **synthetic** unity of the manifold. The representation of this unity cannot, therefore, arise from the combination; rather, by being added to the representation of the manifold, it first makes the concept of combination possible ... We must therefore seek this unity someplace higher, namely in that which itself contains the ground of the unity of different concepts in judgments, and hence of the possibility of the understanding, even in its logical use.[46]

There is unity that precedes all concepts of combination *a priori*. Unity is not a consequence of experience; it does not point to a regularity that governs the manifold of objects in our world, nor is it included in the concepts of the understanding that concern the forms of combination and unification. Rather, unity is posited by all of the above as a representation that is not included in the manifold. Unity is posited by the very operation of the understanding, but it precedes any mode of combination. It is posited by intuition but is prior to acts of intuiting. The wish for unity is the wish for what enables experience itself and underpins this experience, although the phenomenal world is in practice a manifold world that requires forms of combination to be given to our apprehension. Despite being heterogeneous to the objects that stem from it, unity is the unconditioned rule that makes the phenomenal world conditional upon it.

The basis for the unity of cognition, is a principle of unity that neither overlaps with nor is contained in the unity that appears in the operation of the powers of cognition, is equivalent to the eroticism that is supposed for the body, which neither overlaps with nor is contained in the eroticism of each and every body organ. If we did not understand erotic in the Kantian way, we would not see how we are able to sense our body as our own even though we know nothing about it. The eroticism, of course, is not an eroticism of the body independently of thought. The Kantian principle of unity enables us to identify eroticism as a prior principle and cause that is manifested (but not exhausted) in psychosomatic events: dreams, affects, disturbing thoughts that do not cease – to identify these as ours, although we can know nothing about the origin or the cause of their appearance.

Kant's decisive formulation in the above quote about the constitutive role of the *a priori* unity serves Lacan, who requires a similar reasoning when dealing with the concept of identification. Unity constitutes the possibility of combination but is not included in its operations; yet synthetic modes by which the manifold is unified are marked by striving for the One, by the necessary presence of "I think" that accompanies all my representations. Indeed, Lacan's solution to the fundamental question of identification follows this spirit of Kant. In essence, the One of identification is not accessible and cannot be embodied, because identity is underpinned by identification, yet no identification or object of identification carries the subject's identity. The subject locates herself in a mode/object of identification that cannot exhaust nor manifest subjectivity per se.

In the seminar on identification, Lacan says that psychoanalysis teaches us that identity and identification are one and the same, not in the sense that they overlap, but in the sense that the identity of the subject is conditional upon the identification of being with what is distinctly different from it. What determines the subject's so-called self-identity is identification with an Other (an Other that is not external to the subject but is the bedrock of subjectivity itself). In a very similar manner, for Kant all of the syntheses that combine representations enable something to appear as an object of intuition under an *a priori* condition that provides the objective basis for the possibility of synthesis.

But in what sense is it "in precisely the same manner"? Just as for Lacan the identity of the speaking being depends on (non-coordinated) being in accordance with an alien element located in the Other, without which identity would not be constituted, so for Kant the possibility of synthesis depends on a (never guaranteed) accordance with a prior and determining element: "But how should we be able to establish a synthetic unity a priori if subjective grounds of such a unity were not contained a priori among the original sources of cognition in our mind, and if these subjective conditions were not at the same time objectively valid, being the grounds of the possibility of cognizing any object in experience at all?"[47] What determines the unity that conjoins the manifold of phenomena is a different unity, one that is embodied by this combination without being identical, overlapping with, or equivalent to it. In order to understand this equivalence, we can say that for Kant, the relation between the pure element of unity that precedes any experience and the object given to the unity of synthesis (grounded on a transcendental unity) is like the relation between pain and the body, because saying that "this pain is mine" requires a One that will accompany all my pains and thus allow me to say: this is my body in pain, even if the one that precedes my representations does not coincide with the one of "my pain."

Pain, as Freud's narcissism taught us, is an auto-erotic phenomenon[48] rather than a sign of injury. Auto-eroticism means that it is through pain that our body becomes an object for us. That is, the sensation of pain is (among other things) what constitutes the unity of *my* body. The proof that pain is not attributed to the manifold but to the one is that it is impossible to feel two pains at the same time. One pain is driven out by the other, since eroticization belongs to the One. Pain as a mode of cathexis (i.e., libidinal charging), of the eroticization of the body, hence precludes the possibility of multiple pains. Pain demonstrates our body's *a priori* unity, *a priori* and outside experience, given that what enables us to say that this body is "mine" does not come with any knowledge of this body. While in its manifestation pain appears to be an expression of partiality (i.e., we sense pain in a particular place and allay it by avoiding certain objects), pain is an embodiment of the One that enables me to say "I'm in pain" and thus posit the unity of the body as prior to any pain. Just as Kantian space exists without an object, prior to any intuition or cognition of objects in space, so the pain I feel in a particular body part is in effect pain that exists beyond any body part, beyond the multiplicity of my sensations as a prior condition for my identifying with my pain. The object of pain does not exist as an object of cognition but is rather the condition for pain appearing as pain in what is my body.[49]

It should be said, even before we see to what extent this conception of unity is common to Kant and Lacan, and how deeply Lacan embeds himself in Kant's approach, that Lacan's notion of unity neither disconnects the body from the One nor disconnects the One from the body; that is, Lacan claims that the existence of a body in Kant cannot be doubted.

Although it seems that for Kant, the body has no place at all and unity is measured by cognition alone, the effect of the encounter between cognition and experience is that of alienation and difference, although its end result is synthesis and combination. In other words, the drive towards the primordial oneness does not mean that experience is cut perfectly to the measure of the pure unity of apperception. This is made clear by the "transcendental deduction," the part in the *Critique* that deals with the way in which an object that can be known empirically only through sensible intuitions can be derived from an object that can only be thought (through intellectual categories).[50] That is, unity is not derived from the structure of cognition, but is rather equivalent to *the unity of the body* – the only site in which there is difference where all differences have been erased. As we will see presently, Kant's body is a necessary outcome of pure reason, because without it, the unity that is entailed by every act of cognition could not come to be.

C. Identity and Identification

Lacan does not immediately reveal how close identification is to the transcendental dimension of the Kantian unity. At first, under Lacan's approach, identification requires using the operational logic of *the signifier* (and not, according to Lacan, that of an imaginary principle of collectivity, as Kant establishes). "For the unity of a thought consisting of many representations is collective, and, as far as mere concepts are concerned, it can be related to the collective unity of the substances cooperating in it."[51]

In Kant, unity, *Einheit*, is an *a priori* synthetic function that is restricted to the imaginary plane, thus reflecting a kind of myth that had existed in philosophical thought since Plato and reached its pinnacle and perfection with Kant.[52] The *a priori* principle that is posited with the Kantian unity can be illustrated, Lacan says, by a "circle which gathers together,"[53] a gathering together that goes beyond all intuitions and erases the difference between them. Conversely, for Lacan the One is the one of the unary trait, a trait that cannot be located, that is an "aporia of thinking."[54] The unary trait (already discussed in the chapter on Descartes) is, it should be said, the impossible point of encounter between the universality of common concept and absolute difference. For example, the notches the hunter carves on the butt of a gun are a universal mark of a series of hunting events, but each trait, despite being similar to the next in every respect, marks the absolute difference between one hunting event and another – between one animal that was caught and another that escaped and thwarted the hunter, between a hunt that took place in winter and one that took place in the spring, and so on.

While Kant points to the gradual erasure of difference the farther the synthesis gets from experience, Lacan claims that "the more everything which belongs to the diversity of appearances is effaced from it, the more it supports, the more it incarnates ... difference as such." Here we are already dealing with *Einzigkeit*, that is, with unicity rather than unity. This is because we have passed "from the virtues of the norm to the virtues of the exception."[55] We can understand this Lacanian diagnosis, which sees Kantian unity as a norm or a rule and psychoanalytical unicity as deviating from the rule (as concerning the exception that, contrary to common stupidity,[56] does not prove the rule), if we think about the Kantian unity as an *a priori* assumption of *relation* between different intuitions, while the unary trait strives for the *absence of relation*, where the difference that refuses any collectivity appears. Thus far, is seems that the philosophical drive for unity and the psychoanalytical drive for unicity are patently different.

But what starts as a clear affinity then moves to criticism of the distance between the psychoanalysis of the unary trait and Kant's transcendental analytic, quickly makes way for Lacan's claim that if we "repunctuate"[57] Kant's text, we will find that the One in Kant, which is based on the distinction between universal and singular judgment (between *a priori* unity of understanding and the synthesis of the manifold), already marks the beginning of their inversion. Kant, in other words, prefigures the unicity that Lacan wishes to signify through the unary trait: Lacan says that the unary trait does not necessarily appear *through* man, but is rather that *from which man appears*. In other words, Lacan suggests that man appears from pure difference rather than from the universal signifier that goes beyond difference. Lacan's claim, then, is that rather than negating the discrete singularity of the one by one, the Kantian unity makes it possible. How does Lacan arrive at this conclusion?

Lacan concludes this from the fact that it is not enough for Kant to gather together all the singular judgments in order to attain the universal, the *a priori* rule that is beyond the manifold of representations. In Kant, the singular phenomenon retains a kind of independence, while the universal rule does not retain the same autonomy. The universal does not derive from the collection of representations, nor does it enjoy its own autonomy, since Kant says explicitly that the unity of apperception in itself has no content, and time, a major element in the conjunctive existence of phenomena, cannot be sensed.[58] The one of *singularity* must be taken into account so as not to fall into mistaken inferences of the kind Kant analyses in the paralogisms and antinomies. This points to the logical reversal that takes place in the One, *which passes from the status of a universal to the status of uniqueness, the carrier of difference* – which explains the place Kant occupies for Lacan in this context.

   In Kant's first paralogism of pure reason, we can see why Lacan claims that the pure principle of the unity of apperception is connected to the one by one rather than to the universal. The paralogism is a wrong inference that ascribes objective reality to an object that cannot be known (even if this object is posited as an object of thought). Thus the first paralogism is based on the fact that the "I think" that accompanies all my representations is perceived as an object that it is possible to know and characterize (as substance or self-subsistent being). The general condition of the unity of apperception, Kant says, does not involve experience and therefore does not allow us to consider self-cognition as an object. The unity is merely logical, a formal unity of thought and nothing more.[59]

   If we go back to the way Kant presents the unity of apperception in the transcendental deduction, the question that arises concerns the way the fundamental condition of unity turns into a unifying synthesis applied to the sensible manifold, given that the unity of the apperception as a condition for the possibility of thought does not even assume the existence of a manifold. These are two separate concepts of unity, according to Kant: "The consciousness of oneself is therefore far from being a cognition of oneself, regardless of all the categories that constitute the thinking of an object in general through combination of the manifold in an apperception."[60] The cognition of consciousness and the cognition of the manifold in me, the faculty for combination as inner sense, are distinct operations. Yet even if the Kantian unity does not unify (unity can just be an inner sense of mineness), it does *inscribe* the manifold without cognizing it; the unity inscribes the one-by-one whose appearance it enables and conditions. We can see why the logic of this move posits a signifying status for thought: the doctrine of the unity of apperception is neither an ontological thesis about the cognitive apparatus nor a psychological thesis about the structure of cognition, but rather a logical move that gives content to cognition through a signifier, *one*, that determines the necessary affinity between singular

cognition ("inner sense of unity") and its modes of connecting operations. In this way Kant inscribes the singular difference through the *a
priori* universal.

However, the Lacanian move that establishes this reading of Kant has
another stage, in which Lacan wishes to show that the unity that Kant
affirms grounds the unity of apperception on something that has been
subtracted but that is given vital place as part of this unity:

> One could manage to reduce the Kantian schema to *Beharrlichkeit*, to per-
> manence, to the holding [*la tenue*], which I would describe as empty, but
> the possible holding of anything whatsoever in time. This intuition which
> is pure by right is absolutely required by Kant for the functioning of the
> categories, but after all that the existence of a body, in so far as it is the
> foundation of sensoriality – *Sinnlichkeit* – is not required at all, no doubt,
> for what one can validly articulate as a relationship to reality. This will
> take us no further since, as Kant underlines, the use of these categories of
> understanding will only concern what he is going to call empty concepts;
> but when we say that this will take us no further, it is because we are
> philosophers, and even Kantians, but once we no longer are that, which
> is the most common case, everyone knows precisely that on the contrary
> this goes very far because the whole effort of philosophy consists in coun-
> tering a whole series of illusions, of *Schwarmereien* as it is expressed in
> *philogophique* [philosophy + Goya] and particularly Kantian language; bad
> dreams – at the same epoch Goya tells us: "the sleep of reason engenders
> monsters."[61]

In this understanding of Kant and the synthetic function, the senso-
rial reality, the reality of the bodies, seems to become negligible and
unimportant with respect to the apparatus of categories. That is, Kant
seems to describe the permanence of the One as neither conceptual
nor real or tangible since the body has been omitted from all forms of
synthesis. When the body had been subtracted from consideration, the
sensible has in fact been radically cut from the unity of consciousness
as permanence.

Kant indeed indicates that the body is dispensable with regard to the
power of cognition – for example, when he illustrates the existence of
an *a priori* origin for the concepts through the conception of the body: "if
from your experiential concept of a body [*Korper*] you gradually omit
everything that is empirical in a body – the color, the hardness or soft-
ness, the weight, even the impenetrability – there yet remains the space

that was occupied by the body (which has now entirely vanished), and this space you cannot omit."[62] What we have here is the removal of the body as an object or a material thing (rather than as a carrier of sensibility, perceptions etc.); but Lacan puts the emphasis on the fact that Kant stops at this stage in which he posits an empty category as a basis for his concepts. Significantly, Kant stops at the *a priori* space as a container or an empty form, because this gives rise to the possibility of an intuition or a representation of a supersensible object (the unconditioned) – in this case space, as it is beyond any intuition – which is a possibility that must be avoided. Lacan, however, claims that Kant stops at this point only because he is a philosopher, because the whole philosophical endeavour consists in countering any illusion, any *Schwarmereien*, that is, any delusional sentimentality that may accompany the extrication of reason from deception.[63]

But something else occurs with the disappearance of the body. The disappearance of the body forces us to acknowledge that *a priori* space is real, that is, to see the convergence to a point, the gradual reduction of everything into one empty point, as a topological occurrence, that is, an occurrence that has effects in space, as will be presently explained.

What characterizes Kant's position, as it is formulated in the transcendental aesthetic, is that it ignores the real effects of the reduction of inhabited space to empty space, making it necessary to re-examine what this subtraction implies. In order to explain the effects of eliminating the bodily object from the space that coordinates its positioning as phenomenon, Lacan uses, in a kind of analogy to the Kantian understanding, the example of the cosmonaut in his capsule, when his body is in a state of weightlessness but he is still capable of "correctly pushing the buttons."[64] In this state of weightlessness, the cosmonaut's body appears as a material object subtracted from space. The cosmonaut's rational machine, his ability to implement pure combinatorics, materializes where the intuitions of time and space suspend the presence of the body that is located by means of, and on the basis of, this combinatorics. The suspended body is not simply the body that is the vehicle of the cognitive apparatus (the body of the person who possesses cognition), but is something material that belongs to the phenomenal dimension and that is subtracted so that cognition-without-a-body can appear. By subtracting the body, pure intuition, intuition presupposed by our perception of an object or state, appears as a universal form. The question is whether what Kant wishes to show is that forms of intuition are abstracted from outer perceptions and for this purpose the cosmonaut's body should become unreal. Does the subject have to become a disembodied machine in order for his intuition (and understanding) to operate in the most distinct fashion, without disruption? The question, therefore, is whether the cosmonaut is the Kantian embodiment of the synthetic function of cognition as liberated from the presence of a material body. According to Lacan, this is *not* what Kant wanted to prove.

The Kantian cosmonaut is capable of correctly pushing the buttons "without having recourse to their schematism," that is, where the body itself is free of the pure forms of intuition that condition the correct operation of the rational machine. The cosmonaut demonstrates the subtraction of body and sensibility to the extent that he cannot say what time is, or how his body is located in space, and this subtraction allows the pure forms of intuition to appear under the principle of synthesis, allowing the understanding to appear as unity. But when we think of the unity of apperception as conditioned upon the body turning into a weightless body, we realize that the body of the Kantian cognition is not outside the cognitive apparatus embodied in the act of pushing the button, but is rather present in the pure intellectual act itself. Not in the simple sense that the pushed button creates some kind of connection with the bodily/sensory organ, but in the sense that the situation of a weightless body is real and is by no means alien to our lives on *this* earth. Lacan, in other words, wishes to show that Kant's subtraction of the body from his transcendental logic, aesthetic, and analytic does not mean that the body can return only as part of the empirical sensible world; rather, the body is caught in the wheels of the cognitive machine from the start.

What happens, for example, Lacan asks, in the weightless state to the sexual drive? Here, in the absence of weight that so evidently characterizes the masculine fantasy about the phallus, it is precisely the organ that is not subject to gravity that inscribes the presence of the body. Perhaps the body is what cannot be subtracted precisely where its presence appears without gravity, without the burden of sensibility. If so, then it is precisely the subtraction of sensible presence in aspiring for the first element, the One, that can alone inscribe the body as indispensable for the cognitive apparatus. *The Kantian unity, Lacan claims, creates a necessary eroticization of the cognitive apparatus,* where it takes on the weightlessness of the body, a loss of gravity that has been forced on it by the pure forms of intuition and the pure concepts of understanding.

It is the weightless unity of the body that seems to reject the singularity of the subject, while in fact the weightless body, alien to sensibility and outside the burden of sensibility, this body is the vehicle of the cognitive apparatus. The weightless body has become the signifier of eroticism in Kant's synthesis.

The body, in other words, is the trait of the One that is revealed once we have completed examining the Kantian cognition with all its ramifications. At this point we can return to the question of the knowledge gained at the moment of subtraction. What has been subtracted from space and time and from the multiplicity of phenomena is the body that, in its subtraction, signifies the place of the One, that is, the principle of the unity of apperception that forms the condition for the very possibility of cognition.

The body relegated to the rank of dispensable materiality is exactly what is needed for the eroticization of the cognitive apparatus so that it can meet again the body as sensible object. Even if Kant did not grasp it in these terms, he understood that it is by virtue of pure understanding which encounters a body which it cannot enlist on its side, that the synthetic function can be fulfilled. That is, it is only where intuition is an empty form, from which the body has been excluded, that the body can gain the status of a signifier inscribed in the synthetic move. The body remains, inscribed in the empty form of space. This is why at the end of this session Lacan reaches the conclusion that

> by reversing, as I might say, the polarity of this function of unity, by abandoning the unifying unity, the *Einheit*, for the distinctive unity, the *Einzigkeit*, I am leading you to the point of posing the question, of defining, or articulating step by step the solidarity of the status of the subject *qua* bound to this unary trait ... because it is nothing other than the fact that it is starting from a small difference – and to say small difference means nothing other than this absolute difference of which I speak to you, this difference detached from all possible comparison.[65]

It is the subject that is constituted by (and carries) the unary trait, and Kant was the first to understand the mechanism that enables the universal subject to emerge from absolute difference. Kant understood that the subject, with its faculties of intuition and understanding, emerges in empty space, a space created as a result of subtraction. The cognitive apparatus does not operate where bodily reality has been erased, but is rather embodied in the way in which the empty space or the point,

which is being constructed through subtraction, locates the trait of difference without which the reality of thought and of the unity of self-
consciousness cannot be posited.

This is the point of maximum kinship and utmost distance between
Kant's transcendental aesthetic and the trait of identity in Lacan, a distance revealed at the Kantian method's most extreme point of convergence. Kant's mathematical postulates allow him to think about the pure
intuition of space where a representation of space appears and on the
surface of which every circle or ring we draw can be reduced to a point.
This is the power of the synthesis that exists where anything "can be
reduced to a point ... to the vanishing unity of any point whatsoever ...
of a world whose aesthetic is such that everything can be folded back
on everything, one always believes that one can have all in the hollow
of one's hand."[66] But as we have seen, the hand in which the whole
world converges is slowly opened, and we realize that not everything
has converged to the same point, and as in the topological shape of the
torus, not all the circles have been reduced to the one point of unity. It
is the unreduced circle that reveals the place of difference that, even if
it does not rule out the permanent movement of convergence into the
One, ensures that in the hollow of one's hand there remains a singular
point, a point resisting synthesis and that individualizes each one who
says "I think."

Thus, what in Kant seems at first to be a pure universal, a unity of
all-as-one, turns out to enclose what is revealed at the end of the act of
subtraction, as a kind of hole or circle located in space and inscribing the
possibility of the one-by-one rather than that of The One. Kant's unity
of apperception is therefore revealed to be the universal of pure difference, embodied in the trait of the One, in the unary trait.

To sum up, we have traced with Lacan an aspect of the relations
assumed by Kant between the cognitive apparatus and the world
of experience. Lacan accentuates the *heterogeneous* foundation of the
Kantian conception of cognition and its workings. He also emphasizes
in Kant the *alienation* between unity as a principle prior to any possibility of representing an object, and unity as what establishes the connection of understanding to its object (by synthesizing, for instance,
the manifold of perceptions). We saw how Lacan reconciles in Kant
the *a priori* limits of cognition with the complexity of elements that
infringe on this necessary closeness by revealing the eroticism of the
Kantian text. Lacan's references to Kant hence stress that the striving
for unity as demonstrated in the essential place given to pure *a priori*

principles, categories, and forms, is bound with the object that prob-
lematizes such unification. Hence, with Lacan we come across Kant's
idea of unity as an operation of *subtraction* (rather than of *abstraction*)
of a material/bodily object that remains trapped in pure intuition
and in pure understanding. Reading Kant with Lacan shows that the
striving for unity does not entail unification but just the orientation
towards a one.

Chapter 7

Beyond Good and Evil:
Lacan and Kantian Morality

A. Morality as Transgression

[Lacan] has primarily called ethics of psychoanalysis a doctrine of the super-ego, that is to say, a demand going against adaptation, a demand to return to a primary satisfaction, and hence a demand for a jouissance ... It is to reunite the ·Kantian "you must" and this demand for the return of jouissance. He called the ethics of psychoanalysis a doctrine of the superego that has nothing to do with a morality that is finally but a poultice of adaptation.

    – Jacques-Alain Miller, "Biologie Lacanienne et événement de corps," 22[1]

In this passage, Jacques-Alain Miller touches on two issues that are essential to the ethics of psychoanalysis: first, the connection between the law and *jouissance*, that is, the fact that the law is not a negation of pleasure (where obeying the law is perceived as renouncing enjoyment), but an affirmation of pleasure; and second, the difference between ethics and moral standards, that is, the psychoanalytic claim that moral values are not a sufficient foundation for an ethics and that indeed, morality *conceals* the ethical dilemma. This chapter discusses the ways in which Lacan draws these two foundations of ethics *from Kant*. We will see that the ethics of psychoanalysis, as constituted by Lacan, derives from the Kantian moral law established as an *a priori* law that posits *absolute moral will* as its basis. This absolute status given by Kant to the moral law reveals a gap between what the law demands and what human action can provide. This gap between the law and its outcomes is evident on the level of the moral act – that is, in the effects the law creates in the field of desired and proper human action.

Psychoanalysis located itself precisely in this split created by Kantian morality, showing the real effects that this conception of the law has on the subject's field of action.

One effect of constituting the psychoanalytical ethics on the basis of what the Kantian law implies is a morality that goes *beyond the distinction between good and evil*. Psychoanalysis follows the logic of the Kantian moral law and shows that the affinity between it and the logic of psychic causality can explain why the moral law is indifferent to what is usually included in the concept of "morality" – the value distinction between good and evil.

This indifference of the moral law to values is revealed in its full force when the Kantian morality (as it is formulated in *The Critique of Practical Reason*) is read alongside the psychoanalytic conception of the law. This context reveals the link between the psychic reality of the law and the pleasure principle, a link that explains why moral reason precedes any value distinction. It was Freud who, through the idea of the superego, pointed to the distance between the possibilities of pleasure (enjoyment and non-enjoyment, happiness and misery, satisfaction and frustration) and absolute pleasure, or *jouissance* in Lacan's language. The superego is a psychic agency that restricts and curbs the possibilities of enjoyment in the name of obedience to the law, but paradoxically, the superego acts not in the name of restraint and prohibition, but rather in the name of limitless pleasure. Freud suggests that the superego does not neutralize the pleasure principle's operation or negate enjoyment, but rather that the presence of the prohibition or the restrictive law pleases in a way that transcends the distinction between enjoyment and non-enjoyment. Freud's formulation suggests that the ethics that pertains to the superego concerns pleasure that is not related to a moral choice between enjoyment and non-enjoyment (i.e., that we must renounce enjoyment in order to achieve virtue and good deeds); rather, obeying the command involves satisfaction with respect to what is beyond the pleasure principle – pleasure whose reality transcends distinctions such as between good and evil. Freud, in other words, points to a connection between obeying the law and absolute pleasure, although on the face of it the law seems to negate or enforce a forgoing of the possibilities of pleasure. As already mentioned, and as Miller claims in the above quotation, the point of departure of the ethics of psychoanalysis, as established by Lacan, is precisely this link between the law and *jouissance*, a link that is conditioned upon a necessary renunciation that is nevertheless not a renunciation of *jouissance*: "To have the *jouissance* of something ... is to be able to give it up," said Lacan in 1967, and this statement can be seen as the bedrock on which his ethics stands.[2]

The question remains how this link to absolute pleasure results in a non-distinction between moral values. In *Civilization and Its Discontents* Freud shows[3] that, in contrast to our expectation that the superego eliminates any possibility of gratifying a wish, this psychic authority actually has the opposite function of stimulating wishes and instincts. In the case of the superego, denying the instinct does not involve an external authority from which the presence of the drive can be concealed, and therefore "the wish persists and is not capable of being hidden from the superego."[4] The superego is the psychic representative of an external moral authority, which insists on the subject giving up the pleasure connected to forbidden wishes. An analysis of this psychic authority reveals a reversal of the moral implications of this voice of the superego saying "No!" We may say that the superego commands a denial of the possibilities of pleasure in the name of a different order, the order of a pleasure related to the totality of the demand that the law poses. Under the superego's command, it is exactly the simple principle of forgoing pleasure for the good deed that brings a moral satisfaction – this principle becomes unrealizable. Since the distinction between *doing* something bad and just *wishing* to do it completely disappears in the face of the superego, the internalized law, a forgoing of pleasure for the sake of doing good will not satisfy the internal imperative nor allay its demands. No wonder Freud concludes that the better the person is in his deeds, the more the superego becomes oppressive in its demands, and "it is precisely those people who have carried saintliness furthest who reproach themselves with the worst sinfulness."[5] The distinction between good and evil loses its hold on moral action.

Freud's words suggest that conscience and guilt, which reveal the presence of the moral authority in the subject, stem not so much from insufficiently renouncing a forbidden wish for moral reasons, but rather from the presence of a possibility of pleasure that the prohibition actually makes present rather than eliminates. Freud showed that conscience and guilt are affective states that, rather than serving to deny pleasure in the name of an internalized moral authority, represent the psychic presence of the wish for absolute pleasure. The superego places strict demands regarding the deed and the proper thought, demands that are difficult to fulfil, but it does so in order to make room for a total object of pleasure in whose name the law was formulated to begin with. For this reason Freud claims a great proximity between the superego and the id, the seat of the drives.

For Freud, the beginning of the law, the origin of the moral authority, is found at the moment of the elimination from the scene of whomever the law cannot apply to: the *lawless* exception, the agent whose pleasure is subject to no restriction. That someone enjoys absolute, uninhibited, and limitless pleasure is what makes the formulation of the law necessary. The moral law is designed to prevent pleasure that knows no limit, and therefore the law must correspond in its form of prohibition to this absoluteness. The law must exclude any possibility of pleasure that eludes the law, and thus the law actively eliminates the exception from its realm. The law, ostensibly designed to restrict the possibilities of pleasure, aims in fact to protect from the wish for absolute pleasure. "Love thy neighbour as you love thyself," as an example of such a command, poses an absolute demand (to treat the neighbour as you would treat yourself) that there is no way of fulfilling, so it becomes clear that what lies behind the command is not only the restraint on one pleasure or another (do not eat your bread before you have shared it with your neighbour, do not envy your neighbour).

"Conscience is the result of instinctual renunciation, or that instinctual renunciation (imposed on us from without) creates conscience, which then demands further instinctual renunciation."[6] Conscience, Freud claims, does not appear as a *result* of the refusal of the wish for pleasure; rather, it is the *cause* of such renunciation. That is, conscience is responsible for the presence of totality, of an enduring renunciation of the drives that can never be curbed or satisfied. Conscience is revealed as a primal affect that attests to the presence of a totality that morality refuses and whose presence it camouflages through a prohibition that is broken down into practical details. As already noted, the moral law hints at this totality through the form it assumes: that of a *categorical imperative*. The form of the law leaves something of the forbidden totality present, so that we can say that the strived-for absolute *jouissance* is located precisely in the space governed by the law, which in the name of the moral authority forbids any enjoyment. This is why any obedience to the law, any renunciation of satisfaction, highlights precisely the presence of a transgression.

Let us take for example the subject who says to himself: I must work for the general good rather than for my own personal benefit. First, the view presented by Freud implies that there is no difference between the moral law that gives priority to the general good and the opposite law that seems to affirm the less worthy act of acting for one's personal benefit: regardless of the content of the command, both cases will give rise to a pleasure that is not included in the pleasure that the law forbids. Second, striving for the general good, as well as striving for one's personal benefit, is a moral act only insofar as it is the result of an absolute demand. In order for an act to be moral, it must fulfil a certain condition of uncompromising generality, regardless of the content of the demand that this act seeks to satisfy. In other words, the command included in the law ("Work for the good of the community as much as you can rather than for your own good!") must apply to the entire field of human practice and therefore to any action of any kind performed by the subject. Say that based on the command, the moral person decides to share his bread with others – he is still and necessarily remains a wrongdoer. Thus, although his moral act means that he has renounced the pleasure (i.e., of eating the bread alone), in the act performed in the name of the general rule adopted, the subject will find himself also serving the law's opposite, that is, his own good (i.e., by also eating a little himself, by not feeding everyone, by not also sharing his dwelling, his clothes, and the rest of his property, by secretly enjoying being such a virtuous person, by thinking about the taste of the food in another's mouth, and so on and so forth).

We can see that the demand made from the moral act has repercussions for its status. And it also seems that the command that denies pleasure in the name of striving for the worthy act is not foreign to pleasure but rather sustains it in the name of the law itself, since while in the moral act the person violates the absolute law, he also encounters the absolute thing that the law demands of him. This is because the law embodied in the command "do so and so" includes within it the object of the absolute pleasure that the formulation of the law exposes more than it conceals: you must forgo each and every aspect, each and every detail of your personal good for the community. For the law deals with a total demand, with an unconditioned demand that, although unattainable, is real and present as the basis of the law and as its cause.

It should be said that here – in delineating the status of the superego as Freud describes it[7] and as Lacan develops it[8] – we are already dealing with a Kantian formulation of the psychoanalytic ethics. However, the point of departure that psychoanalysis emphasizes regarding ethics is that the prohibition of pleasure in the name of the moral good and through an absolute imperative does not contrast with the possibility of satisfaction. On the contrary: for psychoanalysis, the presence of pleasure is the first reason why one aims to act morally. Furthermore, the affinity of the law to satisfaction explains why acting according to the law's command leaves the subject guilty and ostensibly trapped in the jaws of the law.

Take for example the subject who wants at any cost to fulfil the demand to repay a debt. It turns out that the obedient submission to the demand to repay a debt not only acts as a powerful mechanism for producing guilt, but also reveals the amount of pleasure that the subject draws from his attempts to obey the demand. A typical such case is described by Freud in relation to the "Rat Man," who faces the command "You must pay back the 3.80 Kronen to Lieutenant A.," but who fails to fulfil his vow (which is based on the mistaken assumption that Lieutenant A. paid the post office clerk for his packet).[9] Freud shows with respect to the Rat Man that this subject, through his failed attempts to repay the debt to Lieutenant A., in fact acts out a refusal to hand the payment to that person. And how does this refusal serve him? Since the rat fantasy is related to Lieutenant A., the obsession with the debt and the obligation to repay it become for the Rat Man a mechanism of pleasure derived from this fantasy, which is preserved and sustained by the command to repay the debt come what may. The unsettling pleasure from the rat punishment fantasy feeds the failed attempts to repay the debt and the guilt that accompanies these failures, as this pleasure is enabled by (not) paying A. back.

Obedience to the law already implies a practice of violation, and not only because obedience touches on the possibility of absolute pleasure and of satisfying the drive. The law demands of the subject something absolute, and Kant himself recognizes that the pure absolute element cannot be fully realized by the sole person who is subject to inclinations and desire. In a certain sense Kant presents the moral law as something that can be neither obeyed nor violated, so far is human practice from what can be considered as fulfilling the demands of the law (even if Kant does believe in an infinite approximation of the moral subject to the possibility of realizing the law). We can say that the law remains detached to some extent from what the human act may capture. Unconditioned obedience is impossible, in part because an absolute law cannot produce absolute rules of action, only rules that aim to approximate the demand of the law. The rule of human action is always relative, because the pure rational volition involves needs and motivations that often contrast with objective reason.[10] For Kant, since the law is *a priori* and precedes any question relating to the possibility of *practising* it, it also precedes any question relating to the possibility of *breaking* it.

As we have seen, Kant claims that it is impossible to completely detach the human act from the human inclination, and therefore any attempt to fulfil the demand of the law will necessarily entail its violation, because human inclination will interfere with the moral practice. But psychoanalysis highlights something else that Kant points to: not only may the command give rise to different rules of action as (necessarily failed) ways of practising the law, but the unavoidable violation also stems from an incompatibility between what the law demands and what it actually embodies. In order to explain this, let us return to the example of "Love thy neighbour as thyself!" (which appears in another version in the Hebrew Commandment: Thou shall not covet!), which means, more or less, that we should be as happy for all others' enjoyments and successes as if they were our own. Both Freud and Lacan refer to this command, emphasizing that it makes a demand that is so foreign to human inclination that the question arises what it means to obey the law. The human inclination towards the neighbour (who is emphatically neither kin nor a friend) is one of malice, aggression, destructiveness, and cruelty, rather than goodwill and love. That is, psychoanalysis emphasizes the total alienation between the law and human inclination. We can say that the command demands a totality that is the opposite of human inclination: love and identification where the tendency is towards aggression and hatred. Freud says: "their neighbor is for them not only a potential helper or sexual object, but also someone who tempts them to satisfy their aggressiveness on him, to exploit his capacity for work without compensation, to use him sexually without his consent, to seize his possessions, to humiliate him, to cause him pain, to torture and kill him."[11] This text, says Lacan, which if we did not know was written by Freud we would willingly attribute to Sade, is the heart and soul of *Civilization and Its Discontents*, and describes man's fundamental position in civilization as a position of aggressiveness, an aggressiveness that attests to the presence of the human drive in any social relationship. So what is the connection between "Love thy neighbour as thyself!" and this aggressive drive towards the neighbour? If aggressiveness towards our neighbour is ingrained in us, is not the demand to love thy neighbour fundamentally impracticable? And if so, what is the purpose of formulating a law that no one can fulfil? While we can make an effort to share our bread with our neighbour or even restrain our deep envy of him, these are still risibly far from the unbearable absoluteness that underlies the command itself, since the command presents the subject with an impossible and irrelevant demand. In this context, Kant emphasizes the need to tame and curb any inclination and desire as we face the law; but psycho-analysis notices something else. The good or bad deed with respect to the neighbour is so evidently far from what the law demands, that not only does it not come close to the total demand embedded in the law "Love thy neighbour as thyself," but the difference between the good and the bad deed becomes negligible (is helping out the neighbour while entertaining bitter feelings towards her a good or bad deed with respect to the imperative?).

So what is the command's role? Lacan answers this question in Semi-nar VII, in the chapter that deals with this command.[12] The aggressive-ness towards the other does not express the dark, primal side of drives; aggressiveness is precisely the flipside of the absolute law. Therefore, as long as the neighbour is as happy as you are, or his happiness resembles yours, there is no problem behaving nicely towards him and even help-ing him start his car on a cold morning. That is, the good deed is possi-ble only when the thing that causes the command is not clearly present. But the moment we believe that the distribution of pleasure is biased in favour of the neighbour rather than us, the moment it seems that the other's pleasure is greater than ours – when, in other words, the ques-tion of *jouissance* appears in relation to the other – then the real source of aggressiveness as the basic position towards the other is revealed. The absolute law is necessary where the object of the drive appears. The law that demands unqualified love is formulated where what is on the table is the absolute drive to do away with the other who is having more *jouissance* than the subject. The moral law is not foreign to man's psyche, because it embodies the incessant demand for unconditioned and limitless *jouissance*, rather than the constant rational aspiration to tame one's desires and inclinations. The moral law is not a foreign pres-ence demanding from man what is alien to his nature; rather, it is a foreign yet intimate presence of what it is impossible for him to attain, but is yet the layer that underlies all his social behaviour.

This interpretation of the moral law and the impossible demand it poses is not foreign to the spirit of Kant. For exactly the same logic, stating that the law embodies an absolute possibility of unconditioned pleasure, also underlies the impossibility of deriving an act that would answer the law's demand. Kant himself devotes much effort to examin-ing the relations between the law and the possibilities of action it gives rise to, and to the ways of knowing whether a certain action is moral. Kant claims that while some maxims[13] can take the form of a universal law, others appear to be insufficient to indulge the law's demand. The maxim can take for example the form of resistance to needs and sensible motivated causes,[14] or affects (such as guilt or satisfaction) may appear that stem from eradicating the sensible inclinations and drives. But the attempt to examine empirical conditions as a criterion for the possibility of deriving a universal law always encounters the basic difficulty that the law of practical reason can never be matched by an actual demand, nor by the powers by which we fulfil it.

Since the connection between the maxim and the universal law cannot be determined from the perspective of experience, it must be determined *a priori*. Kant therefore describes the will as the source of obligation to the law away from maxims of action that are unworthy of the law. The will is prior to any concept or object of experience yet is posited "through the concept of the highest good as the object and the final purpose of pure practical reason."[15] The will, in other words, establishes the necessary link between the concept of the good, the moral law, and possible veins of conduct. In some contexts Kant indeed seems to suggest that the *a priori* foundation on which the moral law is constituted does not permit the deduction of an erroneous rule, that is, of a rule of action that does not correspond to the law, because if rule of action, does not correspond to the spirit of the law, we will find ourselves in effect *outside the sphere of the moral law* given and driven by heteronomous inclinations and desires (according to Kant, when action is guided by an empirical condition rather than a principle of pure practical reason, it means it is determined by an erroneous relation between the will – that here follows a pathologically affected capacity of choice – and a sensation of enjoyment or non-enjoyment). In this sense, if someone acts covetously, it is not a violation of the law but an action excluded from the domain of the law, having lost the concept of the good and the final purpose as directives. A covetous action cannot be deduced from a moral law, but only from principles that are heteronomous to the law; interests, sensory enjoyment, and pathological inclination here take the upper hand. The law is irrelevant where man is driven by these principles.

A more detailed example, which makes it possible to distinguish between human practice on the one hand and pure law and its absolute demand on the other, can be found in Kant's analysis of the case of a deposit made on the mere basis of mutual trust. Kant uses this example to explore what conditions a maxim must fulfil in order to generate actions that accord with the moral law. Let us say, Kant proposes, that

I have made it my aim to increase my fortune by any safe means. What prevents this rule of action from being considered a general practical principle guided by moral will?

> Now, I have a *deposit* in my hands, the owner of which is deceased and has left no record of it. Naturally, this is a case for my maxim. Now I want only to know whether that maxim can also hold as a universal practical law ... everyone may deny a deposit of which no one can prove to him to have been made. I immediately become aware that such a principle, as a law, would annihilate itself, because it would bring it about that there would be no deposit[s] at all. A practical law that I cognize as such must qualify for universal legislation; this is an identical proposition and therefore self-evident.[16]

If the maxim aimed at increasing one's fortune becomes a universal law, making a deposit will become meaningless, because a deposit means a deposited amount that belongs to its owner and is entrusted to another, whether or not this fact is known. Here the demand posed by the universal law, set against the rule of action that is related to a person's inclination, reveals the full distance between the *a priori* law and the rule of action that depends on experience. The universality of the law is analytically based on the concept of a deposit and no experience or inclination can divert from this universality (and include for example the possibility of not returning a deposit whose owner has died). Holding to the deposit would not be the violation of a moral law (that says "return any deposit to its owner!"); rather, it would contradict the very concept of a deposit and thus remain heteronomous to the moral sphere.

The concept of "deposit" is thus foreign to human inclinations, turning any attempt to fulfil the demand imposed by deposits on those who accept them into failure (since who will not think, upon the death of the deposit's owner, of keeping hold of the deposit rather than returning it to his heirs?). The moral law stands as the supreme and unconditioned obligation, without any maxim being directly derived from it. The analytical examination of the concept of the deposit, in its role as the basis for the practical command, shows us why for Kant the moral law is foreign to human inclinations and is therefore bound to encounter the human predisposition to action as an obstacle.

It should not be inferred from this, however, that Lacan criticizes Kant for positing the law at a distance from human inclinations and desires. To be sure, psychoanalysis seems to emphasize the opposite: that the moral law, as Kant conceptualized it, is close to the human inclinations precisely because it formulates the absolute on which all inclinations are based. While Kant presented the moral law as foreign to these inclinations, he also accentuated that moral practice amounts to the ways in which pure practical reason imposes itself on man and woman's practical life, rather than reflecting their withdrawal towards the heavens. Abiding by the law produces moral practices in which human inclinations come incessantly across the absolute demand of the law. The person who chooses his personal happiness as the determining motivation for all his actions, and the one who adopts the public good as a moral drive, are equally motivated by pure practical rules that interfere in practical experience. For Kant, the voice of the law is in any case not found outside the field of human action, "and [it] would utterly destroy morality were not the voice of reason in reference to the will so distinct, so incapable of being shouted down, and even for the commonest human being so perceptible."[17] He goes on to say that the voice of reason makes even the boldest sinner tremble, because esteem for the pure moral law is not the result of a rational choice to leave behind human desires and predilections, but a real compulsion felt by any human being, whether he wishes to adhere to the moral idea or to avoid it as much as he can.

Lacan reads Kant's moral philosophy as indicating the moral deficiency in every moral action (aiming to the highest good) because moral action constitutes the site where the absolute demand of the moral law meets the human demand of enjoyment. Kant does not say so explicitly, but his moral theory suggests there is more than one economy to pleasure: the overt one, and the one that demands to be exposed. In Freud's view, what exposes the other economy of pleasure in relation to the moral law is that the law is so oppressive. The law's oppressiveness is related to that it is a constant embodiment of the presence of an absolute unattainable object, that it is always formulated as an absolute demand for impossible totality. This is an essential point of departure, because Lacan's use of Kant in the context of ethics relies on a truly intimate kinship between Freud's conception of the reality of the superego in psychic (and social) life, and Kant's formulation of the moral law that sets out to answer the question: What ought I to do?[18] In both contexts, the subject of the law is at best a well-meaning lawbreaker.[19]

B. Law without a Subject

Much has been written about the bizarre relation between Lacan and Kant around the ethics of psychoanalysis. This has been greatly due not only to Lacan's well-known if convoluted article "Kant with Sade," but also to the fact that Lacan's Seminar VII, "The Ethics of Psychoanalysis," is one of the seminars most widely read by non-analysts. The present book, which is not coincidentally related to the fact that Lacan is read by non-analysts, must equally address the ethics of psychoanalysis, since the latter draws the kernel of its existence from Kant's conception of morality as relying on an *a priori* and absolute imperative. In a certain sense, and perhaps because the philosophical–psychoanalytical ethical question has been the subject of a fair number of readings by psychoanalysts, there seems to be an almost common acceptance of an obvious affinity between Kant's moral approach and the ethics of psychoanalysis[20] – an affinity we began to outline in the previous section.

According to Kant, as long as we are in the realm of experience where we desire the representation of an object, any action undertaken will be measured against this representation and the enjoyment or nonenjoyment that can be drawn from the object. A rule formulated in this context will be conditioned upon experience. Since the moral will takes us away from the realm of actual actions, wishes, and inclinations, the moral demand it assumes must be prior to any question regarding its possible satisfaction in reality. Similarly, the principle of pleasure in Freud demands absolute satisfaction regardless of the possibility of its practical fulfilment. Both contexts assume an absolute and necessary principle (moral will in Kant; absolute satisfaction in Freud; *jouissance* in Lacan) that is judged neither by its results nor by its fulfilment – yet the absoluteness of the object of demand present at the place of the law, has considerable effects on the human being in the realm of action.

But the essential analogy between the ethics of psychoanalysis and the Kantian moral doctrine does not end here. If up till now we have examined the parallel way in which Kant on the one hand and Freud and Lacan on the other show how the absolute law necessarily encounters the human subject in the field of moral action (by creating for example a necessary effect of guilt), in both cases we also encounter an ideal conception of ethics as based on an *a priori* principle that the human sphere of action cannot satisfy. Kant expresses the distance between the law and its practices in two ways. First, the law is objective (indifferent to differences between beings), and in this sense "would have to contain the same determining basis of the will in all cases and for all rational beings."[21] That is, even if the law does not explicitly oppose one's well-being, the law is indifferent to the finite nature of humans and to their longing for happiness. Second, the law is only a form (whereas the desire for happiness is only matter). The practical law is unconditioned, and therefore the will is determined by it in an absolute and immediate way. "The will is thought as independent on empirical conditions, and hence, *qua* pure will, as determined by *the mere form of the law*, and this determining basis is regarded as the supreme condition of all maxims."[22] Thus, the *a priori* position of the moral law determines not only its absoluteness but also its imperviousness with respect to the subject. The law is mere form, and no content that is connected to material experience or to personal desire is relevant to it (pure practical reason does have an object, the highest good, but no material object or any object of volition[23]).

Indeed, such a conception of the moral law in some sense *vacates* the individual subject from the domain of the law. But this vacating of the individual does not in itself suffice to show that the universal form of legislation can supply the practical conditions (under which moral action will be produced). The radicalness of vacating the subject from the domain of the law is related to the fact that the law is only a form, and this fact means there are no reliable correlations between, for example, virtue and the wish to be moral, or moral action and happiness or any other desired outcome. This lack of correlation is the basis for *the antinomy of practical reason* as formulated by Kant: while virtue and happiness are viewed as necessarily linked if we are to obtain the highest good that is practical for us, this link appears to falter in the *Critique*, and "no necessary connection, sufficient for the highest good, of happiness with virtue in the world can be expected [to come about] through the most meticulous observance of moral laws."[24]

While Kant is out to resolve (and annul) the antinomy, the derivation of the antinomy from the way the moral law is qualified is what should interest us. Since the moral law commands us to further the highest good by acting according to practical rules, if such a furtherance is impossible, the moral law may turn out to be fantastic and empty. This is the situation portrayed in the antinomy, and Kant resolves it by indicating the modes of interference of moral considerations in practical rules and actions. For instance, as the moral law transcends the differences between human beings, this fact is reflected in its mode of application and in the very structure of the practical rule.

Consequently, this is how Kant defines the supreme criterion for determining whether a rule is moral or not: "So act that the maxim of your will could always hold at the same time as a principle of universal legislation."[25] The practical rule oversteps the difference between subjects (it has a general applicability), and it further reflects the fact that the moral demand is unconditioned and is independent of experience. The generality required by the moral law hence "interferes" with actual moral practices by completely erasing the individual's inclination: action is morally valid to the extent that it works as a general criterion, "a principle of universal legislation." That is, the generality required of the law does not lie in the law being equally applied to everyone, but in the manner in which this generality is structured: the law is a pure form, one that erases the individual will by turning it into pure will. This is the radical sense of the law having no subject, of the law being a form with which nothing connected with subjective practical life coincides yet which applies to human practice.

In a Kantian vein, Lacan claims that the universality of the moral law expresses a demand for general applicability that is taken to the limit.[26] What makes the law general is not that it imposes itself on everyone identically, but that if it is not valid in *every* case, it is not valid in *any* case.[27] We can say that the moral law is requisitioned from the realm of the subject so that the subject can act morally in relation to the law. Lacan interprets this impossible presence of the law in practical life as that which imposes itself on the subject, but as a foreign presence; and he does so by distinguishing between the subject *as predicate of the law* and the subject as *object of the law*.

The "eviction" of the subject from the realm of the law, therefore, occurs both in the sense that the law negates anything that is "pathological" in Kant's terms (i.e., anything that concerns inclinations, wishes, and desires); and in the sense that the law is found outside what is contained in, derives from, or is conditioned on experience; as well in the sense that the law implicates the subject as its spokesperson and as its victim. Even if the subject – with his wishes, petty desires, and inclinations – does not concern or influence the status of the law itself, the Kantian subject, as Lacan notes, is implicated in the law. This universal logic is revealed as a logic that does not detach the moral principle from human practice; on the contrary – it makes the two inextricably intertwined. The subject, who wishes to act according to the command of an unconditioned law, faces a structural gap that cannot be bridged. This gap that is opened up is illustrated in a somewhat humorous way through the Sadean version of the law, which states: "I have the right to enjoy your body ... without any limit."[28] The law commanding limitless enjoyment must engage the body of the other, and it satisfies all the conditions Kant sets for moral legislation. The Sadean law effectively exposes the masked structure of the law and the way in which it fatally implicates the subject. Through the call for absolute freedom to enjoy, the subject appears as the one on whose behalf the pure practical law is formulated; but the subject is also the one who is supposed to realize the law's demand, since "act so that the maxim of thy will can always at the same time hold good as a principle of universal legislation" – that is, act so that the rule you have set can apply both to you and to anyone else – means that the subject is not just the one who enunciates the law's call, but also the one who undertakes its consequences. The Sadean law grants absolute licence in using the other to obtain enjoyment. But the same absolute licence must also be afforded to the other, who can enjoy the body of the subject himself without restrictions. This is why, with any command that is formulated so that it applies to "thou" ("Thou shall not ..." or "Thou shall ..."), the subject is included as object in the domain of the command's effectiveness. Accepting the Sadean imperative means agreeing to exploitation by the other, and not only gaining total freedom to obtain enjoyment from the other's body.

In a similar spirit to Sade, accepting the Kantian imperative means agreeing to be subject to all that the totality of the law implies. Kant expresses this moral trap in his attempt to specify under what condition the happiness of others becomes a determining factor for the pure will. The condition cannot be found simply by assuming that everyone wishes for the well-being of the other, since there is no basis for making such an assumption. Rather, the condition for the maxim that one must care for the welfare of the other is found in the fact that

the mere form of a law ... restricts the matter ... Let the matter be, for example, my own happiness. This happiness, if I attribute it to everyone ... can become an objective practical law only if I include in it also the happiness of others. Therefore the law to further the happiness of others arises not from the presupposition that this is an object for everyone's power of choice, but merely from the fact that the form of universality, which reason requires as condition for giving to a maxim of self-love the objective validity of a law, becomes the determining basis of the will. Hence not the object (the happiness of others) was the determining basis of the pure will, but this determining basis was solely the mere legal form by which I restricted my maxim – which was based on inclination – in order to impart to the maxim the universality of a law and thus to make it adequate to pure practical reason.[29]

The only condition that underpins the moral demand is the one that turns my self-love into a universal law – that is, gives the form of universality to a personal inclination. Universal love can become a practical rule only when I am willing to impose a condition of universality on my self-love. The Kantian principle formulated here highlights what we have already seen about "Love thy neighbour as thyself!," that by making the inclination general, the moral law restrains the human inclination to aggressiveness towards the other's enjoyment. What can further be learned from this case, which points to the structural way of reconciling between self-love and universal love, is that this universality has considerable effects both on the rule of action that will be considered moral (a rule that will turn a personal inclination into a general principle) and on the situation of the subject who wishes to act according to what the law demands. The law's universality is therefore not the result of the general validity attributed to a specific demand, but the result of giving universal form to an individual cause, by extracting the individual from where her demand for satisfaction can be fulfilled.

But the difficulty raised by the moral law does not stem only from the fact that the subject is entangled in it, despite the law being indifferent to her existence. The difficulty also stems from the fact that the single subject's wish to obey the law turns out to be impossible. Thus, when Lacan claims that Sade embodies the Kantian moral principle of an absolute and total demand that can be formulated as "Enjoy as much as you can!," we learn of this command where it makes the pleasure of the subject – in this case of Sade himself – impossible. For Sade suffers from sadistic impotence, and none of his fantasies is realized in full.[30] Kantian morality similarly posits super-sensible ideas – that is, ideas that are neither drawn from experience nor apply to it – and tries to give them practical content. We can say that practical reason, to which Kant dedicated his second critique, allows us to examine the meaning of categories such as freedom, and the ways in which freedom can be embodied in the human act, and thus see that the human act is always lacking in relation to the practical law and in relation to the ideas that accompany the sphere of the law.

As already mentioned, Lacan describes this perplexity of the moral subject in terms of a split between what the law states and the content of the law. The subject enunciating the law cannot be the subject enacting the law, or in Lacan's terms: the subject of *utterance* is different from the subject of the *statement*. The subject can voice an absolute imperative, can carry the voice of the law as if the law speaks through him, but cannot be the subject of the law, the one who in his action actualizes and fulfils what the law commands. There is no practice that a subject can employ and that satisfies the commandment "Enjoy as much as you can!" – there will always be something else that has not been tried yet, a possibility that has not been made use of, a practice that has not yet been imagined. But just as there is no practice that allows the subject absolute pleasure, neither is there a practice that allows absolute morality (beyond any inclination or desire). The subject of the commandment "Love thy neighbour as thyself!" will always, and necessarily, find himself distinguishing momentarily between himself and the neighbor, and calculating or feeling jealous of the other's advantage. Since the subject is included in the content of the law only as someone who will always break it, we can say that the absolute commandment already includes the impossibility of obeying it. The absoluteness of the law applies only insofar as the "commandment requisitions us as Other"[31] – that is, the subject of the law is annihilated when the absolute measure of morality is recognized.

The law precedes experience, but it also precedes any *idea* of practical reason (such as freedom or will). The law is not conditional upon anything, nor is it a condition from which the subject's action is derived. Nevertheless, the moral law is not located beyond human practice. The fact that the law's absoluteness is foreign to the subject's ability to act in an absolutely moral way does not even for a moment eliminate the certainty and reality that characterize the law's presence in practical life. Indeed, Kant is occupied not only with establishing the foundations of an *a priori* moral doctrine, but also with the ways in which the subject learns of these foundations in actual moral practice. For example, when he refers to the special feeling of respect towards the moral law (which unlike other feelings is brought about not *pathologically* but *practically*), Kant claims that respect is a tribute that we do not choose to feel but that we cannot refuse: "we cannot help feeling it inwardly."[32] Even if respect for the law is a duty rather than a free awakening by choice, respect is not an antecedent feeling attuned to morality, and sensible (pathological) feeling is the condition of what is called respect for the law. Being subject to the law means that the law *participates in the life of one's inclinations and feelings*, and it is in light of its boundless presence in the life of every "finite rational being" that the voice of morality appears in the sphere of action and makes "even the boldest offender tremble and compels him to hide from his sight."[33] The certainty of the law's presence in one's life is not a matter of choice by reason even if freedom of the will is the *a priori* condition for the moral law to apply.

This is the dual nature of the moral law, which on the one hand does not involve a practical precept or a material or empirical condition, for "the law of the pure will, which is free, brings the will into a sphere quite different from the empirical; and ... the necessity involved in the law... can only consist in the formal conditions of the possibility of a law in general"; however, on the other hand, "it is indeed undeniable that every volition must have an object, and therefore a matter; but it does not follow that this is the determining principle..."[34] In other words, for Kant, although the law is merely formal, it is only in applying the law to experience – in the ways in which the law imposes its presence – that the form of the law can become clear to us: "any volition must have an object and hence a matter."[35] Only when my wish for happiness is put to a practical test in relation to an object of experience, can it become clear that this wish lacks the universality required of the pure practical will. But note also that once *matter lays bare the form of the law*, is it revealed that the moral will operates in a sphere entirely different from the empirical one. Thus, although the wish for general happiness is morally preferable to the wish for self-happiness, experience reveals that even universal happiness is based on matter, on human beings' (changing) beliefs and understanding of what desirable happiness is.

Psychoanalysis reverts to the demand for pleasure as one that does not distinguish general happiness from subjective well-being. The real embodiment of the demand for pleasure is in civilization and its discontents, that is, in the split between the subject and his pleasure that the presence of the other entails. Discontent is the matter ethics is made of, and it attests to the presence of an *a priori* and absolute principle – exactly in the spirit of Kant.

C. The Good, the Evil, and the Moral

Well-being [*das Wohl*] or *bad* [*das Übel*] always signifies only a reference to our state of *agreeableness* or *disagreeableness*, of gratification or pain; and if we desire or loathe an object on that account then we do so only insofar as it is referred to our sensibility and the feeling of pleasure and displeasure that it brings about. But *good* [*das Gute*] or *evil* [*das Böse*] always signifies a

reference to the will insofar as the will is determined by the law of reason
to make something its object – as, indeed, the will is never determined
directly by the object and the presentation of it, but is a power to make a
rule of reason the motivating cause of an action (through which an object
can become actual).[36]

For Kant moral action is produced by a moral will that is tied with
the practical law in its formal, prior constitution. This will that aims
at the law of reason by which it can be actualized in an object must be
free. Free will is independent of empirical conditions and the empirically given object of practical maxims, and is yet the determining basis
of the law and of the sense of autonomy that guides the rational being
when acting morally. The relation between the will and *freedom* raises
a suspicion of circularity, though (that freedom just names the cause
that generates the will in the subject of practical reason who acts in a
way that must be free). Kant solves this circularity by distinguishing
the negative sense of freedom (freedom as cause) from a positive sense
(that ties freedom with an *idea* of freedom that exists in every rational
being).[37] In any case, for Kant, the will is not the result of intellectual
power, of temperament or character; it is measured neither by what
it causes nor according to what it manages to achieve. The will in the
moral subject is not drawn from experience but rather from an *a priori*
conception of pure practical reason.

This Kantian position regarding the *a priori* status of the moral will
as free is the basis for Lacan's distinction between morality and ethics,
a distinction that is not found in philosophy in these terms. For Lacan,
while **morality** is subject to experiential concepts (rules of action, moral
actions, the possibility of realizing the will and implementing the maxims), to the test of results and to non-absolute values (such as the values
of good and evil), as well as to the subject's adaptation to the demands
of the law, **ethics** concerns the subject's position towards the absolute
demand and this position must be free so that a moment of moral *decision* can be distinguished. In the human domain the two become mixed,
because free will, even if it is produced by the moral law alone (autonomous of all sensible interests), is already entangled in matters of moral
values and in questions of practicality. The human wish for happiness
and enjoyment touches the domain of moral action, which means that
the moral law may be contradicted by a volition that is affected by desire
and wish. All that can be supposed is that a sufficient intelligence, unaf-
fected by subjective causes, would be capable of drafting a maxim that

can at the same time be objectively a law.[38] Yet this intelligence can serve only as an archetype that ensures the progression *ad infinitum* of our maxims, while "virtue itself ... can never be complete."[39] We can see the distinction that Kant requires between two dimensions of practical reason (paralleling the distinction between morality and ethics) as the reason for his critique of Epicurus, for example, who saw virtue as deriving from enjoyment. Kant believes that the will, as the source of moral duty, is a higher power of desire, which exists by virtue of pure practical reason and therefore does not involve any presentations of the agreeable or disagreeable as relevant causes.[40]

But there are consequences to the fact that the moral law is indifferent to the possibilities of enjoyment. For Kant, even when the subject asks himself what is the right thing to do in a certain situation, what will seem to him decisive in determining the worthy deed may turn out to be a rule of action that does not fulfil the moral demand at all, for we tend to see good and evil as means to pleasure and displeasure.[41] Only when action is determined directly by the practical rule can we say that the action that corresponds to it is "in itself good," that is, "good absolutely in every respect";[42] but even in such a case the concepts of good and evil result from the moral law rather than precede it. One cannot even presuppose the concepts of good and evil when addressing the moral law. This is how Kant establishes the grounds for the psychoanalytic distinction between the morally good and the ethical, and between the concepts of good and evil and the moral law in its *a priori* sphere of absolute demand.

Since the moral law is merely formal, it abstracts from all matter and from any object of volition. Therefore, since even the highest good is the *object* of our pure practical reason, it cannot serve as a determining basis for pure will. Assuming the good as prior to the moral law will make an object the determining factor, that is, it will "bring about heteronomy and displace the moral principle."[43] Hence, even if for Kant, the highest good is a concept that may already include the moral law in perfect harmony, the order of priority should not be conflated: "The concept of good and evil must not be determined prior to the moral law ... but only after it and by means of it."[44]

For Kant, then, there must be an uncompromising distinction between the concept of good, even the highest good, and the law that precedes any such concept. This essential distinction necessarily influences the subject's relationship with the absolute thing that the law demands of him, for the origin of the law is not heteronomous (external to the will) but autonomous (stemming from an internal source of reason's pure will). It now becomes clear why the moral law must be indifferent to the subject's happiness, to his inclinations and to his objects of volition in practice. We can say that the moral *thing* participates in one's practical life by constituting another order of things within it. This is how Kant answers the difficulty of assuming a *consciousness* of the moral law when the latter is ascribed an immediacy but is also contradictory to any sensibility. And he replies: "We can become conscious of pure practical laws just as we are conscious of pure theoretical principles, by attending to the necessity with which reason prescribes them to us, and to the separating [from them] of all empirical conditions, to which that necessity points us."[45] This idea of a marked split within practical reason that the law produces, a split between the pure form of law and the empirical conditions under which the law is implemented, has inspired Lacan's distinction between morality and ethics.

Kant marks a shift within philosophical thought itself regarding the relation of the good to practical reason, when he refers to the perplexity that practical reason introduces to speculative reason. This shift can be indicated through the radical distance between Aristotle's morality and Kant's. Morality, says Lacan in his 1969 Seminar, is based on the idea that there is somewhere a good and that it is in this good that the law resides.[46] Aristotle's ethics is based on such a correlation between well-being (pleasure) and the good, and on the idea "that following a correct channel in this register of pleasure will lead us to the conception of the sovereign good."[47] Aristotle bases the relationship between enjoyment and the supreme good on the *ethos*, that is, the set of customs "brought together in a Sovereign Good, a point of insertion, attachment or convergence, in which a particular order is unified with a more universal knowledge, in which ethics becomes politics, and beyond that with an imitation of the cosmic order."[48] Aristotle thus emphasizes the enjoyment and benefit that can be drawn from the ethical order, which he believes is based on a correlation between the *ethos* and the supreme good. It is to this correspondence that Miller's "poultice of adaptation" refers, in the quotation that opens this chapter. That is, correlating morality with the pleasure principle prevents the fundamental encounter with the ethical question from perplexing us. Against the poultice of adaptation stands the conception of the moral law as merely *form* (without empirical or sensible content or object), and faced with such a law, the subject experiences great perplexity.

The shift to Kant's moral doctrine marks a significant turning point in the history of ethics and the moral law, for Kant undermines the correlation between the moral law and the morally good and relocates the law's absoluteness with regard to the cognition of the moral subject.

Lacan thus refers to Kant's distinction between the subject's well-being (*das Wohl*) and the moral good (*das Gute*) as a key to ethics, identifying Kant's moral theory as the heart of the ethics that can take us beyond the crisis point of morality. For Kant, the distinction between the good and well-being is necessary because the subject's happiness and the concept of the supreme good are incompatible; furthermore, he shows that happiness, enjoyment, or the satisfaction of an inclination may allow the subject to camouflage the existence of a moral conflict. In his critique of the ancient Greek philosophers (the Epicureans and the Stoics), Kant even repudiates their attempt to compare the concepts of happiness and virtue, which are "two extremely heterogeneous notions" whose unity can only be artificial.[49] Lacan claims that the necessary separation between the moral law and the quest for happiness and well-being (i.e., for enjoyment or what is called in Greek *hedone*) is influenced by the changing conceptions regarding the human act and takes on different forms.

The intricate relation of the subject to moral principles is not solved by distinguishing well-being from the question of the moral or worthy act, and this insolubility emerges in Lacan's teaching on ethics. The distance between the question of the good and the presence of the moral law in practice,[50] between one's happiness and the effect of acting morally, pertains to many facets of modern ethics, as Lacan points out. For example, capitalist and post-capitalist society is trapped in this same ambivalence regarding the right action to take in order to gain maximum enjoyment (profit). In capitalism this impossible sphere of the law is revealed in the attitude towards work (as distinct from enjoyment and profit). Capitalism, which deals with profit and its maximization, does not place its mechanisms in the service of enjoyment; that is, what is proper to do from a capitalist point of view (work to increase capital, for example) is irrelevant to the intensification of enjoyment and does not necessarily lead to satisfaction or pleasure. Although there are attempts to connect the worthy deed to enjoyment by representing enjoyment as naturally stemming from work (i.e., work more to increase your enjoyment from life!), this connection leads to the subject's obvious entrapment. The capitalist subject soon discovers the lack of correlation between work and enjoyment. Thus hedonism turns out to be just the flipside of asceticism: one can heed the admonition either to work less in order to pursue enjoyments *or* to work less in order to answer just the most basic needs. In both versions, however – the hedonistic as well as the ascetic – one will find that there is no correlation between work and enjoyment (enjoyment does not correlate with reducing work and non-enjoyment is not correlated with more work) and that indeed, the pursuit of enjoyment involves considerable effort.

In this sense, capitalism openly exposes the intricate connection between enjoyment and work, as well as the fact that it is easier to labour for enjoyment than to enjoy oneself. The capitalist reality has thus turned the struggle to "work less and make do with little" into a struggle whose goal is more and more difficult to achieve, when as part of it, for example, a workers' union is required to hold not only work strikes but also to parade in the heat of high noon in order to achieve a situation in which less work will suffice to earn a living. This indicates that the idea of the capitalist good, in which the law finds its justification, is not overtly compatible with the practice of work and its profits; and that work is a duty that turns even "leisure" into a kind of work. In the capitalist and post-capitalist world, a relation between the right and proper deed and the profit of enjoyment it entails is blatantly absent. Thus, in the ancient world, for Horace for example, leisure was considered something closely related to proper education; whereas for the citizen of the metropolis who is willing to work hard and sweat properly on his holiday, the concept of leisure and its relation to work and enjoyment has become inextricably tangled.

The disruption between morality and pleasure is present in the religious world (where the believer is vaguely promised happiness in the afterlife), as it was among the Greek philosophers (who negated the link between doing good and pleasure). It was Kant who heralded the need for an ethics that recognizes the absence of relation between the good deed and virtue on the one hand and well-being and enjoyment on the other. This ethics stems from his conception of the moral law and acquires its modern significance around the difficulty and anxiety that arise whenever the subject is faced with the compulsion to enjoy himself as the utmost imperative of capitalist life. In the impossibility of complying with the imperative's absolute demand we encounter anew the perplexity that Kant described in his moral theory, a perplexity that is the blatant mark of the split between ethics and morality.

D.   The Topological Space of the Law

The law with its unconditioned demand leaves the subject in great perplexity. Although the moral law is prior, this primacy is not naturally correlated with possible consequences, nor does it coincide with empirical conditions, and it may even contradict the subject's happiness and well-being. This is how Kant illustrates the contrast between the order of concepts created by experience and the order of concepts created by moral freedom. Say that someone is persuaded under duress to bear false witness against an honourable man whom the prince wishes to destroy under a false pretext:

> He might consider it possible to overcome his love of life, however great it may be. He will perhaps not venture to assure us whether or not he would overcome that love, but he must concede without hesitation that doing so would be possible for him. He judges, therefore, that he can do something because he is conscious that he ought to do it, and he recognizes freedom within himself – the freedom with which otherwise, without the moral law, he would have remained unacquainted.[51]

Is it more moral to choose life, or to prevent an injustice? While the practical inclination is to prefer life and do injustice to the other, freedom (of the will from heteronomous principles) does not necessarily resolve the conflict, but rather creates it. It is moral autonomy (freedom) that enables the subject to face a moral dilemma concerning which act would be moral in this situation. The act that will ensue will neither coincide nor overlap with the empirical/practical considerations. We can say that the moral consideration requires an impossible encounter between two separate cognitive orders, an encounter that Lacan diagnoses as one that can only be embodied topologically.

What is the topology relevant to the encounter with the moral law? In Seminar X from 1962–63, which deals with anxiety, Lacan connects the topology required to locate the object of anxiety with ethics – and with Kant. Lacan shows that the status of anxiety is connected to an impossible object, *objet a*, characterized as the *cause of desire*. That is, the encounter with *objet a* is an encounter with an object that is the cause of desire, in the sense that it signifies the cause of the symptom and of the subject's psychic formations. As already noted, Lacan connects the encounter with the psychic cause with an ethical rather than a cognitive possibility (of knowledge or perception), and in this seminar he claims that this encounter is accompanied by anxiety. Lacan finds the evidence for such an encounter precisely in Kant, for whom, as we saw in the previous chapter, the encounter with the object is not possible outside the field of experience, determined by the forms of intuitions (of time and space). Surprisingly, Lacan (as we will see shortly) connects *the ethical dimension of the object-cause* with the transcendental aesthetics, that is, with the forms that *a priori* determine the limits of experience.

This reference to Kant means that we must not ask what is the *meaning* of the object-cause in relation to other objects, but rather what is its *location* in relation to the subject (according to the forms of intuition), and from this derive why the object-cause is an object of anxiety. As Kant says in relation to the status of the cause that precedes all causes (the one that starts the situation in and of itself, spontaneously, and is not subject to the chain of causes): while the representations are connected in relations of time and space *as objects*, "the non-sensible cause of these representations is entirely unknown to us and therefore we cannot intuit it as an object."[52] The cause that precedes all causes is transcendental and is therefore outside experience. It is a cause unknown to us yet posited as the cause of the cause, a causality that has occurred and that determines the totality of experience and is present in thought as "the thought of a possible experience, in its absolute completeness."[53] The cause is not contained in the realm of experience; rather, it determines the possibility of experience as a whole, just as the psychic object-cause is not given to the subject's contemplation but determines the overall psychic reality.

It seems that this is what Lacan is suggesting when he says in Seminar X that space is not merely an attribute of our understanding, beyond which the thing-in-itself will find a totally free field to locate itself; rather, that space is part of the real. Space contains the cause of all the causes, a real cause within space itself and not an object that lies beyond the borders of our intuition. This sentence also explains why Lacan refers to Kant at this point, where he deals with the location of the psychic cause that constitutes a condition for all other causes. This cause is the basis for all the psychic representations but is not contained in any of them. How, then, can the cause be thought as such? This is exactly where anxiety is necessary: it appears precisely because desire is hidden, covered, and anxiety is designed to indicate its presence. Take for example the obsessive person, who leaves the house and a moment later says to himself: I should go back and turn off the tap, lock the door, and so on. The object-cause is not identified with the representations and justifications that the subject has regarding his forgetfulness or the dangers of the surrounding world, but the moment this subject is able to recognize that the symptom has a cause, the moment he can say "this has a cause" – in this place the cause of desire is revealed. The encounter with the reality of the cause that the subject refuses to assimilate as part of the sum of all the representations related as objects in time and space, is what turns the cause into the cause of desire.

Here we can also see why the encounter with the object-cause, like the anxiety that it arouses, is an ethical occurrence. Just as for Kant, causality does not play out solely in the sensible world of experience, but also exceeds the borders of experience and posits a freedom of action that is not subordinate to a prior (heteronomous) cause, so the encounter with the psychic object-cause assumes a free moment of choice that determines psychic reality. The difference between Kant and what Lacan claims here regarding the psychic cause, the cause of desire, is that for Kant, freedom as cause as-it-is-in-itself constitutes a possibility that can be thought even though not experienced, whereas for Lacan freedom assumes a prior cause that the subject encounters in practice through desire: "I mean to transfer this category from the domain that I shall call, with Kant, transcendental aesthetics, over to what I shall call, if you care to endorse this, my transcendental ethics."[54]

In order to turn transcendental aesthetics into an ethics, what is required, says Lacan, is that space not solely determine the limits of subjective cognition, that it exceed the forms of intuition that determine the possibility for an object to become an object of perception or thought (i.e., transcendental aesthetics). The *a* as cause assumes a real space, the space where the subject is willing to recognize the existence of a prior cause, where he is willing to locate the object-cause of his psychic reality, to give it a place as what determines this reality – there the subject takes up an ethical position. Ethics requires that the difference between the psychic cause (which is the cause of causes) and the multitude of psychic causes receive a real status.

The possibility of recognizing the presence of a split between two orders of causality within the psychic realm is provided by topology, because the topological dimension enables us to see the difference between what receives symbolic representation and what it is impossible to represent within the space as intuited. Kant's mistake was that he located the spatial form of intuition in the subject, and the primal cause, the noumenal object (the thing in itself) outside this subjective realm. But if we approach the form of space in topological terms we will see that the object-cause is located within the psychic space itself, and that this object-cause produces a topological cut within this space. On the face of it, the example Lacan gives in this context seems unrelated: he mentions the example of the placenta that envelops the fetus, an envelope that is both the baby's and the mother's (and equally belongs to neither). This unattributed envelope determines the subject's separateness from the object as a fundamental condition and thus serves as a kind of embodiment of an object-cause. The placenta is the impossible representation of the fundamental separateness between the subject (baby) and its object (mother), a separateness that cannot be overcome but can be denied, or camouflaged by various means. The ethical position is a position that does not allow what populates our world to cover the reality of this separateness from the object. That is, the ethical position is a position that includes an encounter with this fundamental separateness, with its causal origin, with the presence of a limit as the basis for every relation with the surrounding world.

The placenta, therefore, enables us to see how the object-cause is part of the *a priori* space that invades the subjective space as a real presence. Kant understood that the only possibility of locating the object-cause is in relation to the limits of the spatial and temporal intuitions, but he left this object beyond these limits (and thus indicated the direction of ethics without really attaining it). What distinguishes the ethical position in relation to this object (i.e., where the transcendental *aesthetics* becomes an *ethics*) is the recognition that even if the object-cause cannot take place or be located in the empirical space of *possibilities* of knowing or perceiving, this object is located in a space that can be topologically represented as a space of *absolute necessity*, a space that is the real space aimed at by ethics, where the kernel of the moral being is located.

Chapter 8

Lacan and Hegel in Three Steps: Otherness, Death, Singularity

Question (J-A Miller): Do you not wish to show, all the same, that the alienation of a subject who has received the definition of being born in, constituted by, and ordered in a field that is exterior to him, is to be distinguished radically from the alienation of a consciousness-of-self? In short, are we to understand – Lacan against Hegel?[1]

Miller's question, asked at the end of one of the sessions of Seminar XI, is enthusiastically received by Lacan, who confirms that indeed, in contrast to what others have inferred from his discussion of the subject in this seminar – namely, that Lacan is "Hegel's *son*" – Miller's positioning of Lacan *against* Hegel is much more accurate. Lacan concludes his response to Miller by saying "of course it is not at all a philosophical debate." This brief exchange poses the two questions that are central to this chapter: In what way is it more correct to say that Lacan is against Hegel, rather than one who follows in his footsteps? And at what point does this rivalry stop being a philosophical one?

The answer to the second question – Where does the rivalry stop being a philosophical one? – will have to be postponed to the end of this chapter. The answer to the first question, on the other hand – Why Lacan against Hegel? – is ostensibly quite simple. From the point of view of psychoanalysis, for which the subject's position is determined by what the subject *does not know (the unconscious)*, Hegel's philosophical belief in states of *consciousness* seems flatly obverse to psychoanalysis. And what state of consciousness contradicts the subject-of-the-unconscious more than the consciousness that knows itself? The one that is called by Hegel *self-consciousness – Selbstbewusstsein*? On the face of it, while Hegel's aim in relation to the constitution of self-consciousness is to attain a consciousness that can say "I know," for the subject of the unconscious of psychoanalysis, subjectivity must be signified through the phrase "I do not know."

On examining Lacan's references to Hegel, however, it seems that while Lacan, as always, uses Hegel in a critical way, he also always uses him *by the letter*, unlike the way he uses Descartes, for example. Lacan reads in Descartes what his arguments *imply*, which sometimes exceeds what Descartes actually says, or what Descartes knows regarding the implications of what he says. Since Lacan's kinship with Hegel is of a different order than that between him and Descartes or Kant, the question of how much the philosopher, were he to encounter the analyst's claim, would say "I didn't know it was so [but retroactively I know it]" arises especially forcefully in relation to Hegel. That is, in relation to the claim on which this book is based – that Lacan *uses* the philosophers – how much is this usage based on something about which the philosopher can say "I didn't know it was so!" or "I knew it was so!"? In other words, if the psychoanalytic reading posits in any case something that the philosopher does not know, is it possible nonetheless to distinguish between different forms of *disagreement* between the analyst and the philosopher he is reading? This question is critical, because it is related to the difference between the philosopher and the analyst, to the way this difference is taken into account and even preserved through the use of one by the other. For usage, as we can see, is not revisionist; that is, it does not allow the conflict between the two positions to be *absorbed into* the psychoanalytic reading. But since we can see different forms of disagreement between Lacan and the philosophers he uses, the question of what, in its usage of philosophy, does psychoanalysis retain of the difference between the analyst and the philosopher can only be answered by examining the different ways of reading that Lacan unfurls before us.

Lacan says in his *Écrits*: "the service we expect from Hegel's phenomenology: that of marking out an ideal solution – one that involves a permanent revisionism, so to speak, in which what is disturbing about truth is constantly being reabsorbed, truth being in itself but what is lacking in the realization of knowledge."[2] The dialectic outlined by Hegel marks out an ideal solution, because it supposes an aim at the end of the dialectic move, one of attaining absolute knowledge. It is a revisionist solution because it absorbs any conflict, any troubling presence in the different states of consciousness, into the next stage of the dialectic. Hegel's dialectic thus delineates moves that obstruct the possibility of attaining ideal knowledge; however, the distance between knowledge and truth will finally be absorbed in the self-knowing consciousness. Lacan's claim with regard to the significance of the overall Hegelian move that Hegel's ideal, where self-consciousness merges with the absolute, merely exposes truth's fundamental otherness to knowledge.

The moves made by desire in relation to consciousness reveal a truth that inherently undermines knowledge. As we will see, the states of consciousness that Hegel is engaged with do not produce understanding or knowledge,[3] and if we adhere to his claims we will find that they "provide the opportunity to always say something Other. Something Other which corrects their fantasmatic link with synthesis."[4] The *Phenomenology* emerges as a testimony to the subject's constant undermining of knowledge; this, however, does not contradict the fact that this subject is under a persistent fantasy regarding an (immanent) synthesis of the states of consciousness, and regarding the final aim of attaining the ideal of absolute knowledge.

This chapter will trace the foundations of the move towards the absolute that governs self-consciousness in Hegel, in order to reveal, with Lacan, what is already inscribed in this move: *les avatars d'un manque,*[5] that is, the avatars of a lack. The history of consciousness is the history of the representations of a lack, of stages of subtraction from what is posited as the ideal of self-consciousness.

Hegel's self-consciousness, as we will see, differs essentially from Descartes's subject, who can say at a moment of primary certainty: "I know that I think," since Hegel's self-consciousness knows only at the end of the whole historical move, and subject to the idea of absolute spirit, that it is where it thinks. We shall see later in this chapter that although for Hegel otherness is present in the very constitution of consciousness through *negation* (as opposed to the Cogito's certainty, which is neither violated nor in any way influenced by the negation implemented by an other), at the end of its formative move consciousness will encounter itself in an immediate way: the self "is like that immediacy and simplicity of the beginning because it is the result, that which has returned into itself, the latter being similarly just the self."[6]

It seems that our initial question, "Is Lacan against Hegel?," refers not only to the idea of self-consciousness that Hegel assumes, but also to the necessary relation between self-consciousness and otherness in the constitution of a subject, when the contrast between Lacan and

Hegel concerns the fate of this otherness. This otherness, which means that the constitution of the subject of consciousness is conditioned upon what does not belong to the subject himself and is even alien to him, this otherness, which is present in both Hegel and Lacan, does not have the same fate. In Hegel's case, alienation leads to an immediate self-present consciousness, whereas for Lacan, while alienation conditions the constitution of a subject, it also cannot be subtracted from the process.

But is it the fate of alienation that determines "Lacan against Hegel"? Or should we perhaps say that the decisive fact is that for Hegel, and throughout the process of constituting self-consciousness, it is always still *not-self-consciousness*, a consciousness that always appears as lacking in relation to what defines its selfhood? Incidentally, even when consciousness completes the process, it is by no means clear that it will still be consciousness (rather than, perhaps, already exceeding the limits of the one consciousness).

In other words, just as it is not enough to locate the *affinity* between Hegel and psychoanalysis in the mere fact that Hegel posits otherness, as present and irreducible, at the moment of establishing and organizing consciousness, so the essential *difference* between Hegel and psychoanalysis cannot be reduced to the mere fact that Hegel posits, on the horizon of consciousness, absolute knowledge as what will eventually eliminate this otherness. In other words, it is possible that in relation to Hegel, the difference between being Hegel's *son* and being *against* Hegel is not so decisive.

It is difficult to separate, in regard to Hegel, between the principles that guide self-consciousness and the aim that is posited with respect to this consciousness. In Descartes's case, Lacan's reading was based on the separation between the consequences of doubting (and the subsequent certainty created for the Cogito) and the stage of constructing clear and distinct knowledge by virtue of God. In Hegel's case such a separation between the two moments is impossible. In Hegel each moment of consciousness is separate from its preceding states but is also imprinted and determined by them. The question whether there is any dimension in which the Hegelian *alienation* differs from the Lacanian one can be answered with both yes and no, and therefore the question must be different: What is posited in the moment of alienation as a constitutive for self-consciousness on the one hand, and as constitutive for the unconscious subject on the other? Only when we answer this will it be possible to examine whether and how Lacan is, among other things, against Hegel.

The key to understanding the kinship between Hegel and Lacan lies in the disconnection of knowledge from thought and in the relation between both and truth. Here the kinship can again be clarified through the difference between Hegel and Descartes. The latter says "I know that I think," since for him thought is subject to and coincides with knowing. In Hegel, however, precisely because for him truth is not present in thought, the consciousness that says "I know that I think" does not actually know. Consciousness's centre of gravity, as we will see in this chapter, is revealed in what is not known; the thinking consciousness knows nothing about its mode of being and needs to posit truth so that at each stage it can know why thought is needed, in order to eventually attain knowledge. In other words, the point of departure in terms of the affinity between Hegel and Lacan is related to the fact that in contrast to Descartes, for whom the cause of thought is known (thought coincides with a certain knowledge about the mental substance), for Hegel and for Lacan the moment of thinking is not a moment of *knowing the cause* but a moment of *missing the cause* of thought. The Hegelian consciousness cannot differentiate itself as a thinking substance because the possibility of knowing does not stem from mere thought. For Hegel the cause of thought lies in absolute knowledge to which thought devotes itself, while for psychoanalysis the cause of thought, what establishes the possibility of thought, is a psychic cause. In both cases the purpose of thought does not lie in thought itself, but is posited in such a way that it is the desire to know that drives the subject. In this spirit Lacan turns to examine the limit of thought in Hegel and in Freud.[7]

Hegel's *Phenomenology*, as Lacan says on the same occasion, is not simply a convenient point of reference but is essential in this context, and not only because the desire to know in Hegel coincides with that of psychoanalysis. Hegel is also necessary for psychoanalysis because through his philosophy we discover how far the proximity between thought and the aim of knowledge goes, since

> the difference between Hegel and Freud is the following. Thinking is not simply the question put about the truth of knowledge, which is already a lot and essential in the Hegelian step. Thinking, says Freud, bars the entry to a knowledge. Do I need to recall what is at stake in the unconscious, namely, how the first access to a knowledge had been thought out? The *Selbstbewusstsein* of Hegel is "I know what I think." The Freudian trauma is an "I do not know," itself unthinkable since it supposes an "I think" dismantled of all thinking.[8]

With these words Lacan sums up the foundation on which the difference between Lacan and Hegel can be considered, that is, on the relation – again – between thought and knowledge. Since for Hegel the beginning (thought) is the means for an end (knowledge), and conversely, since the unconscious is the "creative failure of knowledge," what is revealed here is the truth about self-consciousness: consciousness, says Lacan, thinks as a condition for attaining knowledge (knowledge being the purpose of thought), and therefore can say, in the name of this future knowledge, "I know that I think," that is, consciousness knows itself. But as much as this knowledge of self-consciousness is limited and partial (since no consciousness can say what it itself is), when consciousness becomes knowledge, at that moment it will no longer have any need to think. Conversely, even the Freudian trauma of "I don't know" is not a thought that can be thought, since it posits an "I think" dismantled of all thought, that is, an I that thinks about herself not knowing.[9] This difference is crucial, because it denudes the presence of different reasons to think, the difference between thinking in order to know and thinking in order to know that one does not know. This difference in the *reason* to think is also what reveals the interval that allows the *freedom* to think, since we learn from Hegel, as we will see shortly, that there are some who forgo thought. For Hegel, while the freedom to think does not exist for everyone, but when present, this freedom's only aim is to attain knowledge. Here, the interval that allows thinking or not thinking is measured against the ultimate aim, that is, as an interval between "not-knowing-yet" and "knowing under constraint of the state of consciousness." The freedom to think in the context of the Freudian trauma is the freedom not to think but rather to have someone think in place of the subject. In this sense, knowledge appears only where thought is displaced, where the subject opts for what imposes itself as thinking in (the) place of the subject. Here freedom will be revealed in the place where the subject says "I don't think."

It is not merely Hegel's supposition of self-consciousness (thought that knows itself) that contradicts the unconscious, but also the fact that thought only paves the Royal Road to knowledge and they will merge in self-knowledge.[10] That is, it is not alienation between thought and knowledge in itself that determines the difference between Hegel and the analyst, but rather the contradiction between measures of success and the failure of "knowing" that are posited in the horizon of consciousness. This is the difference between the freedom to think in order to know, and the freedom to not-think in order to know.

A.   Other Consciousness

Phenomenology of the Spirit is a treatise that outlines an entire move, both abstract and historical, in which self-consciousness becomes fully realized. The full realization of self-consciousness is called *spirit* (*Geist*), and the move of consciousness on its way to *Geist* answers this question: How can consciousness become its own object, that is, know itself as an object? In consciousness's attempt to constitute itself as an object of knowledge, it encounters an element of foreignness: it cannot be an object without also continuing to be a consciousness. "the second Subject, viz. the knowing 'I,' still finds in the Predicate [i.e., the subject as the objective and affixed self] what it thought it had finished with and got away from."[11] That is, consciousness wants to know itself and thus finds itself as an object outside itself without being able to stop being consciousness. This problematics occupies the *Phenomenology* as a whole, while the section that deals with the master and the slave – a section that has attracted unusual attention in philosophy after Hegel – concentrates on one aspect of this problematics, the one concerned with difference and unity.[12] The chapter titled "The Master–Slave Dialectic" is not the summary of a move but a segment of it, a segment within a long process through which self-consciousness is realized, a consciousness that be neither primary nor immediately present for Hegel.

Consciousness, before it is self-consciousness, is the consciousness of something else, of an object that is not itself. The relation between consciousness and object begins with consciousness having an immediate relation of certainty with its object, even if consciousness acknowledges that the object is not itself. That is, already in the initial stages, in which consciousness is a perceiving consciousness, it entails negation as part of its relation with the object, as well as a supposition of difference or manifoldness.[13] Consciousness, which sees the unity of the object in itself, recognizes its separateness from it, but also sees itself as responsible for this separateness. "The Thing is a One, reflected into itself; it is *for itself*, but it is also *for an other* ... But the oneness also belongs to the Thing itself as consciousness has found by experience."[14] Consciousness is therefore *for* the object and inseparable from it, but also recognizes its distinctness from it. This movement between *difference* and *unity* accompanies all the stages that consciousness goes through before becoming self-consciousness.

Indeed, consciousness for Hegel is not one thing, and the *Phenomenology* traces the various states of consciousness (a topic we will be concerned with in the third section of this chapter). In the stage of perception, even before consciousness asks itself about the essence of things beyond the realm of the visible, it sees the object as undistinguished from itself, even if the object has its own being, and this unity of consciousness with the object is truth. The truth of consciousness is at this stage the object present in a certain way in the perceiving consciousness.

Thus, the possible existence of something and its opposite in one unity, or the existence of an internal difference, appears in Hegel even before the appearance of self-consciousness. Self-consciousness is the result of a move that has already been established in the *Phenomenology*, in which the contrasting moments that constitute consciousness are revealed in it, since the unity of consciousness itself already contains negation, that is, its internal opposition. The self-same consciousness is therefore a differentiated consciousness, different from itself from the first moment of its appearance. Consciousness turning into its own object therefore lies in the very supposition that every being is the inverse of its way of being determined, and therefore consciousness is fundamentally self-consciousness ("the undifferentiated selfsame being, which repels itself from itself, posits itself as an inner being containing different moments, but for which equally these moments are immediately *not* different – *self-consciousness*").[15] The passages that discuss self-consciousness do not deal with the constitution of consciousness itself as its self-object, but with this question: What does consciousness, being self-consciousness, know about itself?

Hence, self-consciousness is a consciousness whose object is not only the immediate object of perception but also itself. Consciousness must refer to itself from outside itself, since being consciousness it also appears as its own object – that is, as consciousness of itself. But since consciousness first appears to itself as an object external to itself, self-consciousness, where consciousness and object are a unity, will also appear as separate from its object. Indeed, the *Phenomenology*, which moves towards the place where consciousness will absolutely converge with its object, where the absolute aim will be consciousness itself, will reveal in this movement that for Hegel, absolute identity is identity within difference.

The present section deals with *difference* in Hegel as a constitutive element of the individual and society, and in the way in which Lacan makes use of Hegelianism in this sense. Hegelian self-consciousness moves from being only consciousness, through moments of self-consciousness, to its full realization as spirit. Each of the moments of consciousness constitutes a whole array of relations between consciousness and what is being thought through it, and each of the moments differs essentially from what preceded it and what will follow it. The first aspect of difference, which appears even before difference is acknowledged, and certainly before an essential non-identity has been created between consciousnesses, is identified by Hegel with the necessity of negation. By the very fact that reality is considered to be standing outside consciousness it is already negated as being external. Negation and "the portentous power of the negative" is a fundamental principle for Hegel, one that will accompany consciousness all through its development. The very appearance of another consciousness is a necessary condition for the constitution of self-consciousness. "Spirit is this power only by looking the negative in the face, and tarrying with it," and for this reason, negation is essential for the possibility of turning the distinctly other into an object of consciousness (and is therefore essential to all of consciousness's moves).[16] "Self-consciousness is faced by another self-consciousness; it has come *out of itself* ... it has lost itself, for it finds itself as an *other* being."[17]

Otherness, *distinctness*, **and** *negation* designate three necessary aspects in the movement of consciousness. For Hegel, consciousness, like any finite thing, can be in-itself, but in such a case it has no distinguishing nature, there is nothing to know regarding it (for Hegel, unlike for Kant, "the thing in itself" means that the thing is not linked to anything else, and not necessarily that it is not linked to our cognition). Consciousness must duplicate itself, posit itself by means of what is distinct from it, in order to be constituted as consciousness. But once it has found itself outside itself, in what is distinctly other from it, consciousness sees itself in the other. That is, the dialectic in this move is related to the fact that in order for consciousness to face itself and recognize itself in the other, it is not enough for something to appear as distinct from consciousness; also required is its negation as distinct, that is, the negation of what is other to consciousness. Otherness here is the other party (other person) who is recognized as different from consciousness, and for whom this consciousness, the first consciousness, exists as other – but only insofar as its otherness is negated so that consciousness can, through this otherness, reinforce its being for itself. Consciousness's being-for-the-other is a condition for its becoming self-consciousness, consciousness of itself.

But this negation of the other is not absolute, since Hegel goes on to say that being recognized by the other is a condition for self-consciousness.

Recognition does not mean feeling respect or adoration or acknowledging rights,[18] but "recognizing that he is in himself – and therefore also for the other – being for himself." One needs the other's recognition of her own value as self-consciousness in order to be such consciousness herself.

The other party that appears here as other and distinct from the subject is a condition for self-consciousness, because the subject finds herself in the other. "Self-consciousness is faced by another self-consciousness; it has come *out of itself.*" The key to understanding otherness as constitutive for self-consciousness lies in what *directs* consciousness to the other consciousness, and we have already seen that the driving principle is the need for recognition. But even before the need for recognition, which requires a turning outwards, Hegel refers to desire (*Begierde*), which is the first factor in determining consciousness even before it has become self-consciousness.[19] Desire appears in the first moment, which presents the perceiving consciousness as the consciousness of an object, a consciousness to which the object is given with immediacy and certainty. That is, it is desire that connects the object's otherness with consciousness. This absorption of the other, external world is desire.

Desire in Hegel, says Hyppolite, is a movement of consciousness that negates everything it encounters, thus absorbing being and making it its own ("it finds itself in a different essence").[20] Self-consciousness, which is simply for-itself, and which regards its object as a negative element (i.e., as desire), will lose its independence when it learns, through experience, that the object is also "for itself."[21] That is, desire, as it first appears in relation to an object, explains why the movement of consciousness is conditioned upon the presence of the sensible phenomenon, of the perceived object, since desire is the movement towards the object. Desire in itself does not explain consciousness's turning to the other consciousness; rather, it appears as an embodiment of the object that consciousness identifies with its own value, and whose recognition it looks for in the other consciousness. Only in the next phase will desire turn into recognition of the object's otherness. Clearly, then, desire is only one of the moves required for constructing self-consciousness on its way to another consciousness; but desire will take shape as a twofold move: that of finding myself in the other, and that of making this otherness mine. Hegel thus sees otherness and difference as constitutive elements in the long and complex process that leads mere consciousness to the status of self-consciousness.

There is a moment when consciousness of itself and consciousness as its own object merge, when that which constitutes the Thing and distinguishes it from others is now defined in such way that the Thing is in opposition to other things, but is supposed to preserve its independence in this opposition. At this moment "the Thing is posited as being *for itself*, or as the absolute negation of all otherness, therefore as purely *self*-related negation; but the negation that is self-related is the suspension of *itself*; in other words, the Thing has its essential being in another Thing."[22] This moment where the essential being of a Thing is identified with the negation of the other Thing through its opposition to it, indicates a crucial moment in attaining self-consciousness.

Consciousness finds itself in the other and finds the other in itself almost from the moment it is consciousness, and the question is: Who is the other without whom consciousness cannot be "for itself"? For Hegel, from its first manifestations otherness concerns consciousness situating itself as an object outside itself – that is, the alienation that forces consciousness to find itself as an object where this object is recognized outside it. But is this not an alternative formulation of Lacan's famous statement that the subject's "desire is for the desire of the Other"? It is exactly with the suggestion of such an analogy – that is, with the claim that the analytic formula here recalls and parallels the Hegelian formula – that Lacan takes issue in the Seminar on Anxiety (1962–63):

> If, however, there's one point at which it's important to mark the progress, to employ this term – I'd much rather say the leap – that is ours with regard to Hegel, it's precisely concerning the function of desire ... that in Hegel, concerning the dependence of my desire with respect to the desirer who is the Other, I'm dealing ... with the Other as consciousness. The Other is the one who sees me ... and this is what, all by itself, kicks off the struggle, according to the foundations wherewith Hegel marks the start of the *Phänomenologie des Geistes*, on the plane of what he calls pure prestige, and it's on this place that my desire is concerned.[23]

First, we can note in relation to this chapter's point of departure that as long as it is possible to compare Hegel's other with Lacan's, we are still within the realm of a philosophical debate. Second, Lacan's words point to the fundamental principle that defines otherness in relation to the Hegelian consciousness. Self-consciousness requires another, different consciousness to position itself so that the first consciousness serves as an object for it. Later on we will see why Lacan claims that this definition of the other gives rise to the "struggle for life and death" that will take place between the two consciousnesses, but at this stage, Lacan seems to see Hegel's other as another person – a different subject who consciousness imaginarily posits against itself so that this other reinforces its value.

The conception of the other as a consciousness that carries independent value is not immediate in Hegel. When the other is no longer perceived as a hostile, unknown entity that must be destroyed, it will be recognized for itself – and by virtue of that, as consciousness. In other words, recognizing the existence of a different consciousness, of another subject, is an achievement for self-consciousness, which has freed itself from the blindness of consciousness simply for-itself, which sees the object as identical to and overlapping with it and the other as hostile and foreign. But as we will see below, Lacan finds that the doubling of consciousnesses and the appearance of a different consciousness is merely a doubling of the object of cognition (which is the object of desire). Lacan believes that the doubling of consciousnesses is based on the recognition of an object – the one that consciousness finds in the other consciousness and that turns the other into a consciousness. It is this object that, according to Lacan, determines the fate of self-consciousness later in the dialectic:

> For Lacan, because Lacan is an analyst, the Other is there as an un-consciousness that is constituted as such. The Other concerns my desire to the extent of what he lacks and to the extent that he doesn't know. It's at the level of what he lacks, and at the level of him not knowing, that I'm concerned in the most prominent way, because there's no other path for me to find what I lack as object of my desire. This is why for me there is no, not simply access to my desire, but not even any possible means of sustaining my desire that would have any reference to any object whatsoever if not through coupling it, through tying it in, with this, the $, which designates the subject's necessary dependence on the Other as such.[24]

In Lacan the other is not another person – an other that is the subject's double. Thus, while in Hegel the other is a consciousness that sees me as I am, that knows what I lack just as I myself know what is the thing I find in the other's domain, in Lacan the other holds the knowledge about what I know nothing about. The other introduces the dimension of the signifier from which being is derived – that is, *the signifier ties the subject to a different path than the path of learning to know oneself.*

On the basis of this difference Lacan presents two formulas that represent the desire of the other in Hegel on the one hand and in Lacan on the other.[25]

d(a): d(A) < a

This is the formula that represents the Hegelian other, and it should be read thus: the desire (d) towards the object (a) in which self-consciousness finds itself equals (:) the desire of the other (d(A)), since this desire establishes an object. This suggests that the Hegelian other is not just a consciousness, but is itself a site of desire for an object, an object that creates a link with the self-consciousness. The other consciousness, then, is not only another person who sees the subject, but also a site in which the subject's object of desire is located.

Is it in Hegel, then, a matter of an imaginary otherness, an otherness that does not locate the alienation of the impossible object, but precisely mitigates this alienation when consciousness finds itself in the other? Is the other consciousness for Hegel self-consciousness's double? If so, this question arises: Is there, and can there be, some essential kinship between otherness-according-to-Hegel and otherness-according-to-Lacan?

For Hegel, the desire of consciousness is the desire of the other, in the sense that it is the desire that the other consciousness will respond to its call. The desire of the desirer is for the desire *of* the other, rather than *for* the other, and it is indeed in these very words that Kojève explains it as well: for desire to be human, it must be desire for desire rather than desire for the other. "He wants to be 'desired' or 'loved,' or, rather, 'recognized' in his human value, in his reality as a human individual."[26] Humanity comes to light, says Kojève, only where man risks his life to satisfy his desire which is directed towards another desire, towards a value that another desire desires: "I want him to 'recognize' my value as his value."[27] The appeal to the other is then explained by Hegel as the desire for what in the other enables the recognition of the subject in his humanity, his singularity. The subject needs the other's recognition, and this means that the other establishes something that can be signified as *a*, which is what is at stake on the plane of the desire. Desire establishes something in relation to which the appeal to the other consciousness is made – in other words, self-consciousness appeals to the other consciousness – but otherness is not found in the opposing consciousness but rather in that other consciousness's object of desire. And this is how Lacan describes the point at which we arrive with Hegel:

> The whole impasse lies here. In demanding to be acknowledged, right where I get acknowledged, I only get acknowledged as an object, since this object that I am is of its essence a consciousness, a *Selbstbewusstsein*. I can't stand myself acknowledged in the only type of acknowledgment I can obtain. Therefore it has to be settled at any cost between our two consciousnesses. There's no longer any mediation but that of violence. Such is desire's lot in Hegel.[28]

Lacan thus diagnoses something crucial in his reading of Hegel, something that was already hinted at by Kojève. The desire directed towards the other desire is concerned with a common object: it is the same object that self-consciousness and the other consciousness aim at, and that constitutes the possibility of acknowledgment. The imaginary dimension of the other is not connected, then, to the fact that the other is another person or another consciousness, but to the fact that *the desire directed towards the desire of the other is a desire for a desire for the same object*. The subject identifies his desire in the other's desire, and this is unbearable for him because it points at the object desired by the other. The result of this *object-sharing* is that the acknowledgment that self-consciousness aims at in the other is in fact an acknowledgment that the object found in the other originates in consciousness itself (which is the way consciousness is turned into an object, that is, into consciousness-of-itself). As Hegel says, the reality of cognition depends not only on consciousness distinguishing itself from something but also on the way consciousness relates itself to something that exists for consciousness.[29]

Another result of this object-sharing is that the shared object will necessarily lead to a struggle over its possession, a life-and-death struggle. Consciousness finds in the other consciousness an object – a common object for the subject and for its other – and it is here that the shared acknowledgment creates a struggle, a struggle over a "contested object" that cannot be divided in two, just as it is impossible to split the contested baby in the Judgment of Solomon. Precisely for this reason, since there is a specific thing – the desired object that determines the value and essence of consciousness, the object around which self-consciousness's movement towards the other consciousness revolves – precisely for this reason, desire leads to a fateful struggle between the two consciousnesses. The object identified in the other is not an object of unity but an object that it is unbearable for the subject to encounter.

This, then, is the formula that represents desire in Lacan:

d(a) < i(a): d(Ⱥ)

In this formula, which describes the relation between the other and the desire for the object in Lacan, we find that the desire for the object is established through an image that embodies what is subtracted from the Other in his desire. That is, the desire for the object constitutes an Other that lacks that object (Ⱥ), rather than an other that contains the object. Desire constitutes an object that cannot be averaged (between what the subject desires and what the other possesses) because it appears as lacking, as unattainable. Whereas an other that contains the object is an other that supports the transparency of consciousness for itself, an other that the object is subtracted from is an other that supports what psychoanalysis calls "unconscious," that is, the constitution of a subject who does not know what she wants, what she desires.

The colon signifies that desire is what in its supporting image is identified with the big Other's desire for what is subtracted from it (while in relation to Hegel, the colon pointed to the equivalence between the desire for the object and the desire of the other for the same object). Here, the big Other appears as barred (Ⱥ), it is characterized as lacking, whereas in Hegel the object appears in its place in the other as what is present, albeit by virtue of being negated. In Hegel, the subject is signified through a known object, present for consciousness. Kojève locates this difficulty in Hegel in the way in which the philosopher understands desire: desire is directed towards an object, and it is human to desire what the others desire just because they desire it. In other words, in Hegel the difficulty posed by the object of desire is that this object turns the other consciousness into a consciousness that must be engaged with in a life-and-death struggle over the object of desire.

No wonder Lacan concludes this comparison between him and Hegel with the claim that the psychoanalytic formula is more beneficial in the experience of love than the Hegelian one, since from the psychoanalytic perspective the formula amounts to saying: "I desire you, even if I know it not," while the consequence of Hegel's doctrine amounts to this doomed statement: "I love you, even if you don't want me to."[30] Only the first formula can ensure that the desiring subject produces in the Other a lack, that is, posits an Other who will respond to desire.

At this point, after establishing the disparity between otherness in Hegel and in Lacan, Lacan returns to the point of departure and shows the kinship between them, since for both, the point of departure is the object – an object *a* that is the object of desire. For Hegel the point of departure is also the object (as that which consciousness encounters and sets out its movement), that is, something unacceptable in the context of self-consciousness, of the consciousness that knows itself – its finiteness.[31] The object's appearance in the field of the other consciousness means that consciousness has encountered something that places a limit on its infiniteness, which creates an effect of finiteness. This point is common to Hegel and Lacan, since the object is always a stopping point, a sign of finiteness in relation to desire.

But while the finiteness of self-consciousness means that the object consciousness has encountered in the other is already found in consciousness, that it has found itself in the other, in psychoanalysis there is no supposition of transparency in consciousness's relations with itself through the other. The object that signifies the subject in the Other is the unconscious itself; the real presence of what is unattainable or unknowable in the subject is embodied in the field of the Other. In relation to and in reliance on the Other, Lacan says, the subject is inscribed as a quotient (of a division) in the field of the Other. This remainder of the subject is inscribed in the Other as the proof and sole guarantee of the Other's otherness, and this remainder is the object *a*.[32]

For psychoanalysis, the desire of the subject of the unconscious is for something finite but undefined in its appearance. The object is but an embodiment of the fact that the subject is not present to himself, and the object appears – through an image – as a *Repräsentanz*, that is, as a representative of what obstructs the object's transparency. In the analytic context the object's presence is a sign of finiteness, even though ostensibly there are an infinite possibilities to fill the lack with an object. In other words, the desire for the lacking object is revealed as not really infinite but necessarily reduced, although the absence marked in the place of the object can ostensibly be filled with various substitutes. The analyst, says Lacan, knows that there is only one object that can fill this lack, but although it is One, it is an impossible, undefined, unobtainable One. The reality of the object of desire is not related to the possibility of identifying it, appropriating it, or forging a relationship with it. Thus the "dimension of the infinity of desire has absolutely to be cut down to size. In fact, this peudo-infinity is due to one thing alone … But …

this One, to which at the end of the day the succession of signifying elements, in so far as they are distinct, are reduced, does not exhaust the function of the Other."[33]

The desire for the object is the desire of the Other precisely because this desire is constricted to what the signifier in the field of the Other carries, what in Lacan's formula concerns the object's presence through an image. This constriction of the infinity of desire does not stem from the object of desire's actual presence in the Other (as in Hegel, where the object, found in the other, blocks the infinite movement between consciousness and its knowledge about itself), but from the fact that this object appears through an image, through a signifier that creates a necessary disparity, a structural incompatibility, between what the image shows and what the desiring subject desires. For this reason, desire can never home in on a common object. In other words, *the object in psychoanalysis is what prevents rather than enables the relationship between the subject and the Other*; it is what prevents the formation of role play between them around the object.

But why does Lacan claim that the One does not exhaust the function of the Other? We have been inadvertently led to face the fact that the Other, precisely due to its otherness, has been displaced from its function as the field of the subject (the subject finds himself in the Other and thus something, namely the object, is subtracted from this domain) to the function of the One, which produces an image of the subtracted object and thus returns to the subject something of his being:

> Self-consciousness is faced by another self-consciousness; it has come *out of itself*. This has a twofold significance: first, it has lost itself, for it finds itself as an *other* being; secondly, in doing so it has superseded the other, for it does not see the other as an essential being, but in the other sees its own self.[34]

Is it possible that for Hegel too, something of the other's alienation remains as a leftover that constitutes consciousness's being as self-consciousness? Within the present discussion, which seeks to locate the point of divergence between Hegel and Lacan and ascertain why this point occurs where the difference between them stops being a philosophical one, and after seeing a series of points of convergence and divergence between the two, the question that arises is whether the two meanings of otherness in Hegel (the presence of the other in the subject and the presence of the subject in the other) correspond to the two functions that Lacan ascribes to the Other – the function of providing a domain for the constitution of the subject, and the function of establishing the subject's desire precisely through what is subtracted from the Other.

Lacan says:

> I'm telling the other party that, desiring him or her, undoubtedly without knowing it, still without knowing it, I take him or her for the unknown object, unknown to me, of my desire. This means that, in our conception of desire, I identify you, thee to whom I'm speaking, with the object that you lack. In going via this circuit, which is obligatory if I am to attain the object of my desire, I accomplish for the other party precisely what he's seeking. If, innocently or not, I take this detour, the other as such, here object – observe – of my love, will necessarily fall into my toils.[35]

We are back to the practice of amorous life, where the point of divergence between Hegel and Lacan can be rearticulated. This is the point that distinguishes the other of Hegelian consciousness, which turns out to be reduced to *an object the other has*, from the other in psychoanalysis, which marks the *other as lacking an object*, and this divergence has far-reaching effects on the way love and desire are understood. In Hegel, the point we have reached is that the subject's finiteness, which is embodied in the object, is found in the domain of the other. By negating the other consciousness, a reversal occurs through which the object will come to meet and converge with the desiring consciousness (as the lovers who forget their difference). Consciousness will become self-consciousness.

For Lacan, however, the reversal is of a different order: if at first the object is on the side of the Other while the lack is on the side of the subject ("I desire you"), the reversal locates the object on the side of the subject and the lack in the Other. Lacan says, I complete the circle by telling you that this object that I desire is in you (the nature of this object remaining unknown) thereby turning this object into something that you also want to know and possess, that is, into something you desire. The object desired is thus relocated as lacking in the other (you). Otherness is not negated but affirmed as the exclusive place of desire in *this* subject (as I do not know what in the other had answered my quest). Acknowledging the other as the embodiment of the object of desire, receives its constitutive meaning in *the affirmation of that object* (rather than in a negation of otherness).

B. Struggle to the Death

The presentation of itself, however, as the pure abstraction of self-consciousness consists in showing itself as the pure negation of its objective
mode, or in showing that it is not attached to any specific *existence*, not to
the individuality common to existence as such, that it is not attached to
life. This presentation is a twofold action: action on the part of the other,
and action on its own part. In so far as it is the action of the *other*, each
seeks the death of the other. But in doing so, the second kind of action,
action on its own part, is also involved; for the former involves the staking
of its own life. Thus the relation of the two self-conscious individuals is
such that they prove themselves and each other through a life-and-death
struggle.[36]

According to Hegel, self-consciousness (the being that returns to
itself as being for itself) as pure abstraction is conditioned upon the
negation of its objective existence (i.e., the negation of its existence in
the other). To negate this otherness, consciousness engages in a life-
and-death struggle; that is, on the one hand it aims for the death of the
other party, and on the other hand it is ready to risk its life to prove its
freedom in relation to the other consciousness. Risking its life is the
condition for the certainty of consciousness, certainty of its *being for
itself*, while consciousness's *being in relation to the other consciousness*
is decisive in determining its becoming/being self-consciousness. At
this moment of the struggle to death, the consciousnesses separate
into the consciousness of the master and the consciousness of the
slave.

What is it for Hegel that necessitates a life-and-death struggle between
the consciousnesses in order to constitute self-consciousness?

If the other consciousness is at first a hostile entity that must be
destroyed in the struggle over the object, then in the course of constituting consciousness, the need emerges to be recognized by the other
consciousness in order to allow self-consciousness to be for itself –
and this recognition requires an appeal to the other. Later we will see
how the appeal to the other (without the other's recognition, no self-
consciousness is possible) can be reconciled with the readiness to kill
him. At this stage here we can see that attaining certainty about consciousness being for-itself requires a kind of abstraction from the concrete existence of consciousness and its object, an abstraction that takes
place through recognizing the other as consciousness for-itself.

Hyppolite describes this movement between abstraction and recognition as a movement between being in *absolute certainty* and being
immersed in life. Consciousness for-itself is an absolute self-certainty, but
for the other consciousness it is a living thing, an independent entity in
the medium of being. As described by Hyppolite,[37] this difference must
disappear in each of the parties, by the other recognizing consciousness
as what it is for itself (absolute certainty), and by consciousness proving to itself that it is a living thing. What, then, for Hegel, happens to
the difference between consciousness and other consciousness? Since
consciousness finds itself in the other, it appears as alien to itself; it loses
itself as well as the other, since *it sees in the other itself rather than otherness*.
At this point consciousness sees the other consciousness as taking precisely the same action as itself; that is, it is a matter of the twofold movement of two independent consciousnesses whose recognition of each
other is a mutual recognition. In order to be consciousness-for-itself,
consciousness must not be subject to the objectively defined existence in
life, but rather constitute itself as a desire that appeals to another desire,
and this is the basis for the whole dialectic. Since consciousness wants
to show itself as abstracted of the entire objective mode of its existence,
it negates, it refuses to be something that exists independently in the
other, and therefore demands to be recognized as a self-consciousness
that has gone out of itself. This is the source of the struggle for mutual
recognition, which entails negating consciousness's objective existence
in the other and negating the objective presence of the other consciousness in consciousness itself.

All throughout history man has aspired not only to persist as a living
organism but also to gain recognition as self-consciousness, that is, as a
being that transcends life. For this purpose, to achieve this recognition,
consciousness strives for the death of the other consciousness on the
one hand, and acts in this direction by risking its own life on the other.
It is this life-and-death struggle that allows the different consciousnesses to appear as distinct self-consciousnesses. Remember that self-
consciousnesses gain their distinctness in different moments (that do
not reflect each other), and that the completion of the series of moments
will lead to distinctness being cancelled, as for example when the slave
is revealed as the master's master, and the master as the slave's slave.
But since the struggle for recognition is established as a struggle that
determines human experience (and therefore Hegel connects the struggle for recognition to historical life), and since the effect of the struggle
is not uniform, the difference between the distinct consciousnesses is a

critical one. That is, the struggle for recognition reveals unequal positions towards the need for recognition: as, for example, in the unequal positions of slavery and mastery.

Truth means that the reality of consciousness is revealed, and this reality is only revealed in the struggle for recognition and in the risking of life implied in this struggle. For this reason, and in order to raise subjective certainty to the level of universal truth, consciousness must risk its life, that is, show that the reality of self-consciousness is not the immediate, fleeting reality submerged in living experience. Only thus will consciousness be able to be consciousness-for-itself, that is, an autonomous self-consciousness.

As already noted, however, what is needed is not only the act of risking one's life, but also an act in which consciousness seeks the death of another. This is because the presentation of consciousness as the pure abstraction of self-consciousness "consists in showing itself as the pure negation of its objective mode." Since consciousness embodies itself as an other, outside itself, it must eliminate this being outside of itself in order to be pure being for-itself.[38] Consciousness must negate and destroy the thing that is outside it, which conceals the truth about it as consciousness, since it wants to rid itself of any externality, to negate its objective mode. Since consciousness recognizes that the other consciousness is also a consciousness that wishes to be recognized, it is forced to seek its death.

But why is negation likened to death? As already mentioned, to seek the death of the other does not mean to seek its death in practice. For in order to enable the required abstraction, to be relevant to the constitution of self-consciousness, the other consciousness has to be present in practice. The life-and-death struggle is therefore a mode of dialectic overcoming, an act of pure negation, rather than an actual annihilation of the other consciousness. Then why does Hegel identify the negation of otherness with a life-and-death struggle? The answers to this vary. Hyppolite, as already noted, connects death to the fact that for Hegel, the natural position of any consciousness is life, and the struggle for recognition means going beyond this natural state. Life before the absolute negation makes way for a struggle that already posits a different life category of human history, and this is the arena in which the life-and-death struggle takes place.[39]

Kojève claims that the life-and-death struggle is not a passing moment in Hegel, but that in its very orientation, Hegel's philosophy is a philosophy of death. Ontologically speaking, man in Hegel is finite, and phenomenologically speaking he is mortal, that is, he is a being always conscious of its death. Hegel's philosophy is dialectical and anthropological; it does not accept the infinity that is posited, for example, by Christian philosophy. Accepting the fact of death and the finiteness of man means that we are in the realms of a philosophy in which the concept of death fulfils a constitutive role.[40]

Lacan likewise explains the fatal aggressiveness that exists between consciousnesses in Hegel by referring to what lay at the basis of the *Phenomenology* to begin with: namely, *the connection of desire in its primal form to the object*. That is, the life-and-death struggle is not the *result* of acknowledging the other, either as other or as hostile consciousness; rather, it derives from the very irremovable presence of the object *as cause of desire*. That is, it is the nature of the object, rather than the aspirations of consciousness, that can explain why death is necessary to determine self-consciousness.

To learn something about the nature of the object-cause, Lacan turns to the obsessive: the subject who knows how to come to terms with this presence of the object. For the obsessive negotiates with the object-cause: he does not encounter it in itself, nor does he wish to acquire his autonomy from it; rather, he acknowledges the inability of removing it and the need to create a place for it. The obsessive does so by positing the object as an object of value, worthy of appropriation. In the "Rat Man," for example, a stone on which the subject accidentally stumbles in the street receives the status of a significant hazard: it is the stone that his beloved's carriage would strike in the street a few hours later. The external object is a representative (*Repräsentanz*) of the object of his primordial aggressiveness towards the beloved, and the obsessive solution is to give this aggressiveness the status of a categorical dictate that no harm should come to the beloved, and therefore the Rat Man removes the stone.[41]

This granting of value to the object-cause is what in Hegel marks the point osculating the struggle: "it is only through staking one's life that freedom is won";[42] that is, by staking one's life a value is produced for this life, a value that transcends existence itself.

Kojève gives this object-cause, which is not an object of exchange, the status of pure prestige, or of meaning, as Lacan will define it. The obsessive's case shows that the life-and-death struggle is not a means to remove the object but a means to mediate between the object and consciousness, by ascribing it value and meaning. It also implies that this object is present as an object of aggressiveness that constitutes the relation between the subject and the other, even before the question of mutual recognition has been broached. The moment in Hegel's *Phenomenology* in which it is revealed that two self-consciousnesses cannot exist simultaneously is the moment that reveals the presence of this primal object that makes the struggle inevitable. This is because consciousness cannot find the object-cause in itself and therefore wishes to destroy it in the other. At that moment, Lacan says, it is also revealed that the life-and-death struggle is the struggle for nothing (*la lutte pour rien*),[43] a struggle for an object that is not an object of exchange and therefore cannot be eliminated. That is, it is not a struggle for victory, but a struggle that cannot be measured as gain or loss.

Lacan's words suggest, then, that the Hegelian life-and-death struggle reveals the truth about the object-cause that is not present but represented by fatal aggressiveness. Furthermore, this aggressiveness that reveals the necessary presence of an object, enables the subject to appear on the plane of action. The fatal struggle is a struggle in the name of that primordial object that constitutes consciousness and is the cause of the possibility of acting. Hence the struggle reveals what there is to know about the object posited as cause; knowledge that manifests itself through the aggressive act. According to Lacan, in Hegel absolute knowledge is in fact posited through the object-cause, and as such this knowledge can only be posited through the struggle to the death for the object. The struggle, in other words, *places the absolute as cause*, which will later become the aim of consciousness. The subject hence depends on this struggle by which knowledge, knowledge of death, appears as knowledge that must be negated by consciousness so that it returns to it at the end of the dialectic. The knowledge of death, embodied in the life-and-death struggle, is the absolute knowledge that is held in store at the beginning of consciousness's manoeuvres and is sublated in order to return later as the *jouissance* of the master, the one consciousness willing to stake its life for the object-cause.[44]

> This knowledge of death, articulated precisely in this fight to the death of pure prestige, in so far as it grounds the status of the master, it is from it that there comes this *Aufhebung* of enjoyment ... And it is as renouncing enjoyment in a decisive act, in order to make himself the subject of death that the master is established ... It is to the master that enjoyment is supposed to return from this *Aufhebung*.[45]

The action in relation to the other consciousness can only be an action that reveals the knowledge of death, that is, the knowledge about what is beyond the pleasure principle, which has to be negated so that action becomes possible. An object must be renounced, negated, so that self-consciousness is able to acquire its life back, that is, that the struggle will end up reinforcing the existence of being and of the object that was negated in it: "In this experience, self-consciousness learns that life is as essential to it as pure self-consciousness."[46] In this experience, that is, in the dialectical negation that is the experience of a life-and-death struggle that has not ended with the death of one or both of the opponents, life becomes essential to self-consciousness; that is, the place of the absolute object has been recognized, as well as the fact that consciousness is a being-consciousness in the shape of thingness, rather than pure self-consciousness. The struggle is therefore a dialectical overcoming that preserves what is overcome.[47]

Kojève similarly connects the centrality of death in Hegel to the fact that man's being is revealed in the dimension of action, and the first place in which man is revealed in his action is on the plane of struggle. In the world of natural phenomena, man fulfils himself through the negating act, because the negation has an affirmative effect. The negation reinforces the finiteness of being rather than empties it. The act of negation takes place in a historical world that has a beginning and an end, and therefore action in this world is always, and immediately, fatal (but also human). That is, since man is action and action is negative, it means that man exists as a speaking and human being through his death, a death that is rejected but of which man is conscious. Language and the historical world are created from man's struggle with himself and with the natural world, and only the consciousness of finiteness allows him to attain self-conscious wisdom. It is the act of negation that creates the necessary dialectic between the finite being that has been negated (in order to attain the possibility of an abstract consciousness) and the abstract self-certainty, by bringing being to the threshold of annihilation.[48]

What is the affirmation that takes place by virtue of the negating action (a negation that comes to exist through the struggle)? The individual, says Kojève, is a synthesis of the particular and the universal, and man becomes universal even while remaining particular only through acting against the personal particular interest. Individuality posits finiteness and death. The universal is a negation of the particular as such, and therefore in order to turning the particular being universal, being must detach itself from the here and now of its empirical existence. But such a detachment for man means death. That is, the permeation of the universal is the realization of the particular's finiteness, that is, his actual death. Therefore death is the necessary and sufficient condition, not only for man's freedom and historicity, but also for his universality, without which he will not really be an individual.

> It is therefore indeed death – by which is to be understood a death that is voluntary or accepted in full awareness of what is involved – which is the supreme manifestation of freedom, at least of the "abstract" freedom of the isolated individual. Man could not be free if he were not essentially and voluntarily mortal.[49]

Freedom comes to light through the risk of life because by this act the autonomous self-consciousness (of the master) is distinguished from the consciousness in which freedom and autonomy are not realized (of the slave). The essence of the individual's freedom is therefore negation of otherness, which is embodied in its most pure and absolute form in death. But since freedom is essentially negativity, it cannot be realized in its pure state, nor can it be an object of volition in itself. Absolute freedom is absolute negativity and therefore means nothingness and death, and this is already a negation of life and existence, of mere being. Therefore Hegel sees negativity as something rather than nothing, because negativity is mediated by the identity of being, which is preserved even in negation. That is, negation is real only when it creates a *modus operandi* that is connected to the identity of being. Freedom is realized in man only as historical being, but since man exists in history when freely negating (another consciousness, the object, etc.), only mortal being can really be historical. "Man appears therefore (or creates himself) for the first time in the (given) natural World as a combatant in the first bloody Struggle for pure prestige … 'The true being of Man' is therefore, in the final analysis, his death as a conscious phenomenon."[50]

The recognition of particularity introduces the nothingness of death also in relation to the other, since consciousness must know whether the other is consciousness (i.e., man). Every one must necessarily position himself in relation to the other, before him and against him, in order to clarify the other's status as consciousness. One must attack the other in order to know if he is a human being, by pushing him towards his death. Thus every one also shows himself to himself as a totality only by going to his death, by showing himself to the other as someone who is willing to renounce his life. Only thus does one appear for the other, as well as for oneself, absolutely. Calling a halt to the move before death means that consciousness has neither shown itself as totality nor recognized the other as such.

There is an apparent contradiction in the recognition demanded by consciousness: the recognition is of consciousness being-for-itself as totality in the other consciousness. But insofar as the first consciousness is realized objectively, it must destroy the other consciousness in which it is recognized by aiming to kill it. Therefore the recognition is a form of dialectical eradication. Consciousness exists only in the act of it being recognized by an other, and that means it must necessarily have as its goal the death of both the other and itself. Its only existence is through the reality of death. Putting one's life at risk is the condition for being human, and only through risking one's life does man understand that he is mortal in the sense that he cannot exist outside his animal existence, which supports self-consciousness. Therefore the slave is also human, since he recognizes his essential finiteness at the moment he experiences the fear of death, the death that confronts him during the struggle for recognition.

Here we reach a central point in Lacan's use of Hegel, *which aims to substantiate consciousness by the force of negation*. The interpretations of the Hegelian concept of the struggle to the death, then, suggest that death attests to the presence of negation in the moment when consciousness is formed, and that consciousness can position itself in various ways in this moment of formation. In Hegel, the divide between two possible positions vis-à-vis death is not presented as a matter of choice or point of view: in both cases the choice implies death. Lacan stresses this point, connecting the moment of constituting consciousness with the structure of language. Lacan examines the Hegelian position in the face of death by establishing a connection between the life-and-death struggle and the fundamental alienation of the subject of language.

The subject constituted in language decides in favour of a binary signifier that on one side produces meaning and on the other side loses being: "when the subject appears somewhere as meaning, he is manifested elsewhere as 'fading,' as disappearance. There is, then, one might say, a matter of life and death between the unary signifier and the subject, qua binary signifier, cause of his disappearance."[51] The moment a subject is constituted is a traumatic moment of determination and disappearance. Only because the subject is a subject of desire under the rule of language, language signifies the necessary split between what language presentifies and what it compels to disappear. The struggle for life or death is hence the struggle to represent desire by way of the

signifier, which makes something disappear at the moment of its constitution. The binary signifier has a structure analogous to that of the
struggle for death: the struggle is necessary in order to create a *difference* between life and death. Following Hegel and Kojève's reading of
him, we can see why Lacan claims that the struggle is a moment of cut,
an interval in which the living being is distinguished from its immanent death. Equally, one can point to the difference between what is
represented of being in the social relation (here the social relation is
represented through being in language) and what is eradicated in order
for the dialectic of conciousnesses to take place. Death that awaits both
master and slave is needed in order to differentiate between the two
consciousnesses: each is positioned differently in the minimal interval
created between the moment of choice (and constitution of consciousness) and the moment of death.

In order to capture the interval between life and death, in his seminar on "The Hegelian Clinic" François Régnault gives the example of
someone called upon to choose whether to die by a firing squad or on
a guillotine (a choice whose historical meaning Régnault describes as
well).[52] This example shows that at the moment of the decision how to
die, an interval of freedom opens up. What is the nature of this freedom
in the face of death? The moment of choosing a way to die is a moment
in which meaning is chosen over being; in this sense the struggle to the
death is the struggle for meaning through which the difference between
consciousnesses, a difference eradicated by death, is yet sustained.

The struggle creates the freedom to choose at a moment of enforced choice, a
freedom that conditions the separation between two consciousnesses:
the one that chooses freedom without life, and the one that chooses
life without freedom (although the nature of the enforced choice means
that the difference will not be measured by its end result, which will be
death in any case). In other words, Hegel provides the justification for
the binary structure of a disjunction (*the vel of alienation*[53]), of "either/or"
by which the subject's position in language (in relation to the signifier) is
constituted as a position of alienation. For Lacan, the alienation through
which man enters language and civilization is tantamount to the alienation by which one enters the position of master or of slave. This entry
marks the moment of enforced choice: if he chooses freedom, the slave
will lose both his life and his freedom; if he chooses life, he will lose his
freedom. The life-and-death struggle isolates the moment of freedom
in which the subject is forced to choose, because only in this struggle is
the difference between living and dying articulated, when one is willing

to stake one's life and the other refuses. Freedom is marked in the life-and-death struggle, a struggle whose end is foretold: for the slave – no freedom without life, and therefore he is left without freedom but with his life (which hardly makes a life under these circumstances). For the master – no life without freedom, and therefore he is ready to risk his life for freedom. Freedom leads consciousness through death and marks the moment of fatal choice since the subject's fate is always death, the disappearance of being. Freedom is that minimal interval that is not erased under the binary signifier, that is, an interval that exists at the moment one decides between life and death:

> The whole business of this term freedom, which certainly merits the description of phantom, is played out. What the subject has to free himself of is the aphanisic effect of the binary signifier ... it is a question of nothing else in the function of freedom.[54]

There is something fatal in this choice, Lacan says, precisely because, as in the division of chromosomes, the choice is unavoidable. The fatal dimension becomes clear if we put death, as Hegel did, on one side of the equation: death or freedom. The resultant effect is that the only freedom is the freedom to die. That is, the presence of death (a life-and-death struggle) turns any choice into a choice of death – even the slave's choice of life is a choice of life without freedom, that is to say, a symbolic death tantamount to meaningless life. But since death cannot be chosen, the question reverts to being a question about the discussed struggle and about what this struggle attains.[55]

Lacan answers it by ascribing the status of an ideational representative (*Vorstellungsrepräsentanz* – VR) to the life-and-death struggle. That is, what is being represented is representation, since the *object* of the representation, the drive, is repressed. The life-and-death struggle is hence not a struggle about the represented life and death but about their representation and about what is revealed by this representation. Lacan illustrates this conditionality of the representative on the repression of the represented through the example of diplomats who represent their country. In order to be a country's ambassador, the ambassador appears entirely under the aegis of the signifier, and anything beyond his representative position is repressed. In order to be a representative, he must be erased as the person being represented. Therefore VR concerns not *what is* being represented, but *what cannot* be represented because of the intervention of a signifier; likewise, the enforced choice within the logic of alienation reveals the presence of what the signifier cannot represent. Lacan wants to show that the Hegelian consciousnesses' struggling for life-or-death is not related to the fact that they repress or are unconscious of what is at stake. It is a matter of what necessarily stems from the link between consciousness and the object of its desire, an object that is rejected at the moment in which consciousness – be it of the master or of the slave – chooses one of the signifiers. The life-and-death struggle is, therefore, the moment in which we encounter the negated object of desire, demonstrated through the enforced choice imposed on the subject.

As already noted, Lacan describes the life-and-death struggle in Hegel in terms of alienation (the subject loses his being when choosing meaning and freedom). Regarding the binary signifier that makes the represented disappear, Lacan defines the freedom to choose in terms of what is being given away: no-thing without something else. In the slave: no freedom without life, but in fact without freedom he will have no life. In the passage from one signifier to another, the first demand is lost: if you obtain life through freedom, you lose freedom. Lacan says:

> When the subject appears somewhere as meaning, he is manifested elsewhere as "fading," as disappearance ... The *Vorstellungsrepräsentanz* is the binary signifier ... That by which the subject finds the return way of the *vel* of alienation is the operation I called, the other day, separation. By separation, the subject finds, one might say, the weak point of the primal dyad of the signifying articulation, in so far as it is alienating in essence. It is in the interval between these two signifiers that resides the desire offered to the mapping of the subject in the experience of the discourse of the Other.[56]

In order for the signifier of the subject to appear in the field of the Other, the subject as being must be eradicated, given to *aphanisis*. The enforced choice means that this eradication (subtraction) of being is incurred under any choice of signifier/position. But *in the course of this subtraction an interval is created between the signifiers, an interval that signifies the subject himself, alive.* In other words, in this interval appears what is subtracted from the Other at the moment of choice, a part of being, an object. Thus, the subject finds himself again in the interval between the signifier that represents him, and what returns to him from the Other and represents (*Repräsentanz*) what has been subtracted from being. This interval can be illustrated for example by the childhood fantasy of the disappearance or death of the fantasizing child, a fantasy that creates an interval between his being eradicated and what comes back from the Other at that moment. The desire of the Other is discovered by the subject at that moment through the fantasy that answers the question of what will be missed by the other if he himself, the subject, disappears. "It is in so far as his desire is unknown, it is in this point of lack, that the desire of the subject is constituted. The subject ... comes back, then, to the initial point, which is that of his lack as such, of the lack of his *aphanisis*."[57] Insofar as the distance is preserved between the subject's desire and what comes back from the Other (in answer to the question of what will the Other lack of the subject if the latter is eradicated) – there the subject will encounter his subtracted being.

If we return to the different choices of the Hegelian master and slave, we will see that choosing death is common to both. What distinguishes the master is not that he chooses death when he is offered the choice between life and death; rather, what distinguishes him is that the master represents the absolute moment of terror as a moment of freedom. It is the master who demonstrates "how much radical alienation of freedom there is in the master himself."[58] In other words, freedom is the moment of being's intervention in the life-and-death struggle, which is based on an enforced choice imposed on both master and slave. What the Hegelian master reveals is Hegel's preliminary assumption – that at the root of being lies absolute knowledge, knowledge that is attained through the successive syntheses that consciousness undergoes and that will lead it to the place where the radical split of the master will be sutured in a moment of alienation, a moment when knowledge is chosen rather than being, a moment "when no opening remains in the heart of the subject."[59]

Both the master and the slave will eventually die, and this death is the limit of the freedom to die. The death in question is not the death assumed by the master's alienating choice (of knowledge/meaning rather than being), that is, the death of the life-and-death struggle for meaning. The revelation of the master's essence is embodied in the moment of terror, when he faces the choice and is obliged to choose death. At that moment, in which he renounces his very being as living consciousness, the object that remains beyond all abstractions is revealed.

It was Hegel who first brought up the notion that the subject can only appear on the plane of meaning when he is eradicated as living consciousness. In this sense, the life-and-death struggle in Hegel does not present a moment of choice; rather, the struggle is the representative of the force that affirms an object beyond the choice. The object affirmed is the object of absolute knowledge posited at every distinct moment in the dialectic of consciousness: it is the object deferred from one state of consciousness to another, the object remaining beyond all subtractions and yet determining the difference between states of consciousnesses. That is, for Hegel, what emerges in every moment of alienation is the presence of the object in whose name consciousness will go beyond all the syntheses that have guided it. In Lacan, however, the object that is affirmed by virtue of negation of being is precisely the object that is the cause of the split between being and knowledge, rather than the cause of the possible suture between them.

C. Singularity

The point of departure for this chapter was the statement "Lacan against Hegel." We have seen how this conflict should be qualified in the context of the concept of otherness and death. In this section we examine another axis that underpins Lacan's use of Hegel. Lacan uses Hegel to broach a critical issue in psychoanalytical thought: one that concerns the ontological status of the subject. His frequent allusions to Hegel mark out an intermediate point between the universal and the particular, one that is essential to understanding Hegel and crucial for the way in which psychoanalysis locates its subject. I argue that it was Hegel who identified consciousness as a place of *singularity*, a place where consciousness is not subject to the opposition between the universal and the particular, and that the formulation of the place of singularity is one of the tangled issues in psychoanalysis, since only through the logic of singularity is it possible to establish a logic for desire.

While Hegel posits absolute knowledge that, once self-consciousness (becoming spirit) merges with it, will fully overlap with being, the *Phenomenology* deals mainly with a self-consciousness *that has not yet completed* its move. The aim is for spirit to have insight, for knowledge to know itself as absolute, and in order to achieve this aim, "the *length* of this path has to be endured, because, for one thing, each moment is necessary; and further, each moment has to be *lingered* over, because each is itself a complete individual shape, and one is only viewed in absolute perspective when its determinateness is regarded as a concrete whole, or the whole is regarded as uniquely qualified by that determination."[60]

Although it is difficult to conceive of a finite consciousness attaining absolute knowledge, this knowledge is postulated throughout the

Phenomenology as a guiding light, and it outlines the path that self-consciousness follows in each of the stages. For Hegel, it is absolute knowledge that makes it possible for consciousness, in its historical determination, to partake in the universal, and this raises the question: What is consciousness in relation to the universal in each of its different states? Before we examine the meaning of singularity in relation to self-consciousness – singularity as a way of also partaking in the universal – we should highlight an immediate implication that stems from the very supposition of absolute knowledge on the horizon of consciousness. It is precisely when we assume absolute knowledge, when we postulate the possibility of totalizing discourse from the sum of all the stages of alienation that consciousness undergoes, that self-consciousness in each and every stage is positioned in the place of "I did not know it was so," in the place where it necessarily does not know, that is, where consciousness and knowledge *do not coincide*. Lacan hints at this in one of the sessions of Seminar XII from 1964–65, and it will guide us in our present discussion.

The chapter on self-consciousness in Hegel's *Phenomenology* assumes a succession of moments of consciousness, each presenting a specific conflict or split between abstract certainty and a particular consciousness's mode of being. The link that connects these moments, and the difference between the various states of consciousness, suggests that Hegel perceives consciousness as neither particular nor universal. *Lacan seems to develop the concept of singularity on the basis of this status that consciousness receives in Hegel.* Lacan's interest in the concept of singularity and in the dialectic that underpins it touches the kernel of the psychoanalytic thought about the subject. The interest in singularity stems from and concerns the psychoanalytic commitment to the particular case (the patient in the clinical context) and this commitment's relationship with what can be called psychoanalytic knowledge (what Freud called *meta-psychology*, that is, the general foundations by which psychic reality is conceptualized). These require the concept of an individual who is located in between the particular and the universal. As already mentioned, Lacan finds in Hegel a similar orientation in defining the subject's singularity:

> The Individual, for Hegel, is a synthesis of the Particular and the Universal. Particularity would be purely "given," "natural," animal, were it not associated, in human individuality, with the universality of discourse and of action (the discourse proceeding from the action). Now the action

of the particular – and it is always a particular that acts – is truly universal only if it represents and realizes the "general will" of a "community" (*Gemeinwesen*), that is, in the last analysis, of a state. It is only by acting as [a] citizen (against his particular "private" interest) that [a] man is truly and really universal, even while remaining particular.[61]

It is around the issue of knowledge and the subject that, through Hegel, the desire of the subject as a singular rather than a universal or a particular desire will be presented. That is, Hegel provides Lacan with a key to locating the speaking being as a desiring subject, because for Hegel, self-consciousness's desire for knowledge is not universal in the same way that it is for Descartes, for example. It is not the desire that traditionally beats in the veins of the philosopher. The desire that Hegel is concerned with is singular in the sense that while it does not embody the particular conflict of consciousness with knowledge, at no stage is consciousness identified with absolute knowledge. Hegelian consciousness expresses a singular position towards knowledge, and each of the moments of consciousness marks its own unique position. Singularity implies a non-exchangeable relation of irreducible uniqueness; that is, although what is expressed for example by the consciousness of the slave is related to the sceptical position (another state of consciousness in the *Phenomenology*), it is impossible to reverse the roles. Since consciousness's move is divided into several moments, there *is no place for the universalization of consciousness*. None of the moments embody the accomplishment of self-consciousness in full self-realization.

Lacan, then, uses Hegel because the philosopher sheds light on the notion of singularity. The element that constitutes singularity is *difference* that can be formulated (as opposed to the difference between particularities, which cannot be formulated), and in Hegel difference is revealed when the consciousness of the master is distinguished from the consciousness of the slave. The master and the slave are two separate consciousnesses whose divergence embodies a fundamental difference between two different positions, two possibilities of representing the split between being and knowledge: being consciousness is being for-itself but also for another consciousness. This split hence stems from what consciousness does not know (the slave does not know the meaning of consciousness being for itself, while the master knows nothing of the other), although each consciousness is guided by the wish to be pure self-consciousness, that is, to assume absolute knowledge.

The master's consciousness embodies independent being for itself that categorically negates both the other consciousness on which it depends for recognition and the thing that, mediated by the other consciousness, serves it as a source of immediate enjoyment. The slave, on the other hand, embodies a dependent consciousness that cannot categorically negate either what is other to it or the thing that enslaves it. Following the move that stems from this difference between the slave and the master and from the completion of the dialectic that concerns them, Hegel presents two additional consciousnesses: the *stoical* and the *sceptical*.

While the master and the slave represented two different states of consciousness – one the freedom that stems from the removal of any otherness and that manifests itself in pure enjoyment, and the other the freedom that stems from the constitution of a living self-consciousness – each of the additional consciousnesses represents freedom in a different sense. In both it is a freedom based on an illusory overcoming of the split that had already erupted in the distinction between the slave and the master. Unlike the slave, the stoical consciousness is not dependent on one thing or another, but is subject to universal will. However, in seeing pure thought as the be all and end all, and itself as embodied as thought in every last thing, it remains detached and without influence on the differences embedded in life in general and in social life in particular. The content of experience is not influenced in any way by stoical thought. The stoical version of consciousness pushes out anything that is external and concrete by escaping to the internality of thought, to a self-sufficiency that makes no attempt to overcome the internal split. For this reason, stoical consciousness is left with abstract freedom and the stoical idea will later be realized by the sceptical consciousness.

The stoical withdrawal does not allow negation to be applied to the content of consciousness, whereas the sceptical consciousness does act on what is external to it, negating and casting doubt on everything that is not the selfness of consciousness.[62] "It is clear that just as Stoicism corresponds to the *Notion* of the *independent* consciousness which appeared as the lord and the bondsman relationship," writes Hegel, "so Scepticism corresponds to its *realization* as a negative attitude towards otherness, to desire and work."[63] Scepticism complements the abstract consciousness of the stoic, just as the consciousness of the slave complements that of the master, putting into practice the implications of the stoic position.

But the sceptical consciousness has another consequence: it *abolishes difference*, because it has negated anything that is different from it, any singularity that contrasts with consciousness's self-identity. What disappears with the sceptical consciousness is the definite element, or the moment of the split between consciousness and its other, since the distinct being in the other has been utterly negated from this position.[64] Everything that is essential in self-consciousness is subject to "absolute disappearance," and the sceptical consciousness finds itself vacillating between being an abstract and self-identical self-consciousness and being a contingent consciousness in the empirical world – a vacillation of which it is not conscious, but which leads to the appearance of a new consciousness.

We can thus say that the Hegelian difference between consciousnesses is conditioned on the negation entailed by each stage of consciousness, a negation that leads to the appearance of another consciousness, different from its predecessor. The *Hegelian difference* is neither being nor knowledge; it relies neither on particularity nor on universality, but rather on the subtraction of something that was entailed by another consciousness (e.g., the slave negates freedom entailed by the master consciousness, while the master negates the other consciousness, otherness being the constitutive aspect of bondage).

The stoical and sceptical consciousnesses are followed by the *unhappy consciousness*, which retains the split that was found in the master-and-slave dialectic and caused consciousness to be split in two – a split that was unconsciously present in the sceptical consciousness. This split resides in the unhappy consciousness, which is conscious of its presence and of the impossibility of overcoming it.

Each of the consciousnesses thus realizes a different dimension of the split between being and knowledge, and going through the entire move will require additional developments (which will be discussed in the following parts of the *Phenomenology*), before self-consciousness can realize itself to the full. This is because in order to attain such realization, consciousness will have to traverse the dialectical space between self-consciousness and being; that is, self-consciousness does not realize itself simply as I = I, since it had already recognized its otherness in the first stage of the dialectic. It therefore necessarily loses something whenever it appears as self-consciousness confronted with what is different from it.

This brief summary of the Hegelian overall move in the chapter on self-consciousness is intended to bring into focus the way in which the difference between consciousnesses is created by negation. The echo of this delineation of self-consciousness's vicissitudes by Hegel is found in Lacan in the dialectic he constructs for the subject of the unconscious. The dialectic is based on this statement: the signifier represents a subject for another signifier. This formula means that when the subject meets the signifier, something gets lost in this encounter. That is, the subject's relations with the signifier are relations that entail a loss, a loss that must be overcome so that a subject is found at the place of the signifier. "I describe as philosophical everything that tends to mask the radical character and the originating function of this loss," says Lacan. "Every dialectic, and specifically the Hegelian one, which tends to mask, which in any case points towards a recuperation of the effects of this loss is a philosophy."[65] In the Hegelian dialectic, whenever the subject appears as consciousness of a certain kind, something of this consciousness is lost in the other consciousness in order to constitute its own distinctness. The Hegelian consciousness realizes this idea of a necessary loss in every stage or modus of consciousness, but *the Hegelian move as a whole is meant to overcome or find a cure for the loss that has occurred*. This question then arises: How does psychoanalysis, in the spirit of Hegel, come to terms with rather than mask the presence of this loss?

The relation between the subject and the signifier touches on Lacan's constant and continued interest in logic and in the ways in which what is inscribed through universal and particular logical propositions exceeds (creates excess in relation to) these propositions' domain of applicability. Thus for example the universal proposition "all ravens are black" affirms the function and not the existence of what is included under the function (ravens). However, when this universal proposition is negated by "no raven is black," we discover that while the affirmative universal proposition can also be valid if the set of "ravens" is an empty set, the negative universal proposition negates the function (of being black) while affirming the domain to which the function applies (the set of ravens).[66] This is relevant to our present discussion because Lacan was greatly occupied – and not just in relation to Hegel – with the question of how logical negation leads to the affirmation of singular existence, of what belongs neither to the universal order of existence nor to the particular one. If we examine this in the Hegelian context, we can say in relation to Hegel that "all consciousnesses that are self-consciounesses have absolute knowledge," but Hegel also shows that "no self-consciousness has absolute knowledge" (or "for no state of consciousness is there absolute knowledge"). Here, as in the case of the ravens, the general proposition does not posit the existence of a self-consciousness for which the function of having absolute knowledge holds; only the negation of the particular proposition assumes the existence of such a consciousness. What can be inferred from this is that for Hegel, self-consciousness is neither universal (because it contradicts what is posited in the universal proposition) nor particular (to which a particular proposition applies); rather, the states of consciousness reflect a different order of relation between consciousness and knowledge – *the order of singularity*.

The subject of psychoanalysis is characterized as belonging to the order of the lack; it is what the subject lacks that turns it into a particular case. But while the lack of the Hegelian consciousness stems from self-consciousness's incompleteness in relation to the absolute order of *Geist*, in psychoanalysis the lack is inscribed through a trait that is taken from the general reserve of signifiers – through the proper name, the pronoun, or any other form designed to number or name. But if the signifier belongs to the universal order, how does it inscribe the lack of the particular subject – or alternatively, what does the name or trait inscribe, if it does not inscribe the particular being? Lacan suggests that a trait, like a proper name, does not belong to the particular order or to any other order that falls under the binary of the universal and the particular.[67] The trait inscribes something of the particular precisely through universality, just as when we propose that "there are no black ravens," it is by negating the universal ("all ravens are black") that the existence of some indefinite raven that is not black is inscribed, that is, a singular case that does not fall within the function's general domain of applicability, but is also not a specific raven.

When Lacan refers to the position of the analyst in relation to the subject in this seminar (XII) devoted to crucial problems of psychoanalysis, he defines this position as one bound to the empirical element that enables something of the order of singularity to appear, in contrast to the position of the scientist, who is bound to the order of the universal. In line with the principle that states that the subject is represented through one signifier for another signifier, we can say that the signifier itself does not suffice to individualize the field of the subject, since the signifier in itself belongs to the universal order. What emerges of the order of the subject emerges in the interval between signifiers, in the subtraction that occurs in the relation between one signifier and another, a subtraction which is neither of the two but that affirms what exists in the interval between them.

In order to illustrate this Lacan brings the example of a woman who leaves her lover signs about the possibility of a meeting. If the curtain on the woman's window is drawn it means she is alone, and in addition, nearby on the windowsill she places a number of flowerpots to indicate the time when she will be free. These signs, like a code, are meant to be translated in order to summon someone specific to respond to them, although the signs themselves (a flowerpot, a window) have no given significance or uniqueness. What emerges here, then, of the order of the singular subject, and how? The subject manages, through undistinguished signifiers taken from the universal signifying order, to transmit her singular presence, a singularity that is inscribed as such for a specific other who is summoned through the operation. That is, the singular knowledge that is transmitted is not dependent on a private code known only to the subject, nor is it given in the signifier; rather, it is created in the interval between "being alone" and "five o'clock." This is the meaning of a subtraction that constitutes a subject, since it is embodied in the negation of the signifier as representing a particular subject, but also in its negation as a signifier of universal applicability.

Singularity is the order in which the subject locates herself, where there is nothing that stands as the equivalent for the gap that is opened between the signifiers (Who is alone – Seul – at five o'clock? No one in particular). The subject, Lacan says, creates the link between the signifiers just as the code number creates the link between a lock and a key. Without the number the key will not work and the lock will not open, just as without the woman being alone at five o'clock nothing will happen. There is only one number that can make the lock work – the number, or the combination of numbers with which the subject is identified. There is nothing universal in this subject, since either she has the number or she does not, and there is only one subject who has it. The key, says Lacan, plays here a suggestive, even amusing role, because it represents a kind of remainder, something small that sets things in motion, that is not needed in the whole business but is nonetheless indispensable. In practice, the key embodies what supports in a real and effective sense the point of the subject's intervention.[68] This is the way of using the signifier in order to bring the subject to the place where he says "I did not know it was so," that is, to the place where he carries a knowledge that only later will emerge as a knowledge he unwittingly had all along, just as with Hegel's self-consciousness:

> The status of what is articulated there is in a way independent of any fact
> whosoever: it is offered at first as something signified, as this beyond ...

Something emerges which is of the order of the subject only, which does not have, in any way, any real correspondent; as I told you: what is it to be alone, in the real, what is alone.[69]

If the other consciousness created the difference between consciousness and self-consciousness, and the struggle created the difference between living and dying, singularity creates the difference between universality and particularity. Singularity is revealed where the blind spots in knowledge are such that they cannot be negated. "Not all ravens are black" can be understood as a universal proposition of negation, but this negation creates a blind spot with respect to those ravens that are not black, and the latter cannot be subject to negation, nor can it be particularized. Thus, describing the subject's singularity as lying between, on the one hand, the universality of the necessary relation between a key and a lock, and on the other, the particularity of the one code that can serve in this case, clarifies that the knowledge of analysis is the knowledge that appears in the gap between what is known and cannot be articulated, and what is signified/said. This gap is where the place of the subject is revealed, just as in Hegel the singular position of consciousness is revealed in the gap between its self-certain presence, and the question of the knowledge about what is not contained in this self-presence. The status of universal knowledge, the status of knowledge as such, is not independent of the singular place the subject takes in relation to it – and this supposition is common to Hegel and Lacan.

Charting Lacan's use of Hegel reveals that the point of divergence between Hegel and psychoanalysis is located by Lacan much further than it seems, and precisely for this reason we will have to examine where *the difference between them is revealed as irreducible, being the difference between the philosopher and the psychoanalyst*. Hegel's subject is not a subject who has a universal desire for knowledge, but a subject who appears as a singular point of departure in relation to knowledge (therefore each of the states of consciousness that Hegel describes defines a different singularity in the relation between consciousness and knowledge). While Hegel is credited with formulating the foundations of the logic of desire that allows singularity to appear, this is also the point at which the gap between psychoanalysis and Hegelianism opens up:

What is ... what we will call the status of knowledge? For after all ... the psychoanalyst is summoned, in the situation, as being the subject who is supposed to know. What he has to know is not a classificatory knowledge, is not knowledge of the general, is not the knowledge of a zoologist. What he has to know is defined by this primordial level where there is a subject who is led ... to this moment of emergence, which is articulated: "I did not know."[70]

Singularity for Hegel means that at the end of the move, what the subject does not know will still enable absolute knowledge to emerge, even if this knowledge is subject to the rhythm of the moves of self-consciousness. Conversely, the position of the subject of the unconscious is always that of "I did not know it was so"; that is, there is no accumulation of knowledge, but the knowledge of the subject is revealed in the gap between what is known now and the reality of not-knowing prior to knowing:

> This I of the "I did not know," where was it and what was it before knowing? This is indeed a propitious moment to evoke the dimension at which there culminates and tips over the whole classical tradition in so far as there is completed in it a certain status of the subject. All the same, there are many among you here who know where Hegel proposes the completion of history in this incredibly derisory myth of absolute knowledge. What could be meant by this idea of a totalizing discourse, totalizing what? The sum of the forces of alienation through which a subject would have passed, moreover, you know well that it is ideal since, moreover, it is not conceivable that it should be realized as such by any individual.[71]

In Hegel there is no possibility of universalizing the singular consciousness; there is only a vain pursuit of it, through an individual embodiment. Every consciousness embodies the relation with this element singularly, like the unhappy consciousness that finds itself desiring and working without ever finding the certainty of its own existence, only the certainty of the fact that it is split. "But having learned from experience that the grave of its actual unchangeable Being has no actuality, that the vanished individuality, because it has vanished, is not the true individuality, consciousness will abandon its quest for the unchangeable individuality as an actual existence, or will stop trying to hold on to what has vanished. Only then is it capable of finding individuality in its genuine or universal form."[72]

Hegelian consciousness forever falls in the rupture between the accumulation of knowledge into universal knowledge, and unknowing, which prevents the transition or continuity from one moment of consciousness to the next, except through negation. In the seminar "The Names of the Father," Lacan alludes to Hegel in a way that sums up exactly this point: the universal can only be established through accumulation, and the particular appears as contingent. "The entirety of Hegelian dialectic is made to stop that gap and show, in a prestigious act of transmutation, how the universal, by way of the scansion of the *Aufhebung*, can come to be particularized."[73] In other words, Hegel's dialectic is not a description of universal states of consciousness, but an accumulation of contingent situations that create the punctuation, the metrical scansion of what is neither universal nor particular. This is because both the universal and the particular, each in its own way, lose difference as a footing. None of the intermediary stages are considered essential in relation to absolute knowledge, while from the point of view of particularity, consciousness knows nothing about what is other from it. That is, just as pure self-consciousness for which A = A erases the presence of any difference, so the consciousness that settles for only its self-certainty loses the difference that is found in the other. Therefore the stoical consciousness, for example, which sees itself as free self-consciousness guided by thought alone, is fettered with a difference that is not specific. And this, for Hegel, is the way of qualifying the singular blindness, yet essential place, of the stoical consciousness.

We can therefore say that consciousness in Hegel is always a consciousness that does not know how to connect the object of desire, the alien, unchangeable element, for which it aims, with its material being. Thus, for example, the unhappy consciousness does not know that its feeling towards the alienated existence of something inside it is also the substantiation of its own existence. But as we have seen, it is precisely through the specific blindness of each consciousness that Hegel points to the principle of singularity in self-consciousness.

Singularity is a sign of difference inscribed in the universal realm: it appears where the universal element insists on maintaining an irreducible difference for each state of consciousness. That is, singularity appears where a signifier of universal knowledge creates, in relation to another signifier, an interval for a distinct consciousness. We can therefore say with Lacan that the subject who is represented (*Repräsentanz*) through a trait is revealed in the gap between signifiers. The singular trait is like the relationship between fire and smoke: that is, it embodies what eludes both universal knowledge and particularity. Singularity is the appearance of the living being, the appearance of the absolute difference as sign.

Singularity, it should be spelled out, is where the debate between Hegel and Lacan stops being philosophical. Singularity is the psychoanalytic aim, while for philosophy singularity demands to be overcome; therefore in the Hegelian discourse singularity (states of consciousness) will lead to the absolute suture called: spirit.

Conclusion

On the steps of the Pantheon in 1970 Lacan was asked if the ideas he brought from the practice of psychoanalysis gave him something that could not be found elsewhere. His reply was that these ideas can probably also be found in philosophy. Thus, for example, anxiety, which according to psychoanalysis plays a central role in the psychic economy, is a key concept in Kierkegaard. Is it therefore justified to place Lacan in the philosophical tradition? To see his psychoanalysis as a "transcendental psychoanalysis," as someone suggested in response? The difference, says Lacan, is that for him anxiety is not a concept, an idea that can be located in the history of ideas. But then, in what way can psychoanalytic ideas be valid for philosophy? This question is raised by one of the audience members, remarking that he has the impression that Lacan is attacking philosophy.

Lacan's reply to this remark offers a possible formulation of the complex relation between Lacan and philosophy:

> I was asked just a minute ago whether I believed that things I recount may not be problematic. I said I did. My sole motivation for advancing them is because of a precise experience, the psychoanalytic experience. If it weren't for that I would consider that I had neither the right, nor above all the desire to extend the philosophical discourse very much beyond the moment at which it was most properly effaced … That doesn't transform it. It's a different discourse. This is what I am trying to show you by reminding those who have no idea about analytic experience, to the entire extent that I believe it to be so, that this is, all the same, its currency. This is where I start from. Otherwise this discourse would not have an aspect that is philosophically so problematic … The person I was talking about before

places me as a kind of point of emphasis, locates me at the center of some kind of mixture, of fracturing, opening up of philosophical discourse. It's not badly done, it's done in an extremely sympathetic manner, but my initial response – perhaps I will change my views on it – I said to myself, "And yet, to place me in that heritage is quite some Entstellung, quite some displacement, away from the import of what I am capable of saying."[1]

Not only does Lacan locate psychoanalysis in a *necessarily* problematic place in relation to philosophy, he also places psychoanalysis in a position that adjoins and even merges with the interest of philosophy. But the necessity is not one-sided, and Lacan points to two essential layers that determine the necessity of the psychoanalytic gaze for philosophy: (1) it is psychoanalysis that enables the difference between it and philosophy to be a *productive difference*, since (only) psychoanalysis draws philosophy beyond its disciplinary borders; and (2) psychoanalysis is located at the opening that is created when the philosophical discourse is extended beyond its normal borders. All of this makes Lacan conclude that the necessity does not produce reciprocity, nor does it create a *relation* between the philosophical discourse and psychoanalysis; for this reason, Lacan is not a philosopher (nor is he an anti-philosopher) and cannot be placed in the philosophical heritage.

Lacan's words are puzzling, since the claim that he is attacking philosophy is not unfounded. After all, in that same seminar he also claims that the philosophical discourse is the discourse of a master, a discourse adept at stealing knowledge from the slave, since the philosopher himself, as the agent of the discourse, has no knowledge. In this seminar from 1970 Lacan discusses the status of knowledge in relation to discourse, and knowledge appears as especially problematic precisely in the master's discourse, since the master encounters the contrast – which exists in relation to any knowledge – between *know-how* and *episteme* in its strict sense. The slave knows without knowing that he knows, and one can know that the slave knows only if one asks him the right questions.[2] *Episteme*, therefore, is established through the inquiry, by purifying knowledge of the actual toil of the subject. In this context the philosopher appears as a special kind of master, and therefore – as we have already seen in the chapter on Plato – the philosopher wishes to extract knowledge from the slave, in order to turn the slave's *practical knowledge* into *transmittable knowledge*. That is, the philosopher extracts knowledge without becoming the subject who carries it,[3] which explains why the philosopher is the master who creates the (historical and structural) shift from the master's discourse to the university discourse. The philosopher has the role of changing the status of knowledge from knowledge that served the ancient master but was not formulated as knowledge, to knowledge as something that is open to all. But making knowledge itself the end all and be all, as happens in the university, reveals that this knowledge is merely bureaucracy, since it turns out that knowledge is never the knowledge of everyone (*savoir de tout*), but is rather an allegedly all-knowledge (*savoir-tout*), a tyrannical force controlled by a master and producing anxiety for the subject who can never appropriate this all-knowledge.[4]

Now on the steps of the Pantheon, in contrast to these claims, not only is philosophy not presented as procuring truth to be controlled by a master of knowledge, but in a certain way it even regains its traditional place as the mother of the sciences, whereas psychoanalysis's role is defined as providing an opening for truth at the heart of philosophy. Lacan claims here that it is the analyst's position that makes it possible not to forget philosophy when coming to psychoanalysis, since on the face of it these are two contrasting world views. Instead of psychoanalysis being the vanishing point of the philosopher's relevance, it is precisely psychoanalysis that extends the philosophical discourse *beyond* this vanishing point, to the place where this discourse can be heard anew. The suggestion is that without philosophy it is impossible to understand the position of someone who is interested in the analytic experience, because the analytic discourse locates itself in the opening, in the crisis point where philosophy will emerge.

This duality is the crux of Lacan's position towards philosophy. While philosophy is a bureaucracy of knowledge, a procuress of truth, it also stipulates the very existence of psychoanalysis and is dependent on psychoanalysis to reveal what can be a philosophical truth. This duality is also a warning against a too easy diagnosis of the relationship between the psychoanalytic discourse and philosophy. Lacan is responsible for creating an opening in the philosophical discourse, but this does not mean he should be listed as a philosopher, or that the psychoanalytic discourse can be measured as a philosophy, or that the way to diagnose philosophy from the psychoanalytical perspective moves between disciplinary autism and being subject to a psychoanalytic critique and diagnosis.

France, Lacan points out, philosophers travel, like Descartes, for example, who wandered all over Europe; whereas in Germany the philosophers are settled in universities – which may explain how it

occurred to Hegel that the kernel of social revolution can be found in
the slave. Only from the academic armchair can it seem conceivable
that the wretched slaves of the Industrial Revolution, during a period of
hard labour and exploitation unto death, can be gripped by the discovery of the revolutionary truth, by the recognition that it is they who are
making history and that the master is there only to begin that process.

Ostensibly, such a fall into the trap of the truth in ideas cannot occur
in psychoanalysis. Freud spoke about analysis as the love of truth, but
if this truth instils anything in us, it is the signifier "death," where all
concepts fail. Freud tried to describe the radical nature of the truth of
psychic reality, which is inscribed through repetition in language, as
a death drive. Is death the real face of truth, or is truth really about
the slave who is emancipated from his enslavement by the fruits of his
labour? Lacan replies that while it is better not to be carried away by
Hegel's truth, neither should we be carried away by Freud's. Truth has
several faces, and as analysts we must be a little suspicious towards
it, not go crazy for truth, for the first pretty face we encounter at the
curve in the road. We must not forget that Hegel's historical truth was
uttered from the depth of an armchair not so different from the place
from which the analyst Freud uttered his ideas.

Nevertheless, the truth spoken of by psychoanalysis is not a truth
that is revealed, but one that is experienced, and therefore it always
encounters something that cannot be shown through symbolic articulation. This is why the love of truth takes us to government, education,
and analysis – all impossible practices in the sense that it is impossible to formulate their truth or the object of their action. Philosophy is
not counted among the impossible professions because it is concerned
with the articulation of truth, and it will formulate its truth even if this
formulation amounts to nothing more than an attempt to suture the
impossible relation between knowledge and being. This is the limitation imposed on the philosopher's love of the truth.

But the philosopher is not the only one drifting because of her love
of truth; but it is only at the place where she positions herself will the
love of the truth make the real slip between her fingers. For truth always
stands between us and the real, and precisely for this reason, the analyst
cannot avoid the discourse of the master, the philosopher's discourse.

Glossary of Lacanian Terms

affect: we should distinguish between effect and affect. The former refers to a result or a consequence. The latter refers to an affection that has a psychic consequence in the form of a mood that is not an emotion or a feeling, but transcends the distinction between body and psyche: such as anxiety, fear, guilt, shame, and so on – psychic representations of affections that also find their expression on the corporeal level.

    Lacan sees affects as psychic signs of the way in which the subject locates himself in relation to the Other. For example: anxiety erupts where the subject cannot locate himself in the Other; shame and melancholy indicate that the object located in the Other has cast its shadow over the subject; fear is a way to locate anxiety by defining an object for this affect, for example, by replacing the anxiety about death with fear of a certain disease.

agalma: a term whose origin is Greek and that appears in Plato's *Symposium* in relation to Socrates. The literal meaning of the *agalma* is a piece of jewellery or a precious object, and Lacan uses this term to signify the precious object imputed to the Other, which consequently becomes the cause of the Other arousing desire. In the context of Socrates, the precious object is identified with the knowledge attributed to Socrates, this knowledge causing Socrates's interlocutor to desire him as the one holding knowledge. In its general usage the *agalma* is therefore the object that the subject believes his desire is directed to.

    The *agalma* serves Lacan to signify the attraction to Socrates as someone who is loved for his wisdom; but since Socrates often refuses to credit himself with this knowledge or to appear as the owner of knowledge, his *agalma*, the knowledge-treasure he holds, appears as an undefined object whose existence is cast in doubt. This position is analogous in all its aspects to the position of the psychoanalyst.

alienation and separation: "the subject's desire is the desire of the Other," says Lacan, and this condemns the subject to a position of necessary structural alienation. The human organism is not made only of instincts, but is a being whose survival is made possible by the use of language and of the signifier. Such is for example the baby who cries and thereby calls the person who cares for his well-being. The human subject necessarily appears as a speaking being. Speech and the use of signifiers is designed to summon the unknown Other, who governs the language. the signifiers, in order to constitute the field in which the subject can appear. Lacanian alienation is thus the consequence of the subject being the subject of a language from which he is alienated, but that it alone can locate him assigning him a place as a speaking being.

As opposed to alienation, separation denotes the moment in which the human subject qualifies this subjectness and creates an interval between himself and the Other. This is a moment in which the subject can, for example, testify to the pleasure he draws from the seemingly tormenting symptom; a moment that reveals the singularity of being at a distance from the Other, though necessarily in the same field of desire.

anxiety: one of the first affects that Lacan refers to, following anxiety in Freud. Anxiety is an affect in the sense that it does not carry a meaning or refer to a psychic state or an internal emotion, but is a bodily affection (anxiety grips the subject) that is psychically inscribed. Anxiety is a primordial affect in the sense that it does not involve the subject's encounter with the Other, but rather the primordiality of his encounter with the object or with its disappearance. An excessive proximity to the object-cause, or the danger of its appropriation by the Other who determines desire, produces a psychic affect in being, an affect that is identified with anxiety.

castration: a subtraction that conditions and at the same time regulates the possibilities of pleasure for human beings. Lacan distinguishes between an imaginary castration – which has a limited role in Freud in the distinction between the girl's penis envy and the boy's castration anxiety, a difference that is based on the imaginary subtraction of an organ – and a symbolic castration, which means that any actual pleasure is necessarily partial in relation to the possibility of absolute pleasure. Castration in all its senses is inscribed in the psychic reality through the symptom and the other psychic formations.

death drive: this drive refers to every organism's tendency towards the absolute element in its being. In fact, the death drive is the appropriate name for all the drives, since it is contained in any drive (see under **drive**) as the constant force in it that insists on reaching its destination beyond the living being's interest in prolonging its existence.

desire: a fundamental element in the life of the psyche. It exists within a paradox: man's desire is based on an impasse, and it is the impasse that feeds this desire. Therefore, what is impossible for woman – namely, to say what is the object of her desire (which is Lacan's object *a*) – is also what makes this object an object-cause. Thus it is this impossibility that gives rise to different forms of *jouissance* that represent the unique solution that each subject invents for himself in order to nevertheless attain satisfaction. Desire in psychoanalysis is the epistemological and ethical basis of the human being: it is what determines the life force, but also the paths of *jouissance*, which do not necessarily coincide with a person's intentions, benefit, or well-being. The ethical element is embodied mainly in the fact that man does not necessarily want what he desires.

discourse: the structure of the move or the event of an agent/actor's appeal to an addressee/other, when this move or event leads to an encounter with an object that was not given in advance, and to the creation of a truth as its product. A discourse is a move or an event that is linguistic in the broad sense, that is, the discourse can appear in the form of speech, act, or thought, or alternatively be embodied in the position from which a speech event takes place – an event of action or an event of thought. Therefore, discourse represents a social bond: it is a structure that reveals the logic behind the subject's involvement with the Other.

For example: the university discourse is a discourse in which knowledge itself appears as an agent. This knowledge appeals to the student as the addressee who should be taught it. This move encounters a subject that cannot adopt this knowledge, because it is a universal, standardized knowledge, from which the subject is alienated. The outcome of this encounter is not only that the student's being is conquered by knowledge (in relation to which he remains failing), but also that a truth is created from such a dominant position of knowledge – the truth that this knowledge is a master-knowledge – that a master triggered the whole move in the first place.

drive: drive is a Freudian concept by origin indicating that the subject of psychoanalysis appears around a moment in which a bodily element is ascribed with a psychic presence. The drive is the Freudian expression of the fact that the human need is not located in the organic-biological dimension and is forever trapped in a psychic dimension. Thus, the drive captures the movement between the bodily source and the object of satisfaction, such as for example between hunger and what satisfies it; the drive testifies to a link between the two that is no longer purely biological. By assuming the primacy of the drive, the human subject is always already bound with a moment that transcends the distinction between bodily reality and psychic inscription. This stems from the fact that the human being comes into the world incapable of taking care of its needs; this incapacity creates a distance between the need and its satisfaction; and it leads to the inscription of the need as drive.

In his reading of the Freudian drive, Lacan emphasizes that the drive's movement is necessarily deflected in relation to the drive's aim, that is, the force of the drive moves the human being towards a source of satisfaction, yet one is never satisfied. The drive is therefore a deferred movement in relation to the original object of satisfaction: it is impossible to identify the object of the oral drive, only a partial embodiment of such an object can be identified; and it is similarly impossible to point to an object that sums up the genital drive. According to the psychoanalytic approach, this reality of the drive is inscribed in symptoms or in the erotic condition that operates in relations of love, or in any choice of an object that involves desire – all these are representatives of the drive.

empty signifier: this is the signifier in its pure state, a signifier whose effectiveness stems from the fact that it does not carry a specific value or meaning, and can be ascribed with different values, which all together and each separately fail to capture it. This is because the empty signifier, by definition, has no meaning and carries no conceptual content.

Such is, for example, the signifier "Law," which is an empty signifier that can be ascribed with different values and itself has no value, as we learn from Kafka's story "Before the Law." The empty signifier has a crucial role in the Lacanian algebra because it refuses any meaning or thematization, and therefore it always imposes an alien presence in the psychic reality.

ideal: the ideal has two meanings in Lacan: one concerns the image of the ego as whole (the ideal ego, like the I whose image is reflected in the mirror, is unified and whole, and thus serves as an object of identification); that is, the ideal ego is an object of imaginary identification.

The other meaning of ideal concerns the subject's desire for what was subtracted from it and is located in the Other, that is, it is a symbolic identification with an object that always eludes definition or imaginary attainment. The ego ideal can be located in an idea, but is also equivalent to the thing that causes the Other to pose a demand, a requirement, or a desire towards the subject. For example, the teacher's demand from the student posits an object of identification that the student desires to attain. The desire for this object – the desire to attain the ideal of knowledge – is directed at the teacher as the one in whom the object of identification, an undefined and unknown object, is located.

Identification: a psychic mechanism that constitutes identity on the basis of a move in which the subject "finds himself" in the Other, be it in the mirror image or in the alienated, incomprehensible Other, in which the subject locates his identity. Identification in psychoanalysis marks the resolution of the Oedipal complex, since it is through identification with the father, the figure that to begin with is the rival, that the subject's identity is constituted. Identification means that the desire of the Other is identified as the desire of the subject, and the object that causes desire in the Other incites the desire of the subject (*see also* Ideal).

imaginary: one of the three orders named by Lacan (the imaginary, the symbolic, the real) to designate the speaking subject's location in the world of the signifiers. The imaginary order appears in Lacan for the first time in relation to the mirror, when the subject perceives his reflected image as his faithful representation: "It's me over there!" That is, the imaginary order concerns the relationship to an other perceived as one's fellow man. This order is based on the signifier in the dimension in which it maintains a relationship of similarity, reflection or representation with the signified or with meaning. Therefore, in the imaginary dimension the subject can posit a relation of symmetry, reciprocity, or similarity with the other. The imaginary order points to a necessary dimension in language and in any form of thought or action. At the same time, it is also an order that enables the subject to camouflage the fact of her split, to ignore the fact that her consciousness is partly alien to her, that knowledge is not present for her, and that her action conflicts with the intention that was posited at its beginning and with the aim that guides it.

jouissance: *jouissance* designates for Lacan what Freud described as "beyond the pleasure principle," that is, the regular and repetitive element of the drive in Freud, which is a-dialectic. *Jouissance* is therefore what is positioned at the opposite pole of the signifier (since the signifier is trapped in the dialectic of what is said in relation to what cannot be said). *Jouissance* is beyond the pleasure principle mainly because it attests that satisfaction can be found in what appears as suffering, that is beyond the differentiation between pleasure and displeasure. *Jouissance* in Lacan replaces Freud's dualistic formulations and emphasizes the drive's monistic element. *Jouissance*, while marking the element of vitality, is also the carrier of evil, of pain. Within the satisfaction of the drive that it constitutes, it includes what Freud touched on through the dualism of the ego-libido and object-libido, Eros and Thanatos, the life drives and the death drive and so on. In its essence it is therefore the autistic – "headless" – kernel

in any satisfaction of the drive. Any action, thought or speech of a human being are practices of jouissance. Jouissance is thus a fundamental principle that
determines the psychic reality and the trajectories in which being will move.
Jouissance is the principle of psychic regularity.

master signifier: a signifier that constitutes the start of the chain or the beginning of the series of signifiers, but at the same time is not part of this chain
or series, like for example zero in the series of whole numbers, which is the
beginning of the series and therefore part of it, but is simultaneously not
equivalent to other elements in the series, and is an element only in the sense
that it conditions the appearance of the series as a whole. Thus for example
"Justice" is a master signifier of the legal system and its laws, without itself
being able to constitute a concept or part of a conceptual system, being rather
a signifier from which the regulation of all the concepts of justice, law and
judiciary stems. And finally, the "father" is similarly a master signifier of
the Oedipal drama, but is neither given to conceptualization nor points to
a biological or personal identity; the father is the cause of the possibility of
constituting a subject who identifies, distrusts, loves, and desires.

matheme: the formal representation of the psychic logic. The matheme is a
mathematical-thematic unit through which Lacan gives formal embodiment
to the foundation of the psychic reality. Lacan constructs the mathemes by
using fixed elements: $ – for the subject of the unconscious; a – for the object
of the drive or of desire; A – for the big Other; D – for the demand; d – for
desire. In addition, Lacan makes use in the mathemes of forms that express
a relation of containment, exclusion, and directionality. Through the mathemes Lacan tries to generate a form of transmission of an integral knowledge
that is liberated from the imaginary element.

object-cause: one of the values given to object *a*, an object invented by Lacan.
The object-cause is related to Freud's lost object, to the thing that is a cause of
desire – be it a desire for knowledge, for the beloved, or for truth. The combination of object and cause emphasizes that the cause is not a concept or an independent entity, but involves something that is a source of psychic necessity.
The object-cause is, therefore, a constitutive element in any psychic reality.

other, *autre*: the other is the other person who, although appearing as separate
from the I, is located as his double like a mirror reflection. The otherness of
this other is therefore based on relations of similarity, with all the range of
possibilities they offer: symmetry, reciprocity, solidarity, identification, and
communality, as well as rivalry, competition, hostility, and so on. Therefore
in small children, for example, there will be no difference between "I hit
him" and "he hit me."

Other, *Autre*: Other with a capital O is a function in relation to which the subject is inscribed in the social field. The "Big Other" can be the regularity of language and its signifiers, which create a community, a collective, or the law as such; it can also be some absolute element such as justice, *jouissance*, truth. Unlike the other, which is located in the imaginary register, this Other is located as a function in the symbolic dimension, defining and locating the subject on the social plane – for instance, as a man or a woman – and giving him his status as a speaking subject, as having desire, as having a legal status, etc.

pass: a Lacanian concept that denotes the event of assessing the end of an analysis. The Pass refers to the testimony through witnesses that the analysand gives to a "jury" concerning the analysis she has undergone. The Pass denotes the fact that the endpoint of analysis is a movement of separation, where the analysand can testify to her psychic position outside the analytic relationship. The Pass is therefore a way of inscribing the particularity of the subject within psychoanalytic knowledge, which like any knowledge is general and aspires to universality. For Lacan the Pass – confirming the end of the analysis – is also a way to say that the analysand encounters his desire as an analyst and testifies to it, thus adding his analysis to the knowledge of psychoanalysis.

phallic signifier: is also an empty signifier, because the phallus signifies an absence rather than a presence – of an organ, a difference, or a value. Lacan defines the phallus as an empty signifier in relation to which the two sexes function. At the beginning of Lacan's teaching, the phallic signifier is a signifier of the mother's desire beyond the child, that is, the phallic signifier indicates that even in the kinship between the mother and the child – even before the appearance of the father – what is at play is always the logic of a triad, where the third is signified by the phallic signifier. Later in Lacan's teaching, for example around his engagement with the formulas of sexuation, the phallic signifier appears as what those who are located in the masculine position *have* (having) and what those who are located in the feminine position are identified *with* (being).

phallus: see "phallic signifier."

phantasm: designates a psychic scene in which the subject encounters the impossible object that is *the* object of desire. It is therefore through the phantasm that the encounter with the object that the psychic reality locates as missed and impossible is understood. For example, the Freudian dream includes a phantasmatic element, because it allows the dreamer to dream of the possibility of fulfilling a repressed wish. The phantasm is a script or a narrative schema in which conditions are created for the subject's encounter with the object. Outside the phantasm, anything that hints at the possibility of encountering the object of desire, the object of the psychic movement, may provoke terror or anxiety.

real: one of the three orders (imaginary, symbolic, real), which indicates that the order of the signifiers reveals an object that cannot be signified and that resists the operation of the signifier. Since the subject is always in-language, the encounter with the dimension of the real takes place where language encounters impasses – the signs of the presence of an irreducible, irremovable being that is not subject to meaning or to language modes of coherence. The real is what cannot be assimilated or represented in the usual and regulated channels of the activity of discourse and language.

repetition: a psychic mechanism that acts against (or with indifference to) a person's well-being or pleasure principle. Repetition designates a way in which the drive compels itself on the subject. Therefore, the repetition compulsion is indifferent to the difference between the subject's enjoyment and pain. For this reason, repetitiveness – which Freud connected to what is beyond the pleasure principle – indicated for him that the psychic reality is subject to a force that does not distinguish between the borders of the ego-subject and what is beyond these borders. It should be stressed though that repetition itself is not indifferent to the singularity of the subject since its consequence is a certain loss (loss of the repeated, hence infinitely deferred object).

sexuation: defines the human being's position in relation to sexuality as a logical symbolic position. Sexuation is derived from the logical analysis of four formulas: a pair of formulas for each sexual position (feminine or masculine), which maintain relations of contradiction or irreconcilability. For example: feminine sexuation is defined as a partial violation of the formula that defines masculine sexuation. The latter, masculine sexuation, is also defined through two irreconcilable formulas: one claiming that everyone is subject to the phallic function, and the other signifying that there is at least one (the primordial father) who is not subject to it.

We can see that rather than treating sexuality as derived from a biological or gender position, sexuation refers to sexuality as a formal positioning in relation to the presence of the phallic signifier, and accordingly, to different modes of *jouissance*. Sexuation, in this sense, does not distinguish between the sexes in biological or gender terms, but denotes the sexual decision that is open to any being as a decision that determines one's psychic reality.

signified: the conceptual content designated by a linguistic form or by an image and located in the field of meaning.

signifier: the linguistic form or image that stands for something by virtue of its formal and material attributes. For example: the signifier "tree" is a signifier that can be linguistic, visual, or tactile, and by virtue of its formal attributes it can stand for something of a different order. The function of the signifier is connected to its formal presence but not to its content, and therefore a pure signifier has no meaning.

split subject [$]: the subject of the unconscious. This is the subject who says and doesn't know what he says, commits slips of the tongue (thinks and doesn't know what he thinks), dreams, plans, wants, and aspires for certain things, but encounters a reality whose cause is incomprehensible in relation to that intention, wish, or aspiration; that is, a subject who carries a symptom. The split subject is therefore the subject who never knows himself, who is not a self-consciousness, who exists through the order of the signifiers that fails to represent him. The subject of the unconscious is the subject whose representation by an image or a signifier leaves out a remainder of being, and therefore his place in the order of the signifiers is a place of alienation.

superego: Freud sees the superego as the psychic agency closest to the unconscious. In the place where the moral imperative, the absolute prohibition on behalf of a law appears – there the subject is closest to the locus of primordial suppression, to the psychic cause itself. Through the idea of the superego Freud pointed to the distance between the possibilities of pleasure (enjoyment and non-enjoyment, happiness and misery, satisfaction and frustration) and absolute pleasure, or "jouissance" in Lacan's language; it is this absolute pleasure that is the cause for the creation of a law, and the origin of the appearance of the superego's prohibitions in the psychic reality. The superego is therefore a psychic agency that limits and restrains the possibilities of enjoyment in the name of an absolute pleasure, which is possessed by the primordial father, or by any Other that establishes the law as a means to castrate the subject. The superego designates the ethics of the subject of the unconscious. This is an ethics that does not distinguish between enjoyment and non-enjoyment, good and evil, but transcends these signifying distinctions in its targeting on the absolute.

symbolic: in the series of the three orders, the symbolic is the dimension of language in which the psychic reality is made present through substitutive modes. Thus, for example, a symptom should be read not as the representative of a repressed event or the image of a pathological state, but as the making present of a psychic reality, a making present that takes place through an act of subtraction and substitution. The symbolic dimension exemplifies one of the essential differences between a psychoanalytic interpretation and a psychological one, because the symbolic dimension identifies the psychic reality of the unconscious where there is a sign of subtraction or substitution, rather than where we find what has been subtracted or substituted.

symbolic death: symbolic death is the death of the subject in relation to the symbolic order, that is, the erasure of the subject whose appearance/introduction into language was signified through a signifier, out of the network of signifiers. The subject's symbolic death is his death in relation to the big Other, where the subject is no longer taken into account as a memory, a sign, or a trace. The central example that Lacan gives in relation to symbolic death is the tragic figure. Lacan claims that the tragedy of a figure like Antigone stems from her move of transcending the terror of death in order to face the bare meaning of the symbolic dimension. Symbolic death is death in relation to the law and the common legality, the termination of any communal support the subject may rely on. It is standing in the realm of the Other while wishing to encounter the origin of the law – the function that determines the validity of the law, the regularity of language, at the limits of existence. This wish is tragic because symbolic death is the total erasure of the human being from the common order.

symptom: an unconscious psychic formation. The symptom is a sign that appears in the dimension of speech, thought, action, or the body, and expresses a form of discontinuity or disruption in relation to the latter's sequential order and calibrated regularity. For example, an obsessive symptom is a disruption in the continuity of thought, while a hysterical symptom is a disruption in the regulation of body events with regards to the social order.

topological dimension: serves Lacan to exhibit and demonstrate various aspects of the split in the psychic structure that cannot be represented through ordinary spatial forms. The latter rely on a dichotomous logic (on distinctions such as between inside and outside, left and right). Topology, which is concerned with spatial forms that cannot be geometrically represented – such as the torus, the Möbius strip, the Klein bottle, the cross cap, and so on – serves Lacan to exhibit the impossible or paradoxical dimension in the task of representation in any psychic reality.

transference: refers to the structural consequence of the psychoanalyst's presence in the analytic experience. Transference activates the reality of the unconscious of the analysand (i.e., the subject in the analysis). Therefore, transference is the name given to love in the analysis, love ignited already by the first rule of psychoanalysis according to which the analysand is asked to speak in free association ("say whatever"). Transference allows the analysand to encounter the cause that drives her desire, to interpret her fundamental fantasy, and to establish knowledge in relation to her symptom.

unary trait: a trait is a sign that does not signify anything, that does not point to a referent, a meaning, or an object, yet the unary trait carries and embodies the subject's individual, singular identity. The unary trait does not carry the essence of being and is not derived from this being. It has an arbitrary and random dimension in relation to the subject, yet it concerns the subject's individuality, his irreducible and incomprehensible singularity. The unary trait does not represent one's identity or self-knowledge, but is a characteristic of *jouissance*, which always is foreign to the subject. Therefore the unary trait is not the social mask that the subject wears, or an item that identifies him, but a trait is the representative of the singular erotic condition of a particular subject, the encounter with which is one of the tasks of the analysis. Identification with the unary trait is one of the forms of identification available to the subject.

unconscious: for Lacan, following Freud, the unconscious is the general name given to the psychic formations that appear in the wake of what has been repressed or denied. The unconscious formations appear in the subject's thought, way of acting, or speech, as a result of that repression or denial. Rather than being hidden or lying in some "depths" of being, the unconscious therefore concerns the ways in which the psychic reality gives practical expression to what cannot be said (the repressed) and what cannot be thought or identified with.

Vorstellung, **representation**: refers to the alternative expressions of the object that the subject finds in the Other. The desire of the subject of the unconscious is for something finite but undefined in its appearance. The object is merely the embodiment of the fact that the subject is not present to himself, and the object appears – through an image – as *Repräsentanz*, that is, as a representative and a representation of what prevents the subject of the unconscious from being "self-consciousness," that is, a consciousness that is present to itself and knows itself.

Vorstellungsrepräsentanz, **ideational representation**: a Freudian concept that describes the relation between the drive and the psychic reality. Since the object of psychic representation, namely the drive, is repressed, what can appear in practice as represented is the act of representation itself. The drive only appears and is only given to psychic representation through the very movement of striving to represent it. For example: the sucking movements of the baby's lips that continue even after he has been satisfied (fed), these movements are the representative of the drive's pressure, without the object of the drive, that is, the ultimate object of satiation, being represented or embodied through this action. In this way, the body gesture embodies the oral drive's movement towards a partial object, thus marking the psychic sign of the presence of the drive.

Notes

1 Lacan with the Philosophers

1 All the references to Lacan are to the French edition, if an edited version of the seminar exists, along with the seminar's date and the page number. If there is no edited version of the seminar, the reference is only to the seminar's date. In cases where an edited version exists in both French and English, the reference is to the English translation, and the page number of the French edition is given in square brackets.

2 A typical example in this context of obliterating the grounds for distinguishing between diverse discourses would be Richard Rorty's essay "Texts and Lumps," which calls for an almost complete abandonment of the distinction between a material and a textual object. Such lack of distinction implies the removal of any obstacle to the free crossing of disciplinary and historical boundaries.

3 Lacan, *Le séminaire XVI*, 92.

4 It is interesting to note that Derrida refers to both the *with* of Lacan and the philosophers and the *with* of himself and Lacan in similar terms of one of the sides being dead. See Derrida, "For the Love of Lacan," 39ff.

5 Ibid., 43.

6 See, for example, the following studies, which are all attempts to bridge between philosophical concepts and concepts used by Lacan: Juranville, Badiou, Regnault, Ragland-Sullivan, Albin, Milner, and Grigg. Each exemplifies a different approach. For instance, Ragland-Sullivan presents and mediates the various concepts constituting Lacanian thought (about the subject, about consciousness, about linguistic sense, etc.) in theoretical terms, as a theory. Milner's is an attempt to examine what qualifies Lacan's writings and teaching to be considered a system of thought. For this purpose,

Milner portrays a general picture of Lacan's theorems regarding science, language, philosophy, and other humanistic disciplines. Grigg dedicates his study to a few critical encounters between psychoanalysis and philosophy in order to show where Lacan leans, clarifies, or criticizes the philosophical tradition (Kant, Descartes) and how his own work was received by later philosophy (Badiou and Žižek).

7 For an analysis of the productive meaning of anti-philosophy for understanding the position of the psychoanalytic discourse, see Clemens, *Psychoanalysis Is an Antiphilosophy.*

8 Badiou is a contemporary French philosopher (b. 1937) whose thought, perhaps more than that of any other philosopher of our time, is profoundly rooted in Lacan's. Badiou alludes to Lacan, responds to his claims, and points to his importance in relation to philosophy.

9 Badiou, "Lacan et Platon: Le mathème est-il une idée?," 135.

10 Badiou, "Truth: Forcing and the Unnameable," in *Theoretical Writings,* 121.

11 Richard Boothby shows in relation to Freud's philosophical temperament – as manifested in what is called his meta-psychology, that is – the philosophizing that accompanies the formulation of the fundamental concepts of psychoanalysis, such as "the drive," "the unconscious," "repression," and so on.

12 "The Seminar of Jacques Lacan: The Knowledge of the Psychoanalyst, 1971–1972," trans. Cormac Gallagher. http://www.lacaninireland.com/web/wp-content/uploads/2010/06/Book-19a-The-Knowledge-of-the-Psychoanalyst-1971-1972.pdf.

13 The expression in French is "mettre les pieds dans le plat," that is, to raise a question that embarrasses the recipient.

14 Lacan, *Le séminaire IX: L'identification,* 15.11.61

15 Lacan alludes here to Martin Heidegger's *What Is Called Thinking?*

16 Lacan, *Le séminaire IX,* 22.11.61.

17 Lacan, *The Other Side of Psychoanalysis,* 20[20].

18 Ibid., 146[170–1]

19 I-cracy = the rule of the I; a Lacanian neologism based on the model of democracy = the rule of the people.

20 Lacan, *Le séminaire XVII,* 62–3[70–1] (emphasis mine – RR).

21 Significantly, Freud sees the Superego as the agency that is closest to the unconscious. The moral imperative, the absolute prohibition in the name of the law, appears where the subject is closest to the place of the primordial repression, to the psychic cause itself.

22 Lacan, *Le séminaire XVI,* 8.1.69.

23 "The discourse of the university" is the discourse that historically replaces

the "discourse of the master," positioning *knowledge* in the place reserved for the discourse's agent.

24 Note in this context that the analyst disappears from the analytical discourse as "I" but the grammatical-I also disappears when the analyst testifies about his analysis to others. During the procedure of the Pass, which is the analyst's testimony at the end of his analysis, the analyst testifies about himself in the third person. A grammatical choice that can be understood as a means to evade the illusion carried by the I.

2 The Love of Truth: Lacan with Plato

1 Lacan, *L'envers de la psychanalyse*, 26.11.69, 21[21].
2 The university discourse:

$$\frac{S_2}{S_1} \to \frac{a}{\displaystyle\not{S}}$$

3 Ibid., 26.11.69, 22[22].
4 Lacan, "L'étourdit" [Second Turn], trans. Cormac Gallagher, *The Letter* 43 (2010): 1–15 at 2.
5 Plato, *Symposium*, trans. Benjamin Jowett. http://www.gutenberg.org/files/1600/1600-h/1600-h.htm.
6 Ibid.
7 Ibid.
8 Ibid.
9 Lacan, *Le séminaire XIX*, 3.2.72 at 71–2.
10 Badiou, "Lacan et Platon," 144ff; "Anti-Philosophy: Lacan and Plato," in *Conditions*, 332.
11 Badiou, *Conditions*, 208.
12 Lacan, "L'Étourdit," 476.
13 Plato, *Symposium*.
14 Lacan, *Le séminaire VIII*, 25.1.61, 153 [« The Seminar of Jacques Lacan, Book VIII, Transference, » trans. Cormac Gallagher, 25.1.61 IX 2 http://www.valas.fr/IMG/pdf/THE-SEMINAR-OF-JACQUES-LACAN-VIII_le_transfert.pdf].
15 Plato, *Symposium*.
16 Lacan, *Le séminaire VIII*, 25.1.61 at 153.
17 Ibid., 7.12.60 at 67.
18 Plato, *Symposium*.
19 Lacan, *Le séminaire VIII*, 1.2.61 at 176.
20 Sigmund Freud [1915], "Observations on Transference-Love (Further Recommendations in the Technique of Psychoanalysis III)," in Standard Edition [hereafter SE], trans. James Strachey (New York: Vintage, 1999), vol. 12, 157–71.

21 Plato, *Symposium*.
22 Lacan, *Le séminaire VIII*, 25.1.61, at 154.
23 Ibid., 17.5.61, at 362–3.
24 Lacan, *Le séminaire VII / The Ethics of Psychoanalysis*, trans. D. Porter.
25 Ibid., 25.5.60 at 291[248].
26 Plato, *The Republic*, 344 http://www.aprendendoingles.com.br/ebooks/republic.pdf.
27 Lacan, *Le séminaire VIII*, 21.12.60 at 102.
28 Lacan, "Intervention sur le transfert," in *Écrits*, 215–28[176–88].
29 Ibid., 225–6[183–4].
30 Object-cause is one of the values given to the *objet a* in Lacan's work. The object-cause is related to Freud's lost object, which is the cause of the desire for knowledge, for the beloved, for truth. The merging of object and cause highlights the fact that the cause is not a concept or an essence, but what has a logical necessity in the psychic reality.
31 Lacan, *Le séminaire XVI*, 5.3.69 at 215[209].

3 Soulove: Lacan and Aristotle "On the Soul"

1 In Homeric Greek the term refers to what descends into the underworld after death. I would like to thank Dr Orna Harari for this information.
2 Plato, *Phaedo*.
3 In the *Timaeus*, for example, not only is the soul divided (and is therefore created part by part), but it is also not eternal, since Plato claims that it has an age just like the body, that it has a material reality, and that the body is structured within it. See: Plato, *Timaeus*, 34A–36D.
4 "An 'instinct' appears to us as a concept on the frontier between the mental and the somatic, as the psychical representative of the stimuli originating from within the organism and reaching the mind, as a measure of the demand made upon the mind for work in consequence of its connection with the body." Freud, "Instincts and Their Vicissitudes," *SE XIV*, 121–2.
5 "Psyche is extended; knows nothing about it." Freud, "Findings, Ideas, Problems," 1938, 300.
6 To be precise, in the ancient philosophical tradition mind and the body were commonly separated, while other parts of the soul could be connected to the body, and even to specific parts of it (in materialistic schools such as the Stoic school, the mind was also corporeal and is found in the body, and even Aristotle's disciples located the mind in the heart or in the

area around the heart). This was the common view until Descartes reduced
the concept of the soul to the mind and built his dualism on the separation
between the mind and the body.

7 To illustrate the strength of this separateness into two orders from early
modern philosophy, let us quote from Spinoza's *Ethics* illustrating the
parallelism between extension and thought: "Body cannot determine mind
to think, neither can mind determine body to motion or rest or any state
different from these, if such there be." Benedict de Spinoza, *Ethics*, trans.
R.H.M. Elwes, pt 3, prop. 2. https://ebooks.adelaide.edu.au/a/aristotle/
a8so/index.html

8 Aristotle, *On the Soul*, trans. J.A. Smith [University of Adelaide], bk II, ch.
1, https://ebooks.adelaide.edu.au/a/aristotle/a8so/index.html.

9 Ibid., bk I, ch. 5.

10 Lacan, *Le séminaire XX*, 8.5.73, 99[110].

11 The French original reads: "… l'âme, c'est ce qu'on pense à propos du
corps – du côté du manche." Ibid., an idiom that means being on the more
powerful side, on the side of power.

12 Aristotle, *On the Soul*, bk II, ch. 9.

13 Lacan, *Le séminaire XX*, 8.5.73, 100[110].

14 Aristotle, *On the Soul*, bk II, ch. 5.

15 René Descartes, *The Passions of the Soul*. Hackett Publishing Company, 1989.

16 Aristotle, *On the Soul*, bk II, ch. 1.

17 Ibid., bk I, ch. 4. Note that in English translations of ancient texts the Greek
"pathos" (or Pathe – πάθη – in the plural) is translated as "affection" rather
than "affect" to indicate traits that make a thing affectable (changeable or
movable) in some way. Affections are then related to the complex of body
and soul, and even those that are affections of the soul are inseparable
from the material of the living body.

18 Ibid., bk II, ch. 2.

19 While action or activity concerns the very existence of movement or
change, "affect" includes the *cause* of the activity. Affect therefore refers to
what acts or is affected by virtue of something else. In certain senses the
concept of affect transcends the distinction between active and passive.
Thus in Spinoza for example, the body is affected by active or passive
emotions depending on whether the cause of the affection is external
or internal. Spinoza, *Ethics*, trans. W.H. White, pt 3, "On the origin and
Nature of the Emotions." Wordsworth Classics of World, 2001.

20 Aristotle, *On the Soul*, bk II, ch. 2.

21 Ibid., bk II, ch. 4.

22 Lacan, *Le séminaire XVII*, 11.2.70, 70[80].

23 Lacan, *Le séminaire XX*, 100[110].
24 Note that some of Aristotle's commentators claim that the active mind, which is not destroyed with the body and is immortal and eternal, the mind that appears towards the end of the treatise (bk III, ch. 5), should be attributed to the immovable mover, that is, to that divine power of perpetual movement that exceeds the limits of individual existence. By accepting this interpretation, we can say that the contradiction has been resolved, and it becomes possible to say without reservation that Aristotle does not posit any psychic power that is not actualized in the body and its parts.
25 Aristotle, *On the Soul*, bk II, ch. 8.
26 Ibid., bk II, ch. 3.
27 Ibid., bk III, ch. 4.
28 Lacan, *Le séminaire (livre) VIII*, 12.4.61, 261–7.
29 See Lacan's reading of this chapter in "Des Noms-du-père." Éditions du Seuil, 2005, pp. 98–9.
30 Lacan, *Le séminaire (livre) VIII*, 12.4.61, 272–3[XVI 225].
31 Aristotle, bk II, ch. 4, 415b.
32 Aristotle, *On the Soul*, bk III, ch. 3.
33 "The thinking then of the simple objects of thought [objects that do not exist in a specific period of time, for example – R.R.] is found in those cases where falsehood is impossible." Ibid., bk III, ch. 6.
34 Jacques Lacan, *Le séminaire (livre) XX*, 13.3.73, 78[84].
35 Ibid., 8.5.73, 100[110].
36 Ibid., 13.3.73, 81[88].
37 Ibid., 13.3.73, 79[85].
38 Ibid.

4 To Think or Not to Be: Lacan with Descartes

1 Lacan, *Le séminaire X*, 26.6.63, 360[311].
2 René Descartes, *Meditations on First Philosophy*, http://oregonstate.edu/instruct/phl302/texts/descartes/meditations/meditations.html.
3 Lacan, *Le séminaire XVII*, 20.5.70, 178[153].
4 Descartes, *Meditations*.
5 Lacan, *Le séminaire XII*, 9.6.65 (352), http://esource.dbs.ie/bitstream/handle/10788/161/Book-12-Crucial-problems-for-psychoanalysis.pdf?sequence=1.
6 After Bruce Fink's translation of Lacan's famous article as "The *Instance* of the Letter in the Unconscious," I would sometimes use "instance" to refer

to the agency of speech or thought (an instance that is not yet substantiated).

7 Descartes, *Meditations.*
8 Lacan, *Le séminaire XVIII*, 17.3.71, 99. http://www.lacaninireland.com/web/wp-content/uploads/2010/06/Book-18-On-a-discourse-that-might-not-be-a-semblance.pdf.
9 Descartes, *A Discourse on Method*, http://www.gutenberg.org/files/59/59-h/59-h.htm.
10 Lacan, *Le séminaire (livre) XII*, 9.6.65 (353).
11 Ibid., 352–3.
12 A logical necessity would be the case if "therefore I am" was a necessity if it stemmed from the proposition "all that thinks exists, I think, therefore I am."
13 Lacan, *Le séminaire XVII*, 20.5.70, 176[150].
14 Ibid., 20.5.70, 178[152].
15 This word suggests a play on Descartes's "I am" and the Hegelian "master": *m'être; maître.*
16 Lacan, *Le séminaire IX*, 22.11.61.
17 Descartes, *Meditations*, II, 7.
18 "Well, then, what am I? A thing that thinks. What is that? A thing that doubts, understands, affirms, denies, wants, refuses, and also imagines and senses." In ibid.
19 Lacan, *Le séminaire IX*, 22.11.61.
20 Ibid.
21 Lacan, *Le séminaire XII*, 9.6.65 (351).
22 Freud, "Negation," 236.
23 Lacan, *Le séminaire XIV*, 11.1.67.
24 Ibid., 11.1.67
25 Ibid., 14.6.67; 21.6.67.
26 "It is surprising how often people who seek analytic treatment for hysteria or an obsessional neurosis confess to having indulged in the phantasy: 'A child is being beaten.'" From Sigmund Freud, "'A Child is being Beaten': A Contribution to the Study of the Origin of Sexual Perversions," 1. http://www.slideshare.net/341987/a-child-is-being-beaten.
27 The idea of the signified slipping under the signifier and the indeterminacy of meaning appears in Lacan's essay "L'instance de la lettre dans l'inconscient ou la raison depuis Freud," in *Écrits*, 493–530[412–41].
28 Lacan, *Le séminaire XIV*, 11.1.67.
29 Lacan, *Le séminaire XVI*, 20.5.70, 181[155].
30 Ibid., 20.5.70, 176[150].
31 Ibid., 20.5.70, 176[150], 180[154].

5 Lacan Wagers with Pascal

1 Brunet, *Le Pari de Pascal*, 7.
2 *The Standard Edition of the Complete Psychological Works of Sigmund Freud*, ed. James Strachey [hereafter SE], vol. 10, *Analysis of a Phobia in a Five-Year-Old Boy* (London: Hogarth Press and the Institute of Psycho-Analysis, 1962), 37.
3 Lacan, *Le séminaire IV: La relation d'objet*, 27.3.57, 249ff.
4 See attached glossary for a broader explanation of the three notions: Imaginary, Symbolic, and Real.
5 "Man is only a subject full of error, natural and ineffaceable, without grace." Pascal, *Pensées*, trans. W.F. Trotter (New York: Random House, 1941), §83[34].
6 Ibid., §233[79–84].
7 Lacan, *Le séminaire XVI*, 15.1.69, 116 ("un homme en son temps").
8 For instance, Pascal, contrary to the opinion of his predecessors and contemporaries, methodically and persistently argued for the necessity of the existence of vacuum in the world of matter, developed important arguments in the study of probability that anticipate game theory, and formulated a principle that is similar to Karl Poper's refutation principle. Pascal was considered a genius in mathematics and physics during his lifetime and in the history of thought.
9 Pascal, *Pensées*, §233[81].
10 Ibid., §72[23].
11 Ibid., §109[43].
12 Although slightly younger: Descartes died in 1650 at the age of fifty-six, while Pascal died in 1662 at the age of thirty-nine.
13 Descartes, *Meditations on First Philosophy with selection from the Objections and Replies*, trans. John Cottingham (Cambridge: Cambridge University Press, 1986), 31.
14 Kant, *Critique of Pure Reason*, B629.
15 Lacan, *Le séminaire XVI*, 118–19.
16 Pascal, *Pensées*, §77[39].
17 Lacan, *Le séminaire XVI*, 8.1.69, 102.
18 Badiou, *Being and Event*, ch. 21.
19 Pascal, *Pensées*, §4[6] ("Se moquer de la philosophie c'est vraiment philosopher").
20 In the article: "Propos sur la causalité psychique," *Écrits* (Paris: Seuil, 1966), Lacan argues that the danger of madness is blocked by the passion for an image "that imposes its structure on all [man's] desires, even the loftiest ones." P. 188[153].

21 Pascal, *Pensées*, §2.
22 Ibid., §72[23].
23 Ibid., §282[95–6].
24 Ibid., §416[131].
25 Ibid., §233[83].
26 Lacan, *Le séminaire XIII*, 2.2.66.
27 *Le séminaire XVI*, 15.1.69, 119.
28 Pascal, "Preface to the Treatise on Vacuum," in *The Thoughts, Letters, and Opuscules of Blaise Pascal*, 551.
29 Ibid., 11–12.
30 Pascal, *Pensées*, §195[72].
31 Ibid., §219[76].
32 Ibid., §72[23].
33 Ibid., §233[79].
34 Ibid., §194[66].
35 Ibid., §194[71].
36 Ibid., §194[70].
37 Ibid., §200[74].
38 Lacan, *Le séminaire XIII*, 2.2.66.
39 Pascal, *Pensées*, §233[79].
40 Ibid., §233[81–2].
41 Ibid., §233[82].
42 Pascal, *Pensées*, §200[80].
43 Lacan, *Le séminaire XVI*, 22.1.69, 127.
44 This illustration appears in Lacan's Seminar IX that deals with identification.
45 Lacan, *Le séminaire XVI*, 25.6.69, 394.
46 Edward McClennen, "Finite Decision Theory," in *Gambling on God: Essays on Pascal's Wager*, ed. Jeff Jordan (New York: Rowman and Littlefield, 1994).
47 Lacan, *Le séminaire XVI*, 22.1.69, 133.
48 Ibid., 29.1.69, 146.
49 Pascal, *Pensées*, §233[79].
50 Ibid., §233[82].
51 Lacan, *Le séminaire XVI*, 5.2.69, 153.
52 Pascal, *Pensées*, §233[82].
53 Lacan, *D'un Autre à l'autre*, 22.1.69, 135.
54 Ibid., 26.2.69, 194.
55 Ibid., 26.2.1969, 199.
56 Ibid., 21.5.69, 333.
57 Pascal, *Pensées*, §72[22].

58 Lacan, *Le séminaire XIII*, 2.2.66.
59 Lacan, *Le séminaire XVI*, 4.6.69, 342–3.
60 Pascal, *Pensées*, §194[67].

6 The Erotics of the One: Lacan with Kant

1 It is commonly claimed that Lacan returns to Freud "equipped" with post-Linguistic Turn insights (following Frege, Saussure, Benveniste, Jacobson, et al.), and in this sense reads Freud "with language," something that for Freud was not possible.
2 Immanuel Kant, *The Critique of Pure Reason* [hereafter *CPR*], trans. Paul Guyer and Allen W. Wood (Cambridge: Cambridge University Press, 1998), A294, 384.
3 *CPR*, A296, 385.
4 "*A priori*" means deriving from the understanding (or from the fundamental forms of the power of representation, or from the forms of intuition of time and space) and preceding all experience.
5 *CPR*, A297, 386.
6 Lacan, *Télévision*.
7 Kant, B833, p. 735.
8 Lacan, *Télévision*, trans. Dennis Hollier, Rosalind Krauss, and Annette Michelson (New York: W.W. Norton, 1990), 36.
9 "Transcendentality" means that *a priori* rules of cognition determine how certain representations – that do not derive from an empirical source – can apply to the objects of experience.
10 *CPR*, B80–2, 196–7.
11 *CPR*, A57, 196–7.
12 Lacan, *Télévision*, 37.
13 "Objectivity" for Kant means a phenomenon that is given to cognition and that has been created from the process of knowledge itself, having no reality outside it.
14 *CPR*, B124, 223.
15 *CPR*.
16 *CPR*, B223, 304ff.
17 *CPR*, A198, 310.
18 *CPR*, B234, 305.
19 "The house is not a thing in itself at all but only an appearance, i.e., a representation, the transcendental object of which is unknown." *CPR*, A191, B236, 306.
20 "Representation" or "presentation" (depending on the translation)

translate "Vorstellung": "the inner determination of our mind in this or that relation of time" (B242); in other words, "presentation" is any mental image, whether consciously or unconsciously produced, sensual, perceptual, conceptual, etc.

21 *CPR*, B245, 311.

22 Lacan, *Le séminaire X*, 8.5.63, 248–9[214–15].

23 Ibid., 249[215].

24 Ibid.

25 See "The Conflict of the Philosophy Faculty with the Faculty of Medicine," in Immanuel Kant, *The Conflict of the Faculties*, trans. Mary J. Gregor (New York: Abaris, 1979), 175–215.

26 *CPR*, B89, 201.

27 *CPR*, B176, 271.

28 See the table of categories in the *Critique*, which according to Kant includes a *full* list of "all original pure concepts of synthesis that the understanding contains in itself a priori." B106, 211.

29 The understanding is the spontaneous action of thinking concepts and principles, which more narrowly aspires to implement them in the senses. Reason is the pure activity of the spirit outside any sensibility, and more narrowly, the capability that aspires to know supersensible reality and therefore the ability to think the unconditioned (even if not to know it).

30 Presentation translates *Darstellung*: the exhibition of an intuition in correspondence to a concept. Presentation is a central term Kant uses to describe the (complex) synthesis between concept and intuition.

31 *CPR*, B5–6, 138.

32 *CPR*, B174, 269.

33 *CPR*, B218–19, 295–6.

34 *CPR*, B176, 271.

35 Allison, *Kant's Transcendental Idealism*, 204.

36 *CPR*, B89, 201.

37 *CPR*, B131–2, 246.

38 *CPR*, B157–8, 259–60.

39 *CPR*, B153, 257.

40 Lacan, *Le séminaire XVI*, 26.2.69, 194.

41 Lacan, *Les quatre concepts fondamentaux de la psychanalyse* (Paris: Seuil, 1973), 208[106].

42 Kant refers to this difference, between space as a form of intuition and space as a form that involves concepts, in a footnote to the Transcendental Deduction, *CPR*, B160, 261.

43 Lacan, *L'identification*, 21.2.62.

44 Ibid.
45 *CPR*, B176.
46 *CPR*, B130–1, 246.
47 *CPR*, B125–6, 241.
48 Sigmund Freud, "On Narcissism: An Introduction," SE XIV, 82.
49 Lacan, *Le séminaire IX*, 28.2.62.
50 *CPR*, B166–7, 264.
51 Kant, A353, 418.
52 This is how Kant describes the unity of understanding (in opposition
    to the unity of reason): "For pure reason leaves to the understanding
    everything that relates directly to objects of intuition or rather to their
    synthesis in imagination ... Thus reason directs itself only to the use of
    the understanding, not indeed insofar as the latter contains the ground of
    possible experience ... but rather in order to prescribe the direction toward
    a certain unity of which the understanding has no concept, proceeding to
    comprehend all the actions of the understanding in respect of every object
    into an absolute whole." *CPR*, B383, 401–2.
53 Lacan, *Le séminaire IX*, 21.2.62.
54 Ibid.
55 Ibid.
56 "Stupidity" in the present case means for Lacan the seemingly natural con-
    ception that looks for the common in a situation, for the common or shared
    identity. See for example in Seminar XIV, *La logique du fantasme*, 14.12.66.
57 Lacan, *Le séminaire IX*, 21.2.62.
58 "Now in experience our perceptions come together contingently, so that
    no character of necessity in their connection appears, or can appear." *CPR*,
    B219, 296.
59 *CPR*, B404–28.
60 *CPR*, B158, 260.
61 Lacan, *Le séminaire IX*, 28.2.62.
62 *CPR*, B5–6. In this particular case reference is to Werner S. Pluhar's transla-
    tion of *CPR*, as he keeps the original "body" in the translation: 47.
63 Lacan, *Le séminaire IX*, 7.3.62.
64 Ibid., 28.2.62.
65 Ibid., 28.2.62.
66 Ibid., 7.3.62.

7 Beyond Good and Evil: Lacan and Kantian Morality

1 Jacques-Alain Miller, *Lacanian Biology and the Event of the Body*, trans. Bar-
   bara P. Fulks and Jorge Jauregui in *lacanian ink* 18 (Spring 2001): 6–29.

2 Lacan, *Le séminaire XIV*, 31.5.67.

3 Freud, *Civilization and Its Discontents*.

4 Ibid., 125.

5 Ibid., 126.

6 Ibid., 129.

7 In his books *The Ego and the Id* and *Civilization and Its Discontents*.

8 Mainly in the seventh Seminar on Ethics.

9 Freud, "A Case of Obsessional Neurosis," 168, http://mhweb.org/freud/ratman1.pdf.

10 Immanuel Kant, *The Critique of Practical Reason* [herafter *CPrR*] trans. Werner S. Pluhar, Indianapolis/Cambridge: Hackett Publishing Company, 2002, 47–8.

11 Freud, *Civilization and Its Discontents*, 111.

12 Lacan, *Le séminaire VII*, 211–23.

13 A maxim is a subjective principle of practical action. That is, it is a rule that adapts the subjective conditions to the demand of the law. For example, in relation to the command that absolutely prohibits lying, the maxim can instruct a person to lie in a situation of distress, or out of caution.

14 Kant, *CPrR*, 47.

15 Kant, *Practical Reason*, 129[163].

16 Ibid., 40–1.

17 Ibid., 51.

18 Which is the second of the three questions posed by Kant in *Critique of Pure Reason*: What can I know? What ought I to do? What may I hope?

19 Freud, *Civilization and Its Discontents*, 134–5.

20 As exemplified in many of Žižek's works but also, for instance, in Alenka Zupančič's *Ethics of the Real: Kant, Lacan*.

21 Kant, *CPrR*, 38.

22 Ibid., 45

23 "[The moral law] is merely formal, and thus as determining basis it abstracts from all matter and hence from any object of volition. Hence although the highest good may indeed be the *entire* object of a pure practical reason, i.e., of a pure will, yet it is not on that account to be considered the *determining basis* of that will" (Kant, *Practical Reason*, 109[140]).

24 Ibid., 45.

25 Ibid., 45.

26 Lacan, *Le séminaire VII*, 23.12.59, 97–8[66–7].

27 Lacan, "Kant avec Sade," *Écrits*; "Kant with Sade," 787[665].

28 Ibid., 769[648].

29 Kant, *CPrR*, 50–1.

30 "Kant avec Sade," 787[665].

31 Ibid., 770[650].
32 Kant, *CPrR*, 101.
33 Ibid., 104.
34 Ibid., 49–50.
35 Ibid.
36 Ibid., 81.
37 Immanuel Kant, *Groundwork of the Metaphysic of Morals*, ed. and trans. Allen W. Wood (New Haven: Yale University Press, 2002), 4:447.
38 Kant, *CPrR*, 47–8.
39 Ibid., 48.
40 Ibid., 36.
41 Ibid., 79.
42 Ibid., 84.
43 Ibid., 140.
44 Ibid., 84.
45 Ibid., 43.
46 Lacan, *Le séminaire XVI*, 8.1.69, 111.
47 Lacan, *Le séminaire XV*, 17.1.68.
48 Lacan, *Le séminaire VII*, 25.11.59, 31[22].
49 Kant, *CPrR*, 142.
50 Lacan, *Le séminaire VII*, 11.5.60, 260–1[221].
51 Kant, *CPrR*, 44.
52 Kant, *CPrR*, B522–3, 512–13.
53 Ibid., B524, 513.
54 Lacan, *Le séminaire X*, 12.6.63, 326[282]; *Anxiety: The Seminar of Jacques Lacan*, Book X, ed. Jacques-Alain Miller (New York and London: Polity, 2014), 280.

8 Lacan and Hegel in Three Steps: Otherness, Death, Singularity

1 Lacan, *Le séminaire XI*, 27.5.64, 195[215].
2 Lacan, "Subversion du sujet et dialectique du désir," in *Écrits*, 795–8 [673–5].
3 Ibid., 795[673].
4 Lacan, "Position de l'inconscient," *Écrits*, 710[837].
5 Ibid.
6 Hegel, *Phenomenology of Spirit*, 12, para. 22.
7 Lacan, *Le séminaire XVI*, 23.4.69, 271.
8 Ibid., 273(XVII 11).
9 Ibid.

10 "Self-knowledge is self-constituting in Hegel, as we collectively struggle actually to become who we take ourselves to be." Pippin, *After the Beautiful*, 41.

11 Hegel, *Phenomenology of Spirit*, 37, para. 60.

12 Itshaq Klein, *The Dialectic of Master and Slave: A Commentary on One Chapter in Hegel's Phenomenology of the Spirit* (Tel Aviv: Am Oved, 1978). In Hebrew.

13 Hegel, *Phenomenology of Spirit*, 67, para. 112.

14 Ibid., 74, para. 123.

15 Ibid., para. 165.

16 Ibid., paras. 111–12.

17 Klein, *The Dialectic*, 74.

18 Ibid., 75

19 Hegel, *Phenomenology of Spirit*, para. 7.

20 Hyppolite, *Genesis and Structure of Hegel's "Phenomenology of Spirit,"* 159.

21 Hegel, *Phenomenology of Spirit*, para. 168.

22 Ibid., para. 126.

23 Lacan, *Le séminaire X*, 21.11.62, 33[23].

24 Ibid.

25 Ibid., 21.11.62, 34–5[24–5].

26 Kojève, *Introduction to the Reading of Hegel*, 6.

27 Ibid., 7.

28 Lacan, *Le séminaire X*, 21.11.62, 34[24].

29 Hegel, *Phenomenology of Spirit*, para. 82.

30 Lacan, *Le séminaire X*, 21.11.62, 38[27].

31 Ibid., 36[25–6].

32 Ibid., 14.11.62, 23[27].

33 Ibid., [26].

34 *Hegel, Phenomenology of Spirit,* para. 179.

35 Lacan, *Le séminaire X*, 14.11.62, 23[28].

36 *Hegel, Phenomenology of Spirit,* para. 187.

37 Kojève, *Introduction to the Reading of Hegel*, 165.

38 Hegel, *Phenomenology of Spirit*, para. 187.

39 Kojève, *Introduction to the Reading of Hegel*, 168–70.

40 Kojève, "The Idea of Death in the Philosophy of Hegel," 59–60.

41 Freud, "Notes Upon a Case of Obsessional Neurosis," (1909), 189–90.

42 Hegel, *Phenomenology of Spirit*, para. 187.

43 Lacan, *Le séminaire X*, 12.6.63, 330[382].

44 Sublation (*Aufhebung*) in Hegel is a combination of negation, preservation, and elevation, and points to the way in which something that is negated is preserved under a new form. Thus in Hegel, in every dialectic

development previous or inferior content is negated and cancelled out but its meaning is preserved at a higher level; this definition is based on Yirmiyahu Yovel's introduction to *Hegel's Preface to the Phenomenology of Spirit* (Princeton: Princeton University Press, 2005), 28, 86.

45 Lacan, *Le séminaire XV*, 17.1.68.
46 Hegel, *Phenomenology of Spirit*, para. 189.
47 Kojève, *Introduction to the Reading of Hegel*, 15.
48 Ibid., 45–6.
49 Ibid., 53.
50 Ibid., 62.
51 Lacan, *Le séminaire XI*, 3.6.64, 219[218].
52 Régnault, "Clinique hégélienne," 5.6.02.
53 "Vel" in logic is the symbol v used to represent the "either/or" of disjunction.
54 Lacan, *Le séminaire XI*, 3.6.64, 200[219].
55 Ibid.
56 Ibid., 27.5.64, 199[218].
57 Ibid., 3.6.64, 199[219].
58 Ibid., 200[220].
59 Ibid., 201[221].
60 Hegel, *Phenomenology of Spirit*, 17, para. 29.
61 Kojève, *Introduction to the Reading of Hegel*, p. 59.
62 As Hyppolite makes clear, Hegel's scepticism is not that of David Hume. It is not a matter of negating metaphysics in the name of adhering to the impressions and certainties of common sense, but precisely of rejecting determinacies that are based on common sense and whose stability is therefore illusory. Hyppolite, *Genesis and Structure of Hegel's "Phenomenology of Spirit,"* 185.
63 Hegel, *Phenomenology of Spirit*, para. 202.
64 Ibid., para. 204.
65 Lacan, *Le séminaire XII*, 2.12.64.
66 Lacan, *Le séminaire XVIII*, 17.3.71, 109–11.
67 Lacan, *Le séminaire XII*, 5.5.65.
68 Ibid., 7.4.65.
69 Ibid., 5.5.65, 264.
70 Ibid., 266–7.
71 Ibid., 270.
72 Hegel, *Phenomenology of Spirit*, para. 217.
73 Lacan, "Introduction to 'The Names of the Father,'" 74[84].

Conclusion

1 Lacan, *Le séminaire XVII*, 13.5.70, 170–1[146].
2 Ibid., 174[149].
3 In this context of analysing the philosopher's discourse through Plato, Alain Badiou should be mentioned, for he explores the way in which Plato is the one who stands at the root of Lacan's position towards philosophy. Moreover, it is Badiou who claims that philosophy (Plato), just as much as psychoanalysis (Lacan), pointed at an irreducible discordance between being and thought (*Being and Event*, 150), which shifts the whole question of philosophy's relation to truth. Philosophy, claims Badiou, is merely the procuress of truth, and the philosopher cannot be an agent of truth (ibid., 10).
4 Lacan, *Le séminaire XVII*, 17.12.69, 34[31].

Bibliography

Works by Jacques Lacan

–. "L'Etourdit." *Autres Écrits*. Paris: Seuil, 2001.

–. "L'instance de la letter dans l'inconscient ou la raison depuis Freud." In *Écrits*. Paris: Seuil, 1966. / "The Instance of the Letter in the Unconscious or Reason Since Freud." In *Écrits*. First Complete Edition in English, trans. B. Fink. London and New York: W.W. Norton, 2006.

–. "Intervention sur le transfert." *Écrits*. Paris: Seuil, 1966. / "Presentation on Transference." First Complete Edition in English, trans. B. Fink. London and New York: W.W. Norton, 2006.

–. "Introduction to 'The Names of the Father.'" In *Television – A Challenge to the Psychoanalytic Establishment*, ed. Joan Copjec, trans. J. Mehlman. New York: W.W. Norton, 1990.

–. "Kant avec Sade." *Écrits*. Paris: Seuil, 1966. / "Kant with Sade." The First Complete Edition in English, trans. B. Fink. London and New York: W.W. Norton & Co., 2006.

–. *Des noms-du-père*. Paris: Seuil, 2005.

–. *Les Noms du père*. Paris: Seuil, 2005.

–. "Position de l'inconscient." In *Écrits*. Paris: Seuil, 1966. / "Position of the Unconscious." First Complete Edition in English, trans. B. Fink. London and New York: W.W. Norton, 2006.

–. "Propos sur la causalité psychique." *Écrits*. Paris: Seuil, 1966. /"Presentation on Psychical Causality." First Complete Edition in English, trans. B. Fink. London and New York: W.W. Norton, 2006.

–. *Le séminaire (livre) IV: La relation d'objet*. Paris: Seuil, 1994.

–. *Le séminaire (livre) VII: L'éthique de la psychanalyse*. Paris: Seuil, 1986. / *The Ethics of Psychoanalysis*, trans. D. Porter. New York: Routledge and W.W. Norton, 1992.

–. *Le séminaire (livre) VIII: Le transfert*. Paris: Seuil, 2001.

–. *Le séminaire (livre) IX: L'identification*. [Unpublished], 1961–62.

–. *Le séminaire (livre) X: L'angoisse*. Paris: Seuil, 2004. / *Anxiety*, trans. A.R. Price. Cambridge: Polity, 2014.

–. *Le séminaire (livre) XI: Les quatre concepts fondamentaux de la psychanalyse*. Paris: Seuil, 1973. / *The Four Fundamental Concepts of Psycho-Analysis*, trans. Alan Sheridan. London: Hogarth, 1977.

–. *Le séminaire (livre) XII: Problèmes cruciaux pour la psychanalyse*. [Unpublished], 1964–65.

–. *Le séminaire (livre) XIII: L'objet de la psychanalyse*. [Unpublished], 1965–66.

–. *Le séminaire (livre) XIV: La logique du fantasme*. [Unpublished], 1966–67.

–. *Le séminaire (livre) XV: L'acte psychanalytique*. [Unpublished], 1967–68.

–. *Le séminaire (livre) XVI: D'un Autre à l'autre*. Paris: Seuil, 2006.

–. *Le séminaire (livre) XVII: L'envers de la psychanalyse*. Paris: Seuil, 1991. / *The Other Side of Psychoanalysis*, trans. R. Grigg. New York: W.W. Norton, 2007.

–. *Le séminaire (livre) XVIII: D'un discours qui ne serait dus semblant*. Paris: Seuil. 2006.

–. *Le séminaire (livre) XIX: … Ou Pire*. Paris: Seuil, 2011.

–. *Le séminaire (livre) XX: Encore*. Paris: Seuil, 1975. / *Encore, On Feminine Sexuality: The Limits of Love and Knowledge*, trans. B. Fink. New York: W.W. Norton, 1998.

–. "Le séminaire sur 'la Lettre volée.'" In *Écrits*. Paris: Seuil, 1966. / "The Seminar on 'The Purloined Letter.'" First Complete Edition in English, trans. B. Fink. London and New York: W.W. Norton, 2006.

–. "Subversion du sujet et dialectique du désir." In *Écrits*. Paris: Seuil, 1966. / "Subversion of the Subject and the Dialectic of Desire." In *Écrits*. First Complete Edition in English, trans. B. Fink. London and New York: W.W. Norton, 2006.

–. *Télévision*. Paris: Éditions du Seuil, 1974.

Other Sources

Albin, Michel, ed. *Lacan avec les philosophes*. Paris: Éditions Albin Michel, 1991.

Allison, Henry E. *Kant's Transcendental Idealism: An Interpretation and Defense, Revised and Enlarged Edition*. New Haven: Yale University Press, 2004.

Badiou, Alain. *Being and Event*. London and New York: Continuum, 2005.

–. *Conditions*, trans. Steven Corcoran. London and New York: Continuum, 2008.

–. *Handbook of Inaesthetics*. Stanford: Stanford University Press, 2005.

–. "Lacan et Platon: le mathème est-il une idée?" *Lacan avec les philosophes*. Paris: Éditions Albin Michel, 1991.

–. *Ouvertures*. Paris: Librarie Fayard, 2013.

–. *Le Séminaire: Lacan, L'antiphilosophie 3*, 1994–95.

–. *Theoretical Writings*, ed. and trans. Ray Brassier and Alberto Toscano. London and New York: Continuum, 2006.

Boothby, Richard. *Freud as Philosopher: Metapsychology after Lacan*. New York: Routledge, 2001.

Brunet, Georges. *Le Pari de Pascal*. Paris: Desclée de Brouwer, 1956.

Clemens. Justin. *Psychoanalysis: An Antiphilosophy*. Edinburgh: Edinburgh University Press, 2013.

Derrida, Jacques. *Resistances of Psychoanalysis*, trans. Peggy Kamuf, Pascale-Anne Brault, and Michael Naas. Stanford: Stanford University Press, 1998.

Descartes, René. *Discourse on Method, and Meditations on a First Philosophy*, trans. Donald A. Cress. Indianapolis: Hackett Publishing, 1998.

Freud, Sigmund. *The Standard Edition of the Complete Psychological Works of Sigmund Freud*, trans. James Strachey. London: Hogarth Press.

–. "Analysis of Phobia in a Five-Year-Old Boy" [1909]. Standard ed., vol. 10, 1–150.

–. "A Child Is Being Beaten: A Contribution to the Study of the Origin of Sexual Perversions" [1919]. Standard ed., vol. 17, 175–204.

–. *Civilization and Its Discontents* [1925]. Standard ed., vol. 21, trans. James Strachey. New York: Vintage, 1999.

–. "The Ego and the Id" [1923]. Standard ed., vol. 19, 3–66.

–. "Instincts and Their Vicissitudes" [1915]. Standard ed., vol. 14, 117–40.

–. "Negation" [1925]. Standard ed., vol. 19, trans. James Strachey. New York: Vintage, 1999.

–. "Notes upon a Case of Obsessional Neurosis (Rat Man)" [1909]. Standard ed., vol. 10.

–. "Observations on Transference Love" [1915]. Standard ed., vol. 12, 157–71.

–. "On Narcissism: An Introduction." [1914]. Standard ed., vol. 14, 67–104.

Grigg, Russell. *Lacan, Language and Philosophy*. Albany: SUNY Press, 2008.

Hegel, Georg Wilhelm Friedrich. *Preface to the Phenomenology of Spirit*. Translation and Commentary by Yirmiyahu Yovel. Princeton: Princeton University Press, 2005.

–. *Phenomenology of Spirit*, trans. A.V. Miller. Oxford: Oxford University Press, 1977.

Heidegger, Martin. *What Is Called Thinking?*, trans. J. Glenngray. New York: Harper Perennial, 1976.

Hyppolite, Jean. *Genesis and Structure of Hegel's "Phenomenology of Spirit"* [1946]. Evanston: Northwestern University Press, 1979.

Juranville, Alain. *Lacan et la philosophie*. Paris: Presses Universitaires de France, 1984.

Kant, Immanuel. *The Critique of Pure Reason,* trans. Paul Guyer and Allen W. Wood. Cambridge: Cambridge University Press, 1998.

–. *The Critique of Practical Reason,* trans. Werner S. Pluhar. Indianapolis: Hackett Publishing, 2002.

–. *The Conflict of the Faculties,* trans. Mary J. Gregor. New York: Abaris, 1979.

Kojève, Alexandre. "The Idea of Death in the Philosophy of Hegel." In *Hegel and Contemporary Continental Philosophy,* 27–74, ed. Dennis King Keenan. Albany: SUNY Press, 2004.

–. *Introduction to the Reading of Hegel: Lectures on the Phenomenology of Spirit,* ed. Allan Bloom. Ithaca: Cornell University Press, 1980.

Lodge, David. *Small World.* London: Penguin Books, 1995.

McClennen, Edward. "Finite Decision Theory." In *Gambling on God: Essays on Pascal's Wager,* ed. Jeff Jordan. New York: Rowman and Littlefield, 1994.

Miller, Jacques-Alain. "Biologie Lacanienne et événement de corps." *La Cause freudienne: Revue de psychanalyse* 44 (2000): 7–59.

Milner, Jean-Claude. *L'Oeuvre Claire.* Paris: Seuil, 1995.

Pascal, Blaise. *Pensées,* trans. W.F. Trotter. New York: Random House, 1941.

–. "Preface to the Treatise on Vacuum." In *The Thoughts, Letters and Opuscules of Blaise Pascal,* by Blaise Pascal, Henry Rogers, Victor Cousin, Charles Louandre.

Pippin, Robert B. *After the Beautiful: Hegel and the Philosophy of Pictorial Modernism.* Chicago: University of Chicago Press, 2014.

Ragland-Sullivan, Ellie. *Jacques Lacan and the Philosophy of Psychoanalysis.* Champaign: University of Illinois Press, 1987.

Régnault, François. "L'antiphilosophie selon Lacan." *Conférences d'esthétique lacanienne.* Paris: Agalma, 1997.

–. "Clinique hégélienne." Cours 11 du mercredi 5 juin, 2002. [Unpublished].

Rorty, Richard, "Texts and Lumps." *New Literary History* 17, no. 1 (1985): 1–16.

Sartre, Jean-Paul. *L'être et le néant.* Paris: Gallimard, 1976.

Žižek, Slavoj. *For They Know Not What They Do: Enjoyment as a Political Factor.* London and New York: Verso, 1991.

–. *Lacan: The Silent Partners.* London and New York: Verso, 2006.

Zupančič, Alenka. *Ethics of the Real: Kant, Lacan.* London and New York: Verso, 2000.

Index

act, 6, 15, 17, 21, 23–5, 29–30, 35, 39,
    107, 113, 120, 127–30, 136–9, 143–4,
    155–6, 159, 169, 174–8, 181–5,
    199–201, 225–30, 245, 253, 259, 261,
    267, 282
action, 12, 34, 58–9, 67, 78–9, 98,
    107, 128–9, 135, 154, 161, 178–80,
    182–99, 203, 223–4, 227–8, 236, 250,
    253, 255–6, 260–1, 267, 273–5
affect, 55, 60, 62–7, 73, 75–8, 91–2,
    108–9, 124–5, 130, 167, 180–1, 186,
    196, 251–2, 267
affirmation, 65, 96, 99, 105, 178, 222,
    228, 240
agalma, 42–5, 251, 284
alienation, 71, 102, 104, 115, 169,
    176, 184, 205, 208–10, 215–17, 221,
    230–6, 244, 252, 259
Allison, Henry, 184, 282
anxiety, 92, 152, 200–3, 215, 247–9,
    251–2, 258, 276, 282
aphanisis, 233–4
aporia, 38, 141, 169
Aristophanes, 37
Aristotle, 5, 21, 52–82, 139, 198, 266–8

Badiou, Alain, 7, 35, 122, 282
beauty, 10, 26, 38–9, 41–9, 72
body, 11–12, 17, 26–7, 30, 38, 43, 52,
    53–82, 87, 95–8, 113, 154, 164–9,
    172–6, 192, 251, 260–1, 266–8, 274
Boothby, Richard, 264, 283
Burnet, Georges, 111, 283

capitalism, 140–1, 199–200
castration, 69, 70, 72, 252
category, 37, 62, 89, 91–2, 107–8, 157,
    159, 173, 203, 225
certainty, 17, 85–8, 91–106, 113, 116,
    123–7, 131, 137–9, 147, 194–5,
    207–8, 213–14, 223–5, 228, 236,
    244–5
combinatorics, 173
consciousness, 12, 16, 22, 84, 100,
    124, 138, 157–8, 161–2, 171–2,
    176, 198, 205–46, 255, 259, 261,
    263; self-consciousness, 138, 161,
    176, 205–45, 259, 261; unhappy
    consciousness, 239, 244–5; unity
    of consciousness, 124, 157–61,
    172, 212

denial, 71, 97, 100, 111, 125, 130, 180,
    261
Derrida, Jacques, 5, 263, 283
Descartes, René, 5, 15–18, 29–31,
    53–4, 57, 60, 79, 83–117, 121–5, 169,
    206–9, 237, 249, 264, 266–70, 283;
    Cartesian, 14–15, 17, 85–6, 89–91,
    95–9, 102, 108, 122–4; *Meditations
    of First Philosophy*, 16, 83–5, 90, 93,
    268–70, 283; *Passions of the Soul*, 267
dialectic, 40, 44, 49–50, 66, 77, 146–7,
    206–7, 211–16, 224–8, 231–40, 245,
    255, 277, 282
doubt, 15, 84, 90–100, 106–7, 119, 123,
    144, 172, 208, 222, 238, 251, 269
doxa, 28, 34
drive, 20, 22, 54, 65, 77, 81, 87, 118,
    159, 164, 168–70, 174, 180–8, 232,
    250–8, 260–1, 264
dualism, 53–6, 99, 124, 255, 267

empty, 23–4, 38, 40, 88, 98–101,
    104–6, 134–5, 141, 172–5, 190, 240,
    254, 257; empty set, 104, 134–5,
    240; empty signifier, 23, 254, 257;
    empty space, 173–5

faith, 15, 35, 84, 111, 116–17, 120–1,
    125–39, 143
feminine, 4, 68, 73–81, 164, 257–8, 282
free association, 102, 260
freedom, 3, 4, 12, 102, 192–6,
    201–3, 210, 223, 226–33, 238–9;
    of choice, 12

god, 3, 12, 15, 31, 35, 38, 43, 47–8,
    69, 71, 84, 86, 90, 95, 102, 106–7,
    112–22, 125–30, 133, 138, 143–4,
    208, 271, 284

Hegel, Wilhelm Friedrich, 5, 16, 29,
    92, 100, 138, 142, 205–46, 250, 269,
    276–8, 283–4; Hegelian master, 29,
    92, 234
Heidegger, Martin, 4, 5, 16, 264, 283
Hyppolite, Jean, 214, 224–5, 277–8, 283

idea, 4, 6, 16–17, 29–30, 35–9, 43–7,
    51–3, 78, 87, 90, 121, 134, 148–9,
    154, 177–9, 188, 193–8, 200, 207,
    238–40, 247, 250, 259–61, 266, 269,
    273, 277, 282, 284
ideal, 22–4, 31, 43, 51, 109, 122, 189,
    206–7, 244, 254–5, 273, 282
identification, 3, 14, 16–17, 49, 94,
    105, 110, 133, 145–8, 167, 169–84,
    254–6, 261, 264, 271, 273, 282
immortality, 38–9, 45–7, 69, 116–19,
    128–9, 132, 144
imperative, 22–3, 180–5, 189, 192–4,
    200, 259, 264; categorical, 181
infinity, 86, 116–19, 125–8, 130–6,
    137–42, 220–1, 226
instinct, 180–1, 252, 266, 283

jouissance, 4, 54, 80, 99, 138, 141,
    178–9, 181, 185, 189, 227, 253,
    255–9, 261
Juranville, Alain, 263, 283

Kant, Immanuel, 17–18, 100, 121–2,
    139–40, 145–206, 213, 264, 270,
    272–6, 281–2, 284
Klein, Itshaq, 277
Kojève, Alexandre, 217–19, 225–6,
    228, 231, 277–8, 284

Le séminaire VII, 265–6, 275–6
Le séminaire VIII, 265–6

Le séminaire IX, 264, 269, 274
Le séminaire X, 268, 273, 276–7
Le séminaire XI, 276, 278
Le séminaire XII, 268–9, 278
Le séminaire XIII, 271–2
Le séminaire XIV, 269, 275
Le séminaire XV, 276, 278
Le séminaire XVI, 263–4, 266,
    269–73, 276, 278
Le séminaire XVII, 264, 268–9,
    278–9
Le séminaire XVIII, 269, 278
Le séminaire XIX, 265
Le séminaire XX, 267–8
L'Etourdit, 30, 31, 265, 281
"Little Hans," 112–13
Lodge, David, 3, 284

master, 4, 11–13, 19, 25–31, 84, 92,
    107, 133–4, 140–3, 211, 224–39,
    248–50, 253, 256, 265, 269, 277
master's discourse, 11, 27–9, 248–9
master signifier, 23, 27, 107, 256
matheme, 36, 42, 256, 264, 282
McClennen, Edward, 271, 284
method, 25, 35, 40, 48–50, 95–100,
    122, 146–7, 150–3, 159, 161–4, 176,
    269–70, 283
Miller, Jacques Alain, 178–9, 198,
    205, 274, 276, 283–4
mind, 47, 53, 68, 74–5, 84, 99, 102,
    111, 125–7, 161–2, 167, 266–8

negation, 51, 95–107, 120, 178, 207,
    211–15, 222–30, 235, 238–45, 269,
    277, 283

Pascal, Blaise, 111–44, 270–2, 283
pass, 257, 265

pathos, 9, 23, 70–1, 81, 152–5, 161, 267
phallus, 71, 112–13, 174, 257; phallic,
    71, 77–80, 257–8; phallic signifier,
    71, 257–8
phantasm, 52, 76–9, 257–8
Plato, 4–5, 20, 25–37, 42–53, 169,
    248, 251, 264–6, 279, 282; Menon,
    30, 36; Phaedo, 47, 53, 266;
    Republic, 47, 53, 266; Symposium,
    20, 26–9, 32–9, 44–5, 48–51, 251;
    Timaeus, 53, 266
pure intellect, 158–9, 174

Ragland, Ellie, 263, 284
"Rat Man," 183, 226, 275
reason, 12, 57, 87–8, 118–19, 123–5,
    129, 145–8, 152, 155–7, 169, 171–3,
    179, 183, 186–93, 270–6, 281, 284;
    practical, 148, 179, 186–90, 193–8,
    275, 284; pure, 88, 145–8, 152–6,
    169, 171, 270–6, 284
Regnault, François, 231, 263, 278, 284
repetition, 135–7, 250, 258
representation, 36, 70, 112, 139,
    151–76, 189, 202–7, 232, 251,
    255–6, 259, 260, 261, 272;
    repräsentanz, 220, 226, 232–3,
    245, 261; Vorstellungsrepräsentanz,
    232, 233, 261
repression, 97, 105, 232, 261, 264
revolution, 4, 6, 90, 109, 141, 250
Rorty, Richard, 263, 284

Sade, Marquis de, 184, 189, 192–3,
    275, 281
Sartre, Jean-Paul, 20, 284
scepticism, 97, 238, 278
schema, 117, 156–9, 165, 172–4, 257;
    schematism, 156–9, 174

semblance, 11–13, 269
separation, 19, 53–4, 61, 71–2, 80–1,
    84, 89, 105, 156–9, 199, 208, 231–3,
    252, 257, 267
sexuality, 4, 68–73, 81, 146, 258, 282
sexual relation, 51
sexuation, 257–8
Spinoza, Baruch Benedict, 117, 267
superego, 178–82, 188, 259, 264
supposition, 51, 76, 148, 155, 192,
    210–12, 220, 236, 243
symbolic death, 46, 232, 260
symptom, 77, 94, 98–9, 201–3, 252–4,
    259, 260

topology, 116, 173–6, 201–4, 260
transcendental, 22, 146–76, 202–4,
    247, 272–3, 282
transference, 4, 22, 37, 44, 49–50, 69,
    260, 265, 281, 283
transgression, 178, 181

unary trait, 89, 107, 134–5, 166,
    169–70, 175–6, 261

wager, 8–9, 46, 50, 100, 111–44,
    270–1, 284
woman, 50, 69, 78–82, 108, 188,
    241–2, 253, 257